WRITING picture books

Revised and Expanded Edition

A Hands-on Guide from
Story Creation to Publication

Ann Whitford Paul

WD
WRITER'S
DIGEST
BOOKS

Writer's Digest Books
An imprint of Penguin Random House LLC
penguinrandomhouse.com

Printed in the United States of America
10th Printing

ISBN 978-1-4403-5375-8

Edited by Cris Freese and Amy Jones
Cover Designed by Alexis Estoye
Designed by Katelyn Summers and Jason Williams

Dedication

This revised edition is dedicated in loving memory of Sue Alexander, to my special friends and critique partners, Karen B. Winnick and Erica Silverman, who have been with me every step of my writing journey, and to anyone who has ever written or dreamed of writing a picture book.

Proceeds from this book will establish the Ann Whitford Paul–Writer's Digest Award for the Most Promising Picture Book Manuscript. Submission instructions can be found at scbwi.org/the-ann-whitford-paul-writers-digest-book-award/.

About the Author

Reading picture books to her four children inspired Ann Whitford Paul to try her hand at writing them. After all, she thought, they're short. They must be easy.

Wrong!

Much to her dismay, she discovered the fewer words in a book, the more consideration must be given to each word. One day, after a receiving several rejections, she realized she had lots to learn and began reading books about writing, taking classes, and attending conferences (which she continues to do to this day). She has published more than twenty picture books (including board books, early-readers, a poetry collection, plus a variety of fiction and non-fiction, rhymed and prose picture books, including the popular series that began with *If Animals Kissed Goodnight*). Many of her poems have appeared in anthologies and her essays have been published by several newspapers.

Eager to share her hard-earned and slowly-acquired knowledge, Ann has taught picture book writing at UCLA Extension and through webinars and spoken at numerous national and international conferences. She's thrilled to have the opportunity to revise, expand, and update the first edition of *Writing Picture Books*.

When Ann isn't writing, she's knitting, quilting, needlepointing, cooking, enjoying her grandchildren, or reading, reading, reading. She also loves listening to her cat purr, tracing snails' trails, and watching spiders spin their webs. She lives with her husband in Los Angeles and hopes you'll visit her website www.annwhitfordpaul.com.

Table of Contents

PART FOUR

The Language of Your Story

PART FIVE

Tying Together Loose Ends

PART SIX

After Your Story Is Done

Welcome to This Revised and Expanded Book

How can ten years have passed since *Writing Picture Books* was first published? And nearly twelve years since it was written? Just as much has changed in my life and in yours, in our country, and in our world; so, too, has the field of picture books evolved.

Publishers have continued to merge into bigger organizations, and new smaller publishers have opened their doors to manuscripts. Some publishers still want submissions to arrive via snail mail, but others accept only e-mail attachments. Agents are more necessary than ever to break into the business.

And what about the stories themselves? Since the first edition of *Writing Picture Books*, editors have been asking for books that are on the cutting edge and break traditional boundaries. One example might be *I Want My Hat Back* by Jon Klassen, where it appears the thief character suffers a grisly consequence for his crime.

Narrative nonfiction, where plotting and other techniques of fiction are applied to nonfiction, has become a popular buzz phrase. Picture-book poetry collections now need a theme or story format, not just a smattering of different subjects on which the poet focused. In addition, as attention spans have been reduced by television, video games, smartphones, and computers, publishers have begun asking for shorter manuscripts.

Internet sales have skyrocketed, but independent bookstores have struggled. A high percentage of books, instead of being purchased by professional teachers and librarians, are sold to parents. Then there's the phenomenon of self-publishing, which has allowed writers an alternative way to get their stories into the world.

All these developments and more will be addressed in the following pages. If you have read the first edition, you will still find much fresh material here. The recommended published books have been updated, and the examples and quizzes have been rewritten. New chapters have been added, and discussion of the publishing business has been revised to include current information and requirements.

All of this was done with the hope of easing your journey into the land of picture-book publication. May your travels be happy and successful.

Prologue

"I love revisions. Where else in life can spilled milk be transformed into ice cream?"

—KATHERINE PATERSON

Completing a draft of your story isn't the end of the writing process; it's the beginning. Then you must shape your draft into a publishable manuscript. This is the fun part of writing, the time-consuming part of writing, and what separates the amateur from the professional. *Writing Picture Books Revised and Expanded Edition: A Hands-on Guide from Story Creation to Publication* will help you become a professional.

When I first put pen to paper, fingers to typewriter, I made all the mistakes editors groan about. My stories were dotted with characters with cutesy names, like Sammy Skunk. I wrote about putting a child to bed from the *mother's* point of view. I inserted dull directions to the illustrator, saying the character should be walking out the door or skipping down the walk. My characters were perfect children who never misbehaved; my plots were contrived, with an adult conveniently turning up to solve the problem; and my language was duller than an engineering textbook.

Naïvely, I thought my stories were so fabulous that an editor would make an offer of publication as soon as she read one. When, months later, my stories were returned with form rejections, I convinced myself that the editors didn't know what they were missing. After many form rejections (I'm a slow learner), it dawned on me: I had serious learning to do. I signed up for classes, joined several writing groups, attended conferences, and read every book I could find about writing.

The importance of revision (that process between first draft and final submission to an editor) gradually seeped into my brain. I wrote this book to help you and other writers understand this faster than I did.

Writers can have three different kinds of reactions to their first drafts. Which one will be yours?

1. Do you love your draft? Are you so enamored with your text you can't bear to change a thing? I thought my story about Sammy Skunk saving his friends Billy Beaver, Suzy Squirrel, etc. from Coyote Carl by spraying his horrible smell (big surprise there!) was imaginative, original, and perfect. I sent it out immediately.
2. Or do you instead decide your story is hopeless and toss it in the trash? I've done that, too. Once I wrote about a young Italian boy pulling up potatoes. Besides the fact that I had never lived in Italy or grown potatoes, the story felt thin. Convinced my writing was terrible, I tore it up and moved on, not thinking that I could at least plant potatoes and learn more about the process. Maybe if I was fortunate, I could even travel to Italy.
3. The third reaction, which we should all strive for, is a combination of the first two. That's where a writer reads her first draft and decides *this isn't bad.* She knows *it isn't good either*, so she's ready to play around and make it better. But what should she delete? What should she save?

That's the problem. It's hard to be objective about what works and what doesn't in our stories. The key to improving your writing is to learn how to be your own critic, develop ways to pull yourself back from your story, and become an outside reader. How do you do that?

Many writers set a manuscript aside for days, weeks, or months to break through the love-or-hate affair with one's writing. This can help, but few have the self-control to hide a story in a drawer or under a bed for the weeks, months, or years necessary to acquire that objectivity. And there's no guarantee you'll have much of that objectivity even after all that time.

Some writers know what they should look for in a revision—such as a strong opening, good plotting, three-dimensional characters, etc., but this is useless *unless* you know the characteristics of a strong opening, et al. We strive to create well-rounded characters, but few of us can recognize if our characters are flat or behaving inconsistently.

Some writers don't even try to become their own critics. They send their manuscripts to friends or family members or take them to writing groups. Outside readers who understand the craft of writing for children can be helpful. But the process of taking one's story to outsiders can be time-consuming, especially as you repeatedly edit your story and bring it back for further commentary. After too much of this back and forth, outside readers who never liked the story can become less helpful, while others may be so attached to it—and to you—they lose their objectivity.

How much better it is to take responsibility for becoming your own best critic! You'll bring an improved story to your outside critics and shorten the back-and-forth process.

This book offers ways to gain outsider objectivity. The techniques discussed will help turn you into a dispassionate critic of your work and give you the skills to strengthen your writing. The exercises at the end of each chapter will help you see your story more clearly and direct your revisions.

Note that revision is not a one-time event. Every change will call for more changes. Stories rarely jump onto your computer screen in finished form. Instead, they evolve over time. That's one of the pains and one of the pleasures of writing. Something as simple as substituting one word for another (even switching *a* for *the*) may have ramifications throughout the manuscript.

Over the years, I've found being playful while writing and revising makes my work more pleasurable. Although this book discusses serious topics like character development, strong openings, the poetry of prose, page turns, endings, and much more, the revision techniques included here will take you back to childhood. You'll use crayons, markers, scissors, tape, etc. to help you shape your words into a saleable story and give your back and butt a break from your computer. You'll stand and stretch. You'll use muscles that might have grown lazy. Like my students at UCLA Extension and participants in my workshops and webinars, you'll cut, color, paste, and revise your way to publication. You can do it!

WHAT'S NEXT?

Before we turn to specific revision techniques, put on your scholar's cap. It's impossible to write a picture book without understanding its form. That's what our first chapter is about.

BUT . . . Before you go on

Activities in future chapters assume you have a story to revise. If you don't, begin thinking about what you want to write, but read the first chapter before you put pen to paper or type on your keyboard.

Part One

Before You Write Your Story

1

Becoming a Picture-Book Scholar

"Writing is a craft before it is an art . . . ."

—DONALD M. MURRAY

Having your appendix removed doesn't qualify you to then perform an appendectomy, so why should having heard or read picture books qualify you to write one? You wouldn't start creating a software program without first researching computer theory, but some people think they can write a picture book without ever reading or studying contemporary picture books.

Picture books have a unique form and audience. In this chapter, you'll learn what a picture book is and what its audience requires from you the writer. But first I'd like to tell you a true story.

Several years ago, my family was enjoying a pleasant summer supper outside and having an animated discussion about the state of education in this country. With five other eager participants, I couldn't get in a word. Frustrated at being ignored, I pounded my fist on the table: *"Listen to me! I have something to say!"*

My sixteen-year-old son Alan looked at me incredulously. "Listen to you? Why should we listen to you? You write books for people who can't even read."

We all had a good laugh, and I'm happy to say, they did let me speak my piece. Much later, mulling over his comment, I realized Alan had come up with the perfect way to begin defining a picture book.

A BOOK FOR PEOPLE WHO CAN'T READ

Picture books are usually read by an adult reader to a nonreader. To that end, picture books combine words with pictures that entice the nonreader to listen and help her construct meaning from the words. Picture books traditionally find an audience in young children. Today, some picture books and graphic novels are published for fluent readers, even adults, but this book will focus on those aimed at children ages two through eight.

Such picture books are divided into two categories. The first is books aimed at the nonreader. The second is picture storybooks written for emergent or newly established readers. These have more text and more complicated story lines. Hard- and softcover published picture books are usually thirty-two pages long, but your manuscript, double-spaced with one-inch (25mm) borders, will be considerably fewer pages.

A Society of Children's Book Writers and Illustrators (SCBWI) survey found that picture-book manuscripts range from one-half page to sometimes even fifteen pages. Those at the top range would obviously be for independent readers. The length of the manuscript is determined by the age of the audience and its attention span. Manuscripts for children up to two years old (who tend to have short attention spans) should be between one half and one manuscript page. Usually these are published as board books, where pictures are the most important element. There might be one sentence per page, sometimes just one word. Because pictures are so critical to drawing in the listener, early board books are generally written and illustrated by the same person.

Today publishers are increasingly reformatting popular picture books into board books. Although some feel too advanced for the intended audience, I'm not complaining. My story, *If Animals Kissed Good Night*, was originally published as a picture book. When it was reissued as a board book, sales skyrocketed.

Children between the ages of two and five can sit still longer, so their picture-book manuscripts are longer—around two to five pages. With roughly 200 words per manuscript page, that means 400 to 900 words total. When this book was first published, if my manuscripts were in the 700-word range, I searched for ways to cut. Now 500 words seems long to me.

Manuscripts between four and fifteen pages are for older children and even adults. The longer the manuscript, the more likely the book pages will increase, always in multiples of eight. One book might be forty pages; another might be forty-eight and so on. A word of caution: *Books with higher page counts cost more to produce.*

Publishers are wary of spending more money than necessary on an unproven product. And new writers are unproven products. If you've never been published, revise to fit your story into the thirty-two-page format.

Because a picture book is both words and pictures, the writer can limit words to the bare essentials. In *Where Do Pants Go?* author Rebecca Van Slyke asks where certain items of clothing go. She leaves the look of each item to the illustrator, Chris Robertson, thereby eliminating much text (some pages have as few as three words). An added benefit is that she gives Chris control of color, design, and the overall look of the book.

You don't need to describe the house the character lives in, the appearances of his parents, or the breed of his dog. Descriptions, *unless vital* to your story, should be eliminated. That allows you, the writer, to focus on the action and dialogue of your story.

Picture-book writers, even if they're not illustrators, still must have visual images in their minds, particularly when writing for the very young. Your text should allow the illustrator space for a variety of interesting picture possibilities to keep the listener involved in the book. This may be accomplished through one or all of the following:

1. writing scenes with different actions
2. introducing new characters into the story
3. moving characters to different settings
4. changing the emotional intensity of a scene

In picture books for the two- to five-year-old range, the text requires pictures to tell the story. Writers should strive to leave room in their manuscripts for the illustrator to develop an independent picture story line. For example, read the classic *If You Give a Mouse a Cookie* by Laura Joffe Numeroff. On one page in the book, Numeroff writes that Mouse painted a picture but gives no indication of what the picture looks like, allowing the illustrator, Felicia Bond, to create an artist-quality portrait of a mouse family in front of their tree-trunk house.

Sometimes, as in *If Animals Kissed Good Night* illustrated by David Walker, not having all the details in the words allows the illustrator to add his own story. A rabbit never mentioned in the text is frightened by a bear's growl. A little girl in bed, again never mentioned in the text, is illustrated warmly at the beginning and near the end of the book. Good illustrators add their own story so children too young to read can have fun "reading" the pictures. Good writers leave artists the space to do that.

In longer picture storybooks, words can more easily stand on their own. Although they are illustrated, the pictures, while showing aspects of the story, rarely add a new story line. The balance tips from heavy illustration to heavy words; the writer has more room to add details. Often these books have large chunks of text that might take up the entire page. *The Great Moon Hoax* by Stephen Krensky is nearly 1,500 words and contains many imaginings of life on the moon. The illustrations by Josée Bisaillon echo the action and the imaginings but don't add a second story line.

This is true of many historical-fiction and nonfiction picture books. *Noah Webster & His Words* by Jeri Chase Ferris is 1,417 words long. The illustrations by Vincent X. Kirsch enhance the text but do not add a separate story. Regardless of length, picture-book writers keep the reader wondering what will happen next by creating stories filled with action and little contemplation.

THE UNUSUAL TWO-PART PICTURE-BOOK AUDIENCE

This is subdivided into two separate groups: children too young to read and adult readers.

CHILDREN TWO TO EIGHT YEARS OLD

Bearing in mind this targeted audience, it behooves writers to get to know what matters to children. You will have difficulty writing for them if you don't have a strong memory of your childhood or firsthand experience with children. However, you can educate yourself by spending time with nieces, nephews, and neighbors and by visiting parks, nursery and elementary schools, etc. Here are some characteristics of children to keep in mind while you write.

1. **EVERYTHING IS NEW.**

   Adults have been in cars so often our minds travel elsewhere when we're driving, yet children are fascinated by every tree, house, and shop they see from the backseat window. My two-year-old granddaughter Thea is fascinated by puddles, stamping the water, and studying her reflection. A worm? We step right over it. Children squat to watch it squirm. The world is a wonder to children, but most adults have grown blasé about it. As a children's writer, you must tap back into the excitement of discovery. How do you do that?

   Wonder happens automatically when you try something new. Visit a just-opened museum. Walk through an unfamiliar neighborhood. Try a foreign food. Be open to everything around you. In an unfamiliar store, notice the smells from the candy counter. Feel the smooth texture of a satin dress. Listen to the sounds a printer makes as it prints your receipt.

Don't be afraid to be foolish. Put yourself in a child's body. It's not as hard as it sounds. Make yourself small; get down on your hands and knees. (Not in a store. Wait until you return home.) What do you notice at that lower level? Is the floor smooth? Hard? Cool? Does the cat look bigger to you from down here or smaller? Pick up a dust ball. Does it tickle? Outside, touch a snail's trail. Is it sticky? Chase a squirrel. Can you catch it? Dig dirt with your fingers. Is it moist? Dry? Then when you write, put that wonder into your words.

2. **CHILDREN HAVE HAD FEW EXPERIENCES.**

That explains why they scream when a friend won't share blocks. Or sob when ice cream falls off their cone and plops on the ground. Or insist only a hamburger will satisfy them. Adults have lived through many disappointments. We know there will be other times to share blocks and other cones to lick and that sometimes chicken tastes better than a hamburger.

Children don't know these things yet. They cry when left with a babysitter because they're worried their parents might not return—this is *their* high drama. As a writer, look for those seemingly small incidents that matter greatly to children.

The Wrong Side of the Bed by Lisa M. Bakos is a litany of disasters that are not earth-shattering to adults but vitally important to children such as missing one slipper, having trouble making the bed, mismatched socks, and too much syrup on pancakes.

3. **CHILDREN LIVE IN THE PRESENT.**

Anyone traveling with young children knows the question "Are we there yet?" You might answer, "We'll be there in one hour," but ten minutes later, you hear "Are we there yet?" The question gets repeated so often it's like a damaged CD playing the same lyrics over and over again.

The concepts of *an hour from now, tomorrow,* or *next week* are not clear to young children. Therefore, the story lines for this audience usually take place in a few hours, a day, or a night. Books that extend over a longer time are usually for older readers and need a repetitive phrase to help anchor the listener. That phrase can be as mundane as *the next day* or as poetic as *when I dug in the sand with Grandpa.*

- *A Fine Dessert: Four Centuries, Four Families, One Delicious Treat* by Emily Jenkins uses the phrase *What a fine dessert!* to signal the end of one period and transition to another.
- In Virginia Loh-Hagan's book *PoPo's Lucky Chinese New Year*, a fun and fascinating story of preparing for the holiday, whenever the little girl and her PoPo (grandmother) begin a new activity, she signals it with a sound effect related to that activity.

4. **CHILDREN HAVE STRONG EMOTIONS.**

Anatole Broyard wrote "... when you're young, everything matters; everything is serious." If your favorite shirt is at the cleaners, you will probably shrug and put on another shirt. A child might throw a tantrum. A child who doesn't want to go to bed may sob frantic tears.

Misplacing something, like one's favorite toy, is traumatic. If you want to see how upsetting this can be, read Caldecott Honor Book *Knuffle Bunny: A Cautionary Tale* by Mo Willems. Trixie goes with her daddy to the laundromat and accidently puts her stuffed bunny into the washing machine. Her situation is complicated because she doesn't have the words to explain what's happened. Children care deeply. Tap into their strong emotions for your stories.

5. **SOMETIMES CHILDHOOD IS NOT HAPPY.**

Adults look back on childhood as an idyllic time: Children don't have to work for a living, so they have nothing to do but play with toys and eat food someone else cooked. Children should appreciate how lucky they are to not have to pay bills, shop for groceries, or drive in traffic.

It's true that children don't do those things. However, they *do* have to deal with bullies at preschool and struggle to shape the letters of their names. A child may be devastated if the friend he always sits next to during story time decides to sit next to someone else.

Tragic things can happen to children: Pets and grandparents die, and parents get divorced.

- In *Yard Sale* by Eve Bunting, a young girl must deal with a forced move to smaller quarters because of a change in the family's financial circumstances.
- In *Sonya's Chickens* by Phoebe Wahl, a young girl must come to terms with the death of a pet that is killed by a fox.

Print yourself a sign that says *CHILDHOOD IS NOT ALL JOYFUL.* Post it near your computer to remind you of the ups and downs that happen to children.

On the other hand, humor helps them deal with problems, so funny books can be beneficial in times of stress and worry. In Mo Willems's *Knuffle Bunny*, there is humor in the panicked expressions on Trixie's face and in the sounds that come out of her mouth as she tries to get Daddy to understand her.

6. **CHILDREN PERCEIVE MORE THAN WE THINK THEY DO.**

   Sometimes they're smarter than adults. Certainly, children are more intuitive. They read, listen, and observe with their hearts. As much as I tried to hide it, one Mother's Day, my children became extra clingy, sensing my anger at my husband for ignoring the holiday.

   It stands to reason then that children are wise enough to figure out what a story is about without an explicitly stated moral. We're in the business of writing engaging stories, not teaching lessons. Leave that to educators.

7. **CHILDREN HAVE SHORT ATTENTION SPANS.**

   Unfortunately, TV and video games haven't encouraged any lengthening of their attention spans. That's why publishing houses are looking for shorter manuscripts. Don't write long and convoluted stories. Your stories must be so focused that you write not about just one thing but one *aspect* of one thing.

   Suppose you want to write about waking up for our young audiences.

   - You can write a book like Erica Silverman's *Wake Up, City!*
   - Or you can write about a rooster who doesn't want to wake up, like Mike Twohy did in *Wake Up, Rupert!*
   - Alternatively, you could write a book like Mary Casanova's *Wake Up, Island.*
   - Perhaps you want to write a story in this vein that focuses on newborns; that's what Helen Frost did in *Wake Up!*

   Wake-up books seem so popular, I'm thinking of writing some myself—*Wake Up, Aardvark*; *Wake Up, Whale*; *Wake Up, Wildebeest.*

8. **CHILDREN ARE SELF-CENTERED.**

   We're all self-centered, but most adults hide it better. Children don't want to hear stories about teacher or parent problems. They want to hear stories about *their* problems. As a woman, I'm more interested in books with a female lead character than a male lead character. If you're writing for children, make your main characters children or childlike animals, like in the charming book *Pug Meets Pig* by Sue Lowell Gallion. Her main character is a sweet, content pug who is forced to adapt to a new sibling when a pig moves in.

You may rightfully point out that adult main characters appear in picture books, but I would argue that these adults are often children in disguise. The main character in *Old Robert and the Sea-Silly Cats* by Barbara Joosse is shy and afraid of the dark. What child can't identify with those feelings?

9. **CHILDREN LONG TO BE INDEPENDENT.**

Even though deep inside you know they're trying to be helpful, don't you hate it when someone tells you how to do something? Kids are the same. They want to do things themselves; good parents and educators give children the chance to experiment and develop new skills in safe situations. We encourage them to eat with a spoon and hold their own cup even though spills and messes might follow.

In our books, we should strive to give them examples of strong girls and boys who find their own solutions to problems. Our books should empower children. One good example of this is *Imogene's Last Stand* by Candace Fleming. Despite a lack of support from the townspeople, Imogene loves history and wages a fierce battle to prevent the historical society from being demolished.

10. **CHILDREN ARE COMPLICATED.**

They're like adults—not all good and not all bad. Look for that gray area with your characters. Create well-rounded (not flat or cookie-cutter) characters (we'll discuss how to do this in chapter six). Hume Cronyn, the well-known actor, followed one rule in his work that easily applies to picture books: "If you're doing the devil, look for the angel in him. If you're doing the angel, look for the devil in him." Look at *Big Mean Mike* by Michelle Knudsen for an example of a tough dog character who turns out to have a soft side.

11. **CHILDREN HAVE RICH IMAGINATIONS.**

Because they lack experience in the world, children accept the possibility of things that adults know are impossible. A little boy can be carried by a balloon around the world. A frog and a toad can speak. Zoo animals read books. Children's imaginations soar. Let yours soar with them.

For a beautiful book about a child's imagination, look at *Henry & Leo* by Pamela Zagarenski. Henry, a little boy, believes his stuffed lion is real, much to the consternation of his family. Isn't everyone surprised to discover that maybe Leo is alive—something Henry always knew?

12. **ALMOST ANY TOPIC IS OKAY FOR A PICTURE BOOK.**

This is true as long as the author writes in a manner appropriate for the intended audience. For examples, look at

- *I Used to Be a Fish* by Tom Sullivan
- *Everyone Poops* by Taro Gomi
- *Who Has What?: All About Girls' Bodies and Boys' Bodies* by Robie H. Harris

We've focused on the child audience, but since they're too young to read and too young to pay for a book, let's consider our other audience.

ADULT

These are parents, grandparents, relatives, teachers, and librarians who purchase and read our books aloud. This double audience puts picture books in a class by themselves and creates great ramifications for our writing.

1. **LANGUAGE DOES NOT HAVE TO BE BABYISH.**

Because you want to appeal to the adult reader, don't feel constrained to use only simple childlike language. Words like *itty bitty* and *dimple dumpling* are trite, overused, and demeaning. If you want to know what words work for different grade levels, check out *Children's Writer's Word Book*, by Alijandra and Tayopa Mogilner. However, don't limit yourselves to these lists. Part of a writer's job is introducing children to the pleasures of our language. Feel free to use big words like *glittery* or even made-up ones like *fantabulous* if their meaning is clear in the context of your story and if they're not too difficult to read aloud.

The word *segregated*, which a picture-book-aged child might not understand, can still be used in a story if you write something like the following: "Norma was forced to attend a segregated school. There were boys in her class. There were girls, too. But everyone, even her teacher, was black."

When we use big words and help the child see what *segregation* means, we expand the listener's vocabulary.

2. **MAKE BOOKS EASY TO READ ALOUD.**

   Think about the adults reading your books. While one of them might be Jennifer Lawrence or Ryan Gosling, most likely they'll be ordinary people who aren't actors. Your words must give plenty of opportunities for the non-theatrically-trained adult to sound like he graduated from Juilliard Drama School. Avoid words adults have difficulty pronouncing. Don't write humongously long sentences like this one that will make your poor, unsuspecting reader gasp for breath way before reaching the desperately needed punctuation mark that finally, at long last, signifies the end. Remember that it's easier to read characters' dialogue expressively than it is a narrative description. Onomatopoetic words like *boom*, *crash*, and *buzz* are amusing and invite the pre-reader to join in. Another way you can help your reader is by studying poetry and using its techniques in your writing. "Help!" I hear you moaning. "I hate poetry. If I have to write poetry, I'll never do a picture book." Take a deep breath, close your eyes, and tell yourself, "Poetry is my friend." Anyone with the drive and willingness to put in the necessary work can learn the craft of writing picture books *and* poetry. Read each chapter, and do the exercises in the order written. Eventually you'll get to chapters on rhythm and word sounds, and I guarantee you'll enjoy making your stories more poetic.

3. **ADULTS ARE FREQUENTLY ASKED TO READ AND REREAD PICTURE BOOKS.**

   Have compassion for your adult reader. Picture books are meant to be short both for the child *and* the adult. My children often asked me to read their favorite books two, three, even four times. How grateful I was for these stories' brevity!

   Also, picture books are getting more expensive every day. Adults want their money's worth from our short stories. That's why you must give adult readers and their listeners a story that will stay with them. Your writing must strike an emotional chord in both of them that will bring them back to your book time and time again.

As part of your continuing picture-book education, you should always be reading and thinking about them in relation to the topics we cover. After each chapter, one of the assignments will be to read a picture book that is new to you. Read one book after each chapter, and eventually, you'll have read twenty-five and be well on your way to becoming an expert. The more you read and the more you think about what you read, the faster you'll reach your goal of publication.

In addition to picture books, read books about writing. I have several shelves of them that I refer to frequently and sometimes even reread. The bibliography in the back of this book lists my favorites. You may also consider these other resources:

PROFESSIONAL ORGANIZATIONS

The Society of Children's Book Writers and Illustrators (SCBWI) is imperative for anyone interested in writing picture books. It puts on local and national conferences, gives extensive information on the field, and publishes a bimonthly newsletter. SCBWI also updates *The Book*, a must-have reference book available as a hard copy and online. Visit their website at www.scbwi.org.

The Authors Guild advocates for the rights of authors. I love their publication, the *Authors Guild Bulletin*. Besides keeping me up to date on news and actions on our behalf, it also shares quotes from working authors—some of which have found their way into this book. Their website is www.authorsguild.org. The Children's Book Council is a nonprofit organization of publishers and packagers of children's books. Check out their informative publications and their website at www.cbcbooks.org.

PROFESSIONAL PUBLICATIONS

The Horn Book is a bimonthly magazine with articles by librarians, writers, and others involved in the children's book field. They also review new books. It's great for keeping up with the latest trends and with what's being published (www.hbook.com).

Booklist also reviews children's books for librarians (www.ala.org/booklist), as does *School Library Journal* (www.slj.com). *Writer's Digest* (www.writersdigest.com) and *The Writer* (www.writermag.com) are both magazines for all kinds of writers but occasionally have articles regarding picture books.

NEWSLETTERS

Definitely sign up for *Publishers Weekly*'s free semiweekly Children's Bookshelf newsletter (www.publishersweekly.com/pw/email-subscriptions/index.html).

INTERNET RESOURCES

www.underdown.org
www.darcypattison.com
johartauthor.com
12x12challenge.com
writersrumpus.com/category/writing-2/writing-picture-books
www.dlstewart.com/index.htm
www.joshfunkbooks.com/resources-for-writers
www.kidlit411.com

A FEW FINAL WORDS

Now you know about the unique audience for picture books and some of their characteristics. Keeping them in mind will help you create captivating stories that will appeal to both listeners and readers.

WHAT'S NEXT?

In chapter two we're going to look at the wide variety of today's picture books and learn how to write a story that appeals to both adults and children and makes them want to read and hear your story.

BUT . . . Before you go on

1. Read picture books. In most chapters, I'll mention titles related to the topic being discussed. A bibliography at the end includes all books mentioned throughout. Don't just read these books. Think about them. Take notes. Study why one works and another doesn't.

This is good training for beginning writers, and it's a practice you should continue throughout your career.

2. Choose a published picture book you love. Then choose one you hate—one you think is so dreadful that it should never have been published. You might ask yourself, *Why would anyone publish an awful book?* The answer is that publishing houses don't intend to publish bad books. Someone working there loved the manuscript and saw a market for the book.

   Go out and find a best and a worst picture book. Do not buy the worst book. Check it out from the library, or borrow it from a friend. Don't reward bad writing by purchasing it.

   Choose only books published within the last ten years. The styles that are popular in the book world change as fast as in the fashion world. The books published in the year 2000 are far different from the books being published today. If you're exclusively a writer, choose books written by a different person than the illustrator. If you are both an illustrator and a writer, choose books with only one creator.

   Type the good and bad manuscripts into your computer. Using what you have learned about the form and different audiences of a picture book, take note of why they do or do not work. I've assigned you only one good and one bad book (since I do not want to overwhelm you), but over time you will improve your writing immeasurably by reading and typing up many books. Why waste your time doing this? Why not just work on your own stories?

   First, you'll discover why some books are successful and others aren't. More importantly, you'll have manuscripts to compare to your own. In most chapters, you'll be assigned exercises to practice on your story. I encourage you to also do these with the manuscripts you typed up. If you have any questions about the concepts in this book, exploring them within published books should be helpful. If you're fortunate enough to already belong to a writing group—we'll explore how to create and run one in chapter twenty—you might practice these exercises on published books with other members.

3. Ta-Dah! Time to write! You know what a picture book is. You've read some picture books. You've typed up a good picture book

and a bad picture book. If you haven't done so already, write your story. Relax. Have fun. Remember, your first draft will rarely be submission-ready. Just as milk needs churning to become ice cream, your draft will need revision to become publishable. Get your story down, and you'll have something to work with.

4. Check out the picture books mentioned in this chapter.

Part Two

Early Story Decisions

2

Building a Frame for Your Story House

"The story must be short but the idea must be big enough to justify making it into a book."

—ANONYMOUS EDITOR

At the end of the last chapter, your assignment was to write a picture book. Getting that first draft (or as school kids say, "sloppy copy") down can be painful. If you're like me, you have an idea that glistens in your head and already has "bestseller" sparkling in neon lights above it. Then you start writing, and the mundaneness of your plot, the flatness of your characters, and the dullness of your prose hits you like a sledgehammer.

Do not stop. Keep writing. Boring as it may feel, I hope you push on until the very end. That's what you must do in order to have something to look at, to play with, to improve upon until it really does glisten. The majority of this book is about how to make your story the best it can be.

Eric Carle, that amazingly talented writer and illustrator, said, "The hard work goes into the idea—fiddling with it and rejecting it and loving it and hating it. … I probably do fifteen drafts for a book. Sometimes I'm deliriously happy. Other times, I'm just wiped out."

You may do many more drafts of a book; you may do fewer, but rarely is that first draft your finished product. Don't be discouraged by your first draft. Instead, think of all those people who carry ideas around in their heads for years and never do anything with them. Pat yourself on the back for your accomplishment. Then get on with the fun work of revision. Along the way, bear in mind that picture books have two audiences: adults—parents, grandparents, teachers, relatives, librarians who pay money for the books—and children, who listen to the adult reader.

Hopefully, the stories we write will appeal to both so they will want to share the book together frequently. Better yet, children will love the book so much that when they reach adulthood, they will share it with their children. This is how classics like *The Story of Ferdinand* by Munro Leaf, *Where the Wild Things Are* by Maurice Sendak, and *If You Give a Mouse a Cookie* by Laura Joffe Numeroff are born.

Too often, however, picture books appeal to only one audience. As a parent, I couldn't abide many books my children loved. Often, I stooped to immature behavior, hiding an offensive book under a bed or tucking it behind other books on the shelf. Sometimes it mysteriously disappeared forever.

Other books appealed to me but not my children. Because I had control (as the grown-up reader), they had to accede to my wishes. I would foist my choices on their unwilling ears. They tolerated this only because I promised to read one of their favorites afterwards. What child doesn't want to sit a bit longer in an adult's arms while listening to a story, even one they don't like, when there's another, better one waiting to be heard?

Obviously, the ideal picture book must appeal to adults *and* children. The best way to ensure this is to make sure your story resonates with both the reader and listener. How does the writer create such a story?

Enduring picture books must be about something bigger than a series of isolated incidents. Merely writing about Baboon leaping from tree to tree, just above sleeping Lion, has no larger truth. It's merely a string of events, a vignette, a description. The writer must have a theme, or overarching idea, to investigate. He must have something that will turn a set of incidents into a story that stays with the reader long after the book is closed.

The process of building a story is like building a house. A carpenter cannot put up walls until he builds a frame. The frame supports the roof. The frame determines the shape of the house.

Your story frame determines everything—plot, characters, ending, word usage, etc. To discover your story frame, you don't need a hammer or a saw. You don't need tools or expensive gadgets. You require only one thing, and it's free.

STORY QUESTION

It behooves writers to think of a general question about the underlying issue they're trying to unravel in each story.

Let's add something to the plot detail of Baboon swinging from tree to tree. Suppose Baboon has lost her family? Perhaps the writer could explore how she'll find them.

- Does he want to write about how the main character discovers the solution on her own? Then the story question might be *Does Baboon have the resources to find her family?*
- Does he want to explore how working together with friends—Lion, Elephant, and Giraffe—results in Baboon finding her family? Then the story question might be *Can Baboon's friends assist in finding her family?*
- Or maybe he goes in a different direction—that Baboon never finds her family but creates a new life on her own. That story question might be *Can Baboon survive on her own?* To better understand this concept, let's look at the story questions in some well-known published books.

In the popular *Where the Wild Things Are*, the general question might be *How does a child control his anger?* In *We Found a Hat* by Jon Klassen, the question could be *Will two turtles find a way to share one hat?* In *Ella and Penguin Stick Together* by Megan Maynor, the question might be *Can Ella and Penguin conquer their fear so they can enjoy their glow-in-the-dark stickers?*

There are obviously as many ways the story question can be asked as there are people asking it. Another person might word the question in *Ella and Penguin Stick Together* differently: *What happens when two friends have the same fear?* Another person might put the story question this way: *Will Ella and Penguin ever enjoy their glow-in-the-dark stickers?* These questions all pertain to the same general issue. *It's critical that each story implicitly poses a question to the reader.* If it doesn't, the story needs focus.

Notice I said "a" question. Picture books are brief, and your child audience's attention span is too short to explore more than one. Too often writers start out exploring one question and switch tracks to explore another. Don't worry that asking a question might lead to a preachy, didactic story. The question you're exploring is never written directly into your text but kept bold and bright in *your* mind. Trust that the question will be understood by your readers and listeners.

Do you need to know your story question before you start writing? Some writers do. They can't begin unless they have some idea of what they want to say. But for others, writing is a matter of discovery. The story question may not be obvious in the beginning.

That's fine, but sooner or later, you must find and be able to state this question. Your story question is crucial to keeping your writing tight and focused.

It is a set of tracks to keep your story train traveling to its destination. Otherwise, your writing runs the risk of meandering off on detours.

STORY ANSWER

Assume that you know the question you're exploring. Then it's time to answer your question in a manner specific to your story. One sentence should be all that's necessary.

Let's go back to Baboon, who finds herself separated from her family. Try to answer each of the following three questions:

1. **Does Baboon have the resources to find her family?**

   Answer: Baboon retraces her steps, using her memory and her keen senses of smell and hearing to find her family.
2. **Can Baboon's friends assist in finding her family?**

   Answer: Each of Baboon's friends uses its special powers—Lion's sense of smell, Elephant's tracking skills, and Giraffe's unique height and vision—to help Baboon find her family.
3. **Can Baboon survive on her own?**

   Answer: Baboon discovers previously unknown strengths and learns she can and will survive on her own.

What about those published books we asked questions about? What might their answers be?

1. ***Where the Wild Things Are*: How does a child control his anger?**

   Answer: A child controls his anger by mentally traveling to a safe place where he safely expresses his emotions and returns home calm, with supper waiting.
2. ***We Found a Hat*: Will two turtles find a way to share one hat?**

   Answer: Both turtles want to be the sole owner of the hat but realize that's impossible. In their dreams, they each find a way (or a place) to wear the hat.
3. ***Ella and Penguin Stick Together*: Can Ella and Penguin conquer their fear so they can enjoy their glow-in-the-dark stickers?**

   Answer: After trying to see the stickers glowing in dim lighting, they realize that they must see the stickers in complete darkness. They decide to hold hand and flipper and support one another in this endeavor.

Notice the answer is essentially a short blurb about the book. In the movie business, this is called a "pitch." If you cannot describe what happens in your story ***in one sentence***, you may have too much going on. Spend time formulating your question and answer. If you do, writing your book will be infinitely easier.

QUESTION AND ANSWER IN CONCEPT BOOKS

Some writing for children does not tell a story but explores a subject like shadows, hands, or water. We call these "concept books." Does the question-and-answer principle still apply? Absolutely, but as you can see below, the question is expressed more specifically to the book.

1. ***Weeds Find a Way*** **by Cindy Jenson-Elliott: How do weeds survive and thrive?**

   Answer: Weeds survive by sending out thousands of seeds that spread far and near and have special powers to grow in unusual and unfriendly places.
2. ***Suppose You Meet a Dinosaur: A First Book of Manners*** **by Judy Sierra: What happens when you meet a dinosaur in a grocery store?**

   Answer: When you meet a dinosaur in a grocery store, you'll have plenty of opportunities to practice your manners.
3. ***I Used to Be a Fish*** **by Tom Sullivan: Who are our ancestors?**

   Answer: Evolution explains that we started out as fish but became land animals, acquiring adaptations for our new life.

Recently, picture-book biographies have become popular with publishers, and they, too—in fact every book, fiction or nonfiction—must have a story question and answer. Here are a few examples:

1. ***Noah Webster & His Words*** **by Jeri Chase Ferris: Who is Noah Webster, and why is he important?**

   Answer: Noah Webster lived in the early days of our nation and created the first dictionary of American words.
2. ***Brave Girl: Clara and the Shirtwaist Makers' Strike of 1909*** **by Michelle Markel: Who is Clara Lemlich, and how did she make her mark?**

Answer: Clara, a young immigrant girl, organized employees in her shirtwaist factory for better pay and working conditions and led the largest strike of women workers.

3. ***The Music in George's Head: George Gershwin Creates Rhapsody in Blue* by Suzanne Slade: Who is George Gershwin, and what was the inspiration for his famous composition, *Rhapsody in Blue*?**

   Answer: The composer George Gershwin got his inspiration for his music from all types of music and sounds around him.

Whether you are writing fiction or nonfiction or exploring a concept, it's not enough to just know your question and answer. You need to keep them in mind throughout your revisions. They will help you avoid unnecessary detours. Without this map, you might start writing a story about a zebra who wants to make friends with a wildebeest and veer off on a tangent about the lion who wants to eat them both.

When I'm working on a story, I keep my question and answer in a word document on my computer so I can easily refer to it. You might prefer to tack it to a bulletin board or post a sticky note to your wall. Go through your story line by line, and delete anything that doesn't have to do with the story's question and answer. Remember how short and focused picture books must be. Your question and answer will keep you on the right track.

In my book *If Animals Said I Love You*, my question was *If animals could express love, how might they do it?* Keeping this in mind prevented me from writing about animals gathering food or being chased by predators. Those subjects, albeit interesting, had nothing to do with my question and didn't belong in my story.

MULTIPLE LEVELS IN A BOOK

Another way to appeal to your two audiences is to make sure your book has multiple levels. Books that are loved by parents and children and can be employed by teachers to illustrate concepts in the curriculum will obviously result in optimal sales. Years ago, a simple set of objects of increasing quantities was enough for a counting book—e.g., one apple, two cats, three cars, etc. Then publishing houses wanted a theme, such as fruit—one apple, two oranges, three peaches, and so on. Counting books today are required to do more.

My book *Eight Hands Round: A Patchwork Alphabet* doesn't have a story but still has several levels besides the alphabet—the history of how people lived in colonial and pioneer days, an introduction to an art form, and something that completely surprised me, a mathematical application. In addition to the different geometric shapes in the patterns, my book could be used to introduce fractions. No wonder it remained in print for over twenty-five years (that's like a century in the usual lifetime of a book).

Seven Hungry Babies by Candace Fleming includes, beyond the counting element (going backwards from seven to one), the story of the mother's increasing exhaustion from caring for her little ones, which finally spurs her to ask the father for help. That's what I mean by more than one level. Similarly, at first glance, *A Library Book for Bear* by Bonny Becker is about being open to new experiences, but because the new experience is about the treasures to be found in a library, the book has special appeal to teachers and librarians. Likewise, while *City Dog, Country Frog* by Mo Willems is a story of friendship and loss, its organization around the seasons offers an extra reason for teachers to share the book with students.

A FEW FINAL WORDS

No writer should add extra levels if they don't enrich the story. But a story with multiple levels has a better chance of a long shelf life than a story with just one. And isn't a long life what we want for our books?

WHAT'S NEXT?

Now that we've discussed how important it is to have something to say in your story, we're moving on to chapter three, the first of three chapters on determining your approach to storytelling.

BUT . . . Before you go on

1. Write a story question and answer for your manuscript. Ask a friend or fellow writer to do the same. If her question is wildly different than yours, then your writing is unclear or you're exploring something other than what you thought. Either one will force you to rethink your narrative. Once your question and answer are determined to your satisfaction, go through your story and highlight anything that does not relate. Then delete and revise.
2. Write the story questions and answers for your good and bad published books. Then print the manuscript for the bad book, and, using a pen, cross out anything that doesn't relate to that question and answer. Perhaps the reason the book doesn't work is that it doesn't answer any general question and is therefore unfocused.
3. Read a new picture book, perhaps one mentioned in this chapter.

3

Telling Your Story

Part One

> *"... the work of art as completely realized is the result of a long and complex process of exploration. ..."*
>
> —JOYCE CARY

Remember when you were young, how you loved dressing up like Little Red Riding Hood or Superman? Remember how you changed clothes to play? Maybe you put on a firefighter helmet. Maybe you wore a crown. What does playing dress-up have to do with writing picture books? A lot!

In much the same way you changed outfits, you can change your story by telling it in different ways—so many ways I've divided them into three chapters. This first covers point of view (POV). Most picture-book stories are told by an *outside* narrator who speaks of the characters using third-person pronouns such as *he, she, it*, and *they*. In a completely unscientific study of twenty-five books I've typed up since this book's first edition, the majority—seventeen—were written in third person. Five stories were told by a character who was a *participant* in the story—a first-person narrator. That adds up to twenty-three.

And the odd-duck stories? *Smile Pout-Pout Fish* by Deborah Diesen is told in the apostrophe form, where the narrator talks to something that can't talk back. We'll discuss this in the next chapter. *Suppose You Meet a Dinosaur: A First Book of Manners* by Judy Sierra is told in the second person, where the writer addresses the reader and listener. Test picture books on your shelves or in the library to see for yourself. You, too, will find most books are told by an outside narrator—in the third person.

Novelist Willa Cather said, " ... there are only two or three human stories, and they go on repeating themselves as fiercely as if they had never happened before. ..." If we accept her statement, then the only way to differentiate our writing from other stories on the same topic is to write them uniquely. Today more than ever, you *must* make your story so original it will leap into an editor's hands and shout, "Publish *me!*"

To do that, explore different ways of telling your story. You may discard each experiment and go back to your original, but, trust me; no journey is wasted in pursuit of a story.

In this and the following two chapters, we're going to play around with a familiar story by Aesop from 600 B.C.

THE ANT AND THE DOVE

> An Ant went to the bank of a river to quench its thirst and being carried away by the rush of the stream, was on the point of drowning. A Dove sitting on a tree overhanging the water plucked a leaf and let it fall into the stream close to her. The Ant climbed onto it and floated in safety to the bank. Shortly afterwards a birdcatcher came and stood under the tree and laid his lime-twigs for the Dove, which sat in the branches. The Ant, perceiving his design, stung him in the foot. In pain the birdcatcher threw down the twigs, and the noise made the Dove take wing.
>
> ONE GOOD TURN DESERVES ANOTHER.

NARRATIVE VOICE–THIRD-PERSON-LIMITED POINT OF VIEW

This story above is told in the popular, traditional form of an outside observer who relates what happens but doesn't participate in the action. Notice the narrator doesn't go into Dove's head. He starts his story with Ant and stays with her. As you've seen from my informal study, most picture books are told in this manner—by a single outside observer who goes only into the head of the main character.

Jacob's New Dress by Sarah and Ian Hoffman tells the moving story of a boy named Jacob who wants to wear a dress to his preschool. His mother is supportive, his father is slow to accept it, and one boy at school declares that boys don't wear dresses.

Jacob, though, knows what he wants and has the guts to do what feels right for him. The narrator doesn't allow us into any head but Jacob's. We know the other characters' feelings only by what Jacob hears them say. Read this book, not only for voice but for the way Jacob is an active character insisting on what he wants and solving his problems without much adult interference.

CHANGE THE POINT-OF-VIEW CHARACTER

What happens if I tell this story with Dove as the main character?

> One early morning Dove was munching seeds while sitting on the branch of a tree that overhung a river. "Help! Help!" he heard a thin voice squealing. Ant, struggling against the current, was thrashing about.
>
> Dove couldn't let her drown. Thinking quickly, he tossed down a leaf. "Climb aboard," he sang. Ant did as directed and rode safely to shore.
>
> That very afternoon, Dove was enjoying his nap when he was jarred awake by a loud scream and the sight of a birdcatcher hobbling off. Ant, the very same one he had rescued earlier, explained, "The birdcatcher was preparing a trap for you. I bit his foot, and off he ran." Dove was so grateful he sang to Ant.
>
> "I'm not your mother;
> I'm not your brother,
> but I believe one good turn
> deserves another."

This example is still told from only one point of view—Dove's. Switching main characters allowed me to expand on his role and put it in a song (a cheesy one), highlighting his singing ability.

THIRD-PERSON-OMNISCIENT (OR MULTIPLE) POINT OF VIEW

Let's see how this story might read if the narrator jumps between the heads of each character.

> Ant went to the bank of a river to quench her thirst but lost her footing and tumbled into the water. The rush of the stream was carrying her away. She was sure she was a goner.
>
> Luckily Dove was sitting on a tree branch overhanging the water and understood she was in danger. He didn't want Ant to drown,

so he plucked a leaf and dropped it close to her. Ant couldn't believe her good fortune. She climbed onto it and floated safely to the bank.

Shortly afterwards a birdcatcher came and stood under Dove's tree. The birdcatcher, dreaming of dove supper, laid his lime-twig trap. But he didn't see Ant.

A good thing too, for Ant, grateful to Dove for saving her life, wanted to return the favor. Hidden by the grass, she crept, crept, crept closer . . . closer and BIT that birdcatcher.

"Yeow!" he howled. Dove awakened with a jerk just in time to see the birdcatcher hobble away.

In this telling, I'm initially in Ant's head, but then I move to Dove's. I even spend time in the birdcatcher's head.

While older readers can easily move from one character's viewpoint to another's, picture-book listeners, who are new to books, story, and plot, may have more trouble. It's best to make the action easy for them to follow. Staying in one character's head allows the listener to know whom to focus on and identify with.

However, *Extra Yarn* by Mac Barnett is an example of a successful book told in third-person-omniscient point of view. The story starts out with Annabelle, the main character, knitting sweaters from a box of never-ending yarn. She knits sweaters for everyone and then for animals. At that point, the author peers into the minds of the townspeople, who are sure she'll run out of yarn. But she doesn't.

Annabelle knits sweaters for houses, churches, barns, and birdhouses. The author also enters the mind of a jealous archduke who tries to buy her box of yarn. When she turns him down, he hires thieves to steal it. You'll have to read the book to find out what happens next. Being a knitter myself, this book appealed to me, but non-knitters will enjoy it, too. It has the feel of an old tale, and the illustrations won Jon Klassen a Caldecott Honor.

FIRST-PERSON, OR THE LYRICAL VOICE

In this point of view, the narrator is one of the story's participants. *I* and *we* are the key words that let you know you're in a first-person story. What happens when our story is told by Ant?

Danger was the farthest thing from my mind. I was at the bank of a river and thirsty, so I leaned down for a drink. *Splash!* Into the wa-

> ter I fell, and the rushing current carried me away from shore. "Help! Help!" I cried, but we ants are small in body and in voice. No one could hear me. I was a goner for sure.
>
> Lucky for me, Dove was sitting on a branch overhanging the water and tossed me a leaf. I grabbed it, climbed aboard, and floated to shore. Was I grateful?
>
> You bet, and soon I had a chance to show it. A birdcatcher came to Dove's tree and started making a trap for him out of lime-twigs. Time for action!
>
> I stung him badly on the foot. "OWWWWWWWWWWWW!" he howled. The noise warned Dove, who took flight and was saved. Just goes to show that one good turn deserves another.

With this first-person perspective, listeners experience the action and emotion along with Ant. They get into her head and feel her gratitude for her narrow escape. The story's tone changes.

If I'm having trouble getting into my character's head, I write a version in this voice to get to know her better. Perhaps I'll like it and leave it in the lyrical voice, but I may rewrite it again in third person. Either way, my experimentation wasn't wasted because I gained a deeper understanding of my character's feelings.

However, first person has drawbacks. Telling your story this way doesn't allow you an opportunity to write about offstage actions. The main character—the *I*-writer—must be on every page. Also, telling it in this manner lets the reader know that the narrator survives. We might not know in what state, but we're certain he lived to tell the tale.

Check out *Ralph Tells a Story* by Abby Hanlon. Ralph's teacher tells him that stories are everywhere. His classmates always find them, and although Ralph tries and tries, he fails to come up with a story. Since the book is narrated by Ralph, we feel his pain and suffer with him. More importantly, we rejoice in his success when he finally does tell a story.

Now I'm going to tell the story again in first person, but with the birdcatcher as the narrator. Here's the opening:

> I woke this morning with a longing for dove stew. Delicious, delightful, delectable dove stew. I'm not one for inaction. Not me. I gathered string and lime-twigs and set off to make my dream a reality.

You can see how if you wrote this to the end, it wouldn't be the story we started with. That change is what we're after, something to liven up a tired and much-told tale. First-person voices may take several different forms, including letters and journal/diary entries.

One long letter

Dear Mother,

So much has happened since I left your nest, I had to write. Thank you for teaching me to not ignore those in need. Yesterday, I was sitting on a branch in the loveliest of trees, minding my business, enjoying the breeze. The peace was broken by squeals from the stream below. A poor ant was struggling to swim to shore, but the current was too strong. I couldn't swoop down and pluck her from the water. My beak might have broken her in two, so I came up with an alternate plan. I plucked a leaf from the tree and tossed it down. The ant had just enough energy to pull herself aboard and float to safety.

That might have been the end of the story, but after she'd dried off, caught her breath, and calmed down, along came a birdcatcher. I remember your lesson about flying away from those nasty people, and I would have, but I was dozing and didn't realize he was setting a trap for me. Luckily that birdcatcher was wearing sandals. Even luckier for me that ant was nearby and knew exactly what was up! She bit that birdcatcher's foot! I'd be surprised if you couldn't hear his scream from where you live. You can bet it startled me. Off I flew, and off the birdcatcher hopped, clutching his foot, moaning in pain.

I'm so thankful you taught me that we eat seeds, not insects. If that ant hadn't been around to save me, I shudder to think what would have happened. For one thing, you certainly wouldn't be reading this letter.

Your Loving Son,

Featherly

My favorite example of a published book told in a single letter is *Nettie's Trip South* by Ann Turner. In this compelling story, Nettie writes to her friend Addie about her experiences visiting the South just before the Civil War. Among other incidents, she describes attending a slave auction and the horror of watching two young children being separated. She returns home forever changed. Although this book was published in 1987, it remains in print. I urge you to read this beautiful and poignant story.

A more contemporary book that takes the form of one letter is *Love, Mouserella* by David Ezra Stein, where a little mouse writes her grandmother a letter about all she's done since her grandmother returned to her home in the country.

Journal or diary

Monday
Dear Diary,

What an exciting day! If it hadn't been for me, there would have been one less ant in this world. I was minding my own business on a low tree branch overhanging a river when I heard the tiniest of screams from an ant splashing in the water, struggling to reach shore. It was easy to see if no one helped her, she would drown. But no one rushed to the rescue. Where were her mom and dad? Her cries grew more frantic, so I tugged a fat maple leaf off of the tree and tossed it down. That ant had just enough strength to pull herself up onto the leaf and float to shore. She was one grateful ant and thanked me profusely.

Friday
Dear Diary,

Remember that ant I wrote about? Now I'm the one who's grateful and thanking her profusely. Here's why:

I was dozing on my tree branch when a horrific howling awakened me just in time to see that birdcatcher, the bane of my existence, clutching his foot and hopping away. I had no idea what to make of this crazy behavior until the ant I'd dropped the leaf to scampered up the tree trunk and explained how she'd stopped that mean man from laying a trap for me: She bit his foot! Good thing the birdcatcher was wearing sandals and good thing the ant knew this was my tree. I'd saved her, so she saved me.

Diary of a Spider by Doreen Cronin is written in diary form and is a great follow-up to her earlier success, *Diary of a Worm*. Now let's be a bit more daring with the story.

SECOND PERSON

The word *you* is a clue here. Using *you*, the author invites the reader into the story. This is how Aesop's fable might read if written in second person:

> If you saw your neighbor's dog tangled up in its leash, what would you do?
>
> I hope you'd rush to its rescue.
>
> Why?
>
> Because someday maybe that dog could help you. And that day might come as soon as the very next day.
>
> You'll hear that dog bark, bark, barking and after you get over your annoyance at the noise, you'll go outside and see smoke coming out of your trash can. You'll grab a hose and spray out the fire. And you'll know it really is true that one good turn deserves another.

Notice here, I took the story in a completely different direction, getting rid of the dove and the ant and inserting a dog. That's the fun of experimenting. Your story can fly off to places you'd never imagined even though the new version was always where it was supposed to be.

Suppose You Meet a Dinosaur makes use of this point of view, but you don't need to look further than the If You Give a ... series written by Laura Numeroff: *If You Give a Mouse a Brownie, If You Give a Cat a Cupcake, If You Give a Dog a Donut, If You Give a Moose a Muffin*, and on and on. In each of these, the author talks to the reader. Check out at least one of them to see how involving this form of inviting the listener to participate in the action can be.

In all the retellings, notice I didn't switch the voice midstory. This would confuse our young audience. They wouldn't know who the main character was or with whom to identify. Once you start a picture book in one point of view, stick to it.

QUIZ TIME

You've read ways to change how you tell your story. Let's make sure you recognize the voices covered here—third-person limited, third-person omniscient, first-person lyrical, one long letter (first person), diary/journal (first person), and second person. On a separate piece of paper, write the point of view that you think matches each of these examples.

1. When Jimmy arrived at school, he was surprised to find the doors locked.
2. February 1

   Today my dog, Willie, died.

   February 2

   Today I drew a picture of Willie so I'll never forget him.
3. Do you want to be a cat? Easy. All you have to do is get down on all fours and purr. Nap on a windowsill. Squeeze into a closet. All fun things until you have to eat. Mouse might not be your favorite lunch.
4. If only I could fly like a bird.
5. Lora wishes she didn't have a younger sister. Emma wishes she weren't the younger sister. She'd love to be big like Lora.
6. Dear Steve,

   Why did you have to tell the teacher that I copied your homework?
7. Have you ever baked a cake?
8. Dear Diary,

   I hope I never have another day like today.
9. On my way to Grandma's house, I ran into a wolf. He seemed friendly, but I didn't trust him.
10. Piglet snuffled about the garbage, searching eagerly for banana peels and orange rinds.
11. Pete loves broccoli. Sue hates broccoli but loves carrots. Lena loves any vegetable.

ANSWERS: 1. third-person limited 2. diary (first person) 3. second person 4. first-person lyrical 5. third-person omniscient 6. one long letter (first person) 7. second person 8. diary (first person) 9. first-person lyrical 10. third-person limited 11. third-person omniscient

A FEW FINAL WORDS

Isn't it interesting to see how changing the point of view can affect a story so markedly? I hope you'll experiment with this in your story and in any future stories you write.

WHAT'S NEXT?

We've tried out several basic writing voices here. Now it's time to go wild. In chapter four we're going to consider more unusual and dramatic ways to write your story.

BUT . . . Before you go on

1. Rewrite your story's opening paragraph in at least three of these different forms. If you have time, do all of them.

    a. Third-person limited
    b. Third-person, different point-of-view character
    c. Third-person omniscient
    d. First-person lyrical
    e. First-person lyrical, different point-of-view character
    f. One long letter (first person)
    g. Diary or journal (first person)
    h. Second person

    While you're writing, let your imagination soar.
2. Do you like one of these new voices? Then write your story through to the end. But if you're not thrilled with any, don't be discouraged. Turn the page, and see how else you can tell your story.
3. Read a new picture book, perhaps one mentioned in this chapter.

4

Telling Your Story

Part Two

"In baseball you only get three swings and you're out. In rewriting, you get almost as many swings as you want and you know, sooner or later, you'll hit the ball."

—NEIL SIMON

In the last chapter, we covered some basic ways to tell a story, and you experimented with a few of them in your manuscript. Maybe you liked one and continued to write in that voice. Good. But maybe nothing improved your story or took it in a direction you felt comfortable with. Don't give up. As Neil Simon describes above, writers get as many chances as they want or need to perfect their work. In this chapter, we'll look at three dramatic voices you may use to change your story and make it more enticing to that hard-to-please editor.

APOSTROPHE VOICE

In this voice, the writer speaks to something in the story that can't speak back. Let's see what happens when I try this in Aesop's fable.

> You've seen a lot of action recently. First poor Ant being carried down the stream. Thank heavens Dove saw what was happening and acted quickly. If he hadn't torn off one of your leaves and tossed it to Ant, she never would have been able to ride it to shore. They're both grateful to you for your leaf boat.
>
> Later, when that birdcatcher was setting his trap right next to your trunk, you knew what he was after but couldn't help. You must have been relieved that Ant stung his foot and foiled his plan. I'll bet Dove will happily settle forever in the safety of your tree.

I can attest to how this can give new life to a story. In my book *Hello Toes! Hello Feet!*, the first few (okay, I admit it, many) versions were told in third person. Here's the opening:

> These are Jon's toes.
> These are Jon's feet,
> tangled up between his sheets.
> First his feet touch the floor.
> They hop him to the closet door.

The manuscript was done, but I had a niggling feeling the story fell flat. When I expressed my misgivings to my writing group, someone suggested I experiment with having the main character (who was my son Jon) talk to his feet. A lightbulb flashed in my head.

I rushed home and changed the opening:

> Good morning, toes,
> Good morning, feet,
> tangled up between
> my sheets.
> Be the first to touch the floor,
> hop me to the closet door.

Then I wrote in that voice all the way to the end. It worked! The manuscript suddenly became vibrant, and my editor agreed.

The one thing my editor and I differed on was the character's gender. The illustrator, Nadine Bernard Westcott, made her a spunky girl who had a closetful of fun shoes. That's the joy of collaboration. Other people take your words and guide them in new directions. Although I was sad to leave Jon behind, I'm thrilled with how the book came out. Experimenting with different approaches can make a dull story shine. Look at the mini board book *Smile, Pout-Pout Fish* by Deborah Diesen, where the narrator speaks to the fish, wondering why he's so glum. Because it ends with a kiss, it's perfect for our tiniest listeners. Another fun book in the apostrophe voice is *Nellie Belle* by the multitalented Mem Fox. Here the narrator poses questions to a dog who never replies.

I've never seen a writer use the apostrophe voice to talk to more than one character, probably because doing so might confuse young listeners. In picture books, keep this voice simple, and talk to the same character or object throughout the story.

MASK VOICE

In this voice, the narrator becomes an inanimate object, like a tree, desk, or bed, and tells the story from that object's point of view. Writing in this voice has a tendency to unleash one's imagination. No one, for example, knows how a tree feels when it rains, so one can play it for all it's worth. Let's try this voice with our Aesop fable.

> Come, all you creatures. Come live near me. My branches are resting stops for birds. My leaves are boats for ants, and my seeds are food for squirrels. Come, all you creatures. Come live with me.

This voice can be tricky because if the tree is humanized (presumably with a mouth for speaking, plus eyes and ears) the pictures could border on cute, which we want to avoid. Another problem is that an inanimate object like a tree, skyscraper, or bridge usually remains stationary, so the writer can't talk about anything beyond its view, leading to static illustrations.

That said, I urge you to check out *School's First Day of School* by Adam Rex. While this story is not strictly mask voice (it's told in third person by an outside narrator), it stays in the school's mind. We know School's fears about what will happen when students and teachers arrive. We sense School's wonder when he discovers what different parts of him are for and his distress when some children don't like him. This book received numerous starred reviews.

Another book told in third person that delves into the thoughts of an inanimate object is *The Tree in the Courtyard* by Jeff Gottesfeld.

In true mask voice, however, the story would be told in first person and the inanimate object would be the narrator. For example, *Rivers of Sunlight: How the Sun Moves Water Around the Earth* by Molly Bang and Penny Chisholm is narrated by the sun.

Trying out new voices in your story is never a waste of time. Any experimentation you do will enrich your vision. You will be forced to think outside the box, and that can make your story different, distinctive, and saleable.

CONVERSATION VOICE

Exactly as it implies, this voice is nothing more than a conversation between two characters. There's no narrative description, no speaker attribution. It can be between two persons, two animals (assuming they can talk), or between a person and an animal, as long as you write nothing but dialogue.

Pretend Ant and Dove can speak to one another.

> Help! I'm drowning! Help!
>
>   <u>Stay calm, Ant.</u>
>
> Help!
>
>   <u>I'll toss you this leaf. Grab hold!</u>
>
> Got it!
>
>   <u>Hold tight!</u>
>
> I'm scared!
>
>   <u>You'll be fine. Just ride it to shore.</u>
>
> How can I thank you, Dove?
>
>   <u>No need, Ant.</u>
>
> Oh, but I must! One good turn always deserves another.

I like this version because it feels more dramatic. Who knows if that would continue? Maybe problems might appear farther along.

Notice how I differentiated them by underlining Dove's words. In published books, you might see one character's dialogue indented or one character's lines done in normal text and the other's in italics.

When using the conversational voice, keep the different voices distinct. In the above example, Dove is calm throughout. On the other hand, Ant is frantic—as would be natural if one were almost drowning. Each voice must ring true to the character and help define her.

I Don't Want to Be a Pea! by Ann Bonwill is a conversation between Hugo, a hippo, and Bella, a bird. They're planning their costumes for the Fairy Tale Fancy Dress Party. Hugo wants them to go as the Princess and the Pea, but Bella objects because she would be the pea. As they try to come up with an alternative costume, tension increases. This book is well worth reading to see how successful this voice can be.

CORRESPONDENCE BETWEEN TWO CHARACTERS

Letters between two characters is another form of the conversation voice.

> Dear Dove,

I can't thank you enough for tossing me that leaf today. It wasn't the comfiest raft, but it served its purpose. You saved my life.

Dear Ant,

It is I who must thank you. If you hadn't stung that birdcatcher, I would have been trapped, de-feathered, poached, and served up on a platter. Why don't you climb up to my nest and hang out someday? Anyone who saves my life will be my friend forever.

In this tight construction, scenes are summarized and dialogue is compressed because that's what we naturally do in letters.

When creating a correspondence, concentrate on making each letter true to its respective character's voice, and as we do in writing conversation, make each voice sound unique.

My Favorite Pets: by Gus W. for Ms. Smolinski's Class by Jeanne Birdsall takes this correspondence form and turns it into a class report. Gus's report takes up 90 percent of the book. The teacher's response comes on the last page, when she gives him a grade. Gus's voice comes through strongly and clearly; it is humorous and delightful.

Dear Dragon by Josh Funk is a story mostly told through rhyming letters. For a class project, George begins corresponding with a pen pal, who, much to his surprise, turns out to be a dragon. A fun read!

QUIZ TIME

Here's another short quiz to see how well you can identify the apostrophe, mask, and conversation voices.

1. I am Car. Open my door; settle down in my seat. Make yourself comfortable. I will take you wherever you want to travel.
2. Chair, sitting forever by the window, what sights you must have seen! Do you ever wish you could get up and move to a new window?
3. Why haven't you handed in your homework?

   My dog ate my homework. Ripped it into a zillion pieces.

   Don't think I haven't heard that excuse before.
4. Dog, why must you always bark at me? I'm the one who walks you, who feeds you, who bathes you. Why can't you be still?
5. I am the shoe you slip on each morning. If I had a nose, I would hold it because your feet stink.

6. Please open the door.

    Open it yourself.

7. Telephone, why must you ring just as I'm sitting down to write? Couldn't you wait until I finish this chapter?
8. Dear Jon,

    Can you believe the latest news?

        Dear Steve,

        Sadly, nothing surprises me now.

ANSWERS: 1. mask 2. apostrophe 3. conversation 4. apostrophe (in this story the dog cannot talk) 5. mask 6. conversation 7. apostrophe 8. correspondence between two characters

A FEW FINAL WORDS

Experimenting with these different dramatic voices can open your eyes to new story possibilities. Any voice you try will enrich and enliven your vision. Perhaps one of them will cause a blip in your heart that seems to say "Perfect!" Follow that one to the end. The result will lift your story out of the ordinary and create something so unusual and compelling that an editor will see your potential and perhaps offer to publish it.

WHAT'S NEXT?

I hope you've had fun experimenting with these unique approaches to writing your story, but you're not done yet. In chapter five we'll look at ways to open up new illustration possibilities. In addition, we'll consider what happens when you change your story's tense.

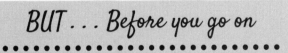

BUT . . . Before you go on

1. Rewrite the opening paragraph of your story in at least three of the following forms:
    a. Apostrophe
    b. Mask

c. Conversation
d. Correspondence between two characters

2. Do you like any of these? If so, rewrite your entire story.
3. Read a new picture book, perhaps one mentioned in this chapter.

5

Telling Your Story

Part Three

"Imagination is more important than knowledge."

—ALBERT EINSTEIN

The more you consider all the routes your storytelling might take, the more likely you are to create a unique and enduring book. Here are a few more options to weigh. Which may be the key(s) to realizing your vision?

CHANGING TENSES

PAST TENSE

We can see from the first sentence in the original version of Aesop's fable (*An Ant went to the bank of a river to quench its thirst and being carried away by the rush of the stream, was on the point of drowning*), that it is written in past tense. One of my favorite recently published picture books that uses past tense is the charming *Sophie's Squash* by Pat Zietlow Miller. Sophie and her mom purchased a squash at the local farmers' market. Her mom planned to cook it for supper. Sophie had a different plan, with funny and tender moments.

Another story that employs this tense is *The Kite that Bridged Two Nations* by Alexis O'Neill. It is a dramatic and lyrically told nonfiction story about how a boy and his kite helped build a bridge across Niagara Falls.

PRESENT TENSE

Let's experiment with Aesop's fable again. How does the reading experience change if we rewrite it in present tense?

> Ant, desperate for a drink, goes to the bank of a river to satisfy her thirst. Oh, oh! She tumbles into the water. "Help!" she cries, struggling against the current. "Help me!"

> Dove, sitting on a tree branch overhanging the water, plucks a leaf and tosses it down. Ant thrashes, trying to grab it.

Writing in present tense can make your story more immediate. The action unfolds as one reads each line. This increases the drama because the reader and listener are living each event along with the characters and no one knows what the ending will be.

There's a Bear on My Chair by Ross Collins is a delightful story told in rhyme by a mouse who wants a bear to leave his chair. The mouse struggles to push the bear off, glares nastily at him, tempts him with a snack, and tries to scare him—all to no avail. Because these events happen as we read them, we share the experience with the mouse, feel his frustration, and sympathize with his despair.

If you think all historical picture books are written in past tense, think again. Michelle Markel turns that logic upside down in *Brave Girl: Clara and the Shirtwaist Makers' Strike of 1909.* Although the events took place in the early 1900s, the book is written from beginning (when the ship carrying our heroine pulls into the harbor) to end (when she determines to keep fighting for workers' rights) in present tense.

Dot. by Randi Zuckerberg is another story told in present tense. Dot knows a lot about computers and keyboards, smartphones, and e-readers, but when her mother sends her outside, she discovers other pleasures.

I also love the gentle telling of *I'm New Here* by Anne Sibley O'Brien. This present-tense story concerns the challenges three children from different countries face as they try to adjust to American culture and a new school.

FUTURE TENSE

Writing Aesop's fable in future tense gives it a decidedly different feel than the past- and present-tense versions.

> When Ant grows thirsty, she'll hurry to the river bank. She'll lean down for a drink. Oh, oh! A wave will lift her off her feet and carry her into the water. Will anyone save her?

Your Alien by Tammi Sauer is a fun picture book that employs future tense and second person. This story tells us what will happen if an alien lands near your house and you take him home and have adventures. The future tense allows for some emotional distance from the actions of the story. It's safer if it hasn't happened yet.

CHANGE YOUR STORY'S TIME PERIOD

If your story is set in present day, you could move it to some time in the past. The original "The Ant and the Dove" is already set in the distant past. What would happen if I moved it to the present?

> Ant quenching her thirst at a lake paused to watch a motorboat speed by. Its wake splashed her into the water. Without a life jacket, she was in big trouble. Why hadn't she ever taken swimming lessons at her local Y?

Setting it in a different time creates all new picture possibilities. Remember: It's not enough to just change the time. The writer must integrate the aspects of this different world into the text.

We could also set this story in the future.

> Ant had never seen anything like this—a driverless boat! She was so shocked she didn't notice the boat was heading right towards her. Its computer must have been broken. She screamed, but nothing came out of her tiny mouth. Fortunately for her, Dove up in a tree saw everything. He grabbed his laser and zapped the boat, splintering it into millions of pieces.

What about setting your contemporary story in colonial times? Earlier we talked about adding levels to a story. A manuscript based in a specific historical period, if written well and accurately, could not only be a compelling story but could be used by teachers when their students study that era.

One example of this would be *The Great Moon Hoax* by Stephen Krensky. The book's theme about the power of words could apply to any time and could have been approached any number of ways, but the author chose to base his story on an actual event that occurred in 1835.

CHANGE YOUR STORY'S LOCATION

Let's see what happens if we relocate Ant to a city.

> Ant was minding her own business, strolling across the walk, when a bike came speeding down the concrete. Directly at her!
>
> Dove swooped down from his place high on a traffic light.
>
> Startled by the frantically flapping bird, the cyclist swerved, just missing Ant. When Ant could finally stop trembling from her near-squashing, she asked Dove, "How can I ever thank you?"
>
> "No need," Dove cooed. "Just pay it forward."

Any relocation will require research to create an authentic setting, but the time may be well spent since such a change can transform your story from ordinary to extraordinary.

You're probably familiar with the old song "Old MacDonald Had a Farm." In Rachel Isadora's book *Old Mikamba Had a Farm*, she moves the farmer character to Africa. Now instead of the sounds of a cow, a horse, and a pig, we have the bleat of a giraffe, the grunt of a hippo, and the snort of a warthog, plus glorious pictures of an exotic location.

Antoinette Portis turns the typical friendship story upside down in *Best Frints in the Whole Universe* by situating the two friends on planet Boborp. The friends are space creatures named Omek and Yelfred. Antoinette must have had great fun making up words for the alien culture depicted in this book. It's a good example of a rather common story line that was made utterly charming by changing the location. But we're not yet done with ways to make your story stand out in this competitive field.

CHANGE HUMAN CHARACTERS INTO ANIMALS OR ANIMALS INTO PEOPLE

In the "The Ant and the Dove," what would happen if I changed Ant into a little boy named Billy and Dove into a teenager named Sam who lives across the street?

> Sam barely nods hello to Billy until the day Billy trips and falls. Sam hears his cries and rushes outside. He cleans Billy's scabbed knee and puts on a Superman bandage. Billy thanks him profusely and promises to do something to help him.
>
> Sam snickers at the idea, but at that very moment, the girl of his dreams walks by. Sam is tongue-tied but not Billy. This girl is his swim-

ming teacher, and they start talking about ways to improve his free-style form, a style that he knows Sam is great at. ...

You can imagine some possible directions this snippet might be headed. It tells a different story than the fable but retains its thematic core. However, when writing picture books, it may be a good idea to use animal characters instead of people. Why?

DISTANCE FROM EMOTIONAL ISSUES

Animal characters allow your listeners to semi-remove themselves from threatening and scary issues presented in the story while still, on some level, facing them. That bit of distance is sometimes useful in helping children overcome emotional obstacles. A fine recent example is *Little Bot and Sparrow* by Jake Parker. Instead of two humans, a robot and sparrow become friends and have adventures together, but they must part ways when the sparrow flies away at the first snow. Similarly, children sometimes must say goodbye to friends who move away or go to a new school. Such difficult transitions can be relived and relieved through a story because it's happening to someone else, which makes them feel less alone in their struggles. Just as important, the listener can learn how the characters survived a situation that is much like his own.

UNIQUE ILLUSTRATIONS

Another reason to switch to animal (or nonhuman) characters is that it allows for imaginative illustrations. I adore the robot in *Little Bot and Sparrow.*

ANIMALS ARE RACIALLY NEUTRAL

They belong to all races and nationalities. In the current environment of attention to diversity, this can be a definite positive. On the other hand, you don't have to make all your characters animals or all humans. In *Ella and Penguin Stick Together,* Megan Maynor chose to pair a human with a penguin, which made for interesting and charming illustrations.

A FEW FINAL WORDS

You can change the verb tense, time period, or location of your story. You can even change the characters from people to animals or vice versa. But as I'm typing this, I've thought of other ways to tell a story ... as a newspaper article, recipe cards, e-mails, or text messages. The possibilities are limited only by your imagination.

Experiment with your story because ordinary works cannot make it in this world of expensive paper and printing, increased competition, and publishing-house cutbacks. You must make your manuscript so distinctive that an editor will forget financial concerns and shout, "YES! YES! YES!"

WHAT'S NEXT?

Now that you know many different ways you can tell your story, let's turn to your characters. Are they flat or three-dimensional? How do you create characters children will remember all their lives?

BUT . . . Before you go on

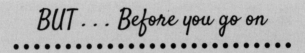

1. Experiment with at least three more ways of telling your story. Write the opening paragraph of each iteration.
    a. Change the time period.
    b. Change the location.
    c. Change the verb tense.
    d. Change your characters to animals or vice versa.
2. If any versions pique your interest, rewrite the entire manuscript.
3. Read a new picture book, perhaps one mentioned in this chapter.

6

Darlings, Demons, or a Mixture of Both

Creating Compelling Characters

"You can never know enough about your characters."
—W. SOMERSET MAUGHAM

Remember when you were the one listening to picture books? Which were your favorites? Did any have a character that continues to live on in your mind?

The best characters stay with readers and listeners long after childhood—like Ferdinand from *The Story of Ferdinand* by Munro Leaf, Peter from *The Tale of Peter Rabbit* by Beatrix Potter, and Madeline from her eponymous book by Ludwig Bemelmans. These characters' books remain in print and have been regarded with warmth and affection for generations. Sometimes people even name a child after a favorite storybook character.

I still conjure up the picture of Ferdinand sitting under the cork tree, Peter Rabbit sneaking into Mr. McGregor's garden, and small, forlorn Madeline in her bed at the orphanage. My children remember how Frances (from *Bedtime for Frances* by Russell Hoban) was terrified of the *thump, thump* of the butterfly's wings on her window and how Curious George (from *Curious George Gets a Medal* by Margret and H.A. Rey) frantically cleaned the ink mess before his friend, the man with the yellow hat, returned. They still laugh over Rotten Ralph (from the book of the same name by Jack Gantos) sawing off the branch that held the swing with his loving owner in it!

Now we have a generation of readers in love with David (from *No, David!* by David Shannon), who day and night hears nothing but "No!" They identify with Olivia (from the book of the same name by Ian Falconer), whose energy wears out everyone, even herself. My granddaughter loves playing dress-up like Nancy in *Fancy Nancy* by Jane O'Connor. These children will grow up to share their special books with their sons and daughters.

No doubt, you have your own favorites. Look again at these memorable picture-book characters. Think about the qualities that make them stick in the minds of picture-book readers and listeners long after the book is closed.

IMPORTANT ATTRIBUTES IN A MAIN CHARACTER

SOMEONE YOU CARE ABOUT

I like a character who follows her dreams without regard for what others think. Wasn't it wonderful how Ferdinand refused to fight the bulls? He gave me confidence to stand up for my convictions. Perhaps you're fond of a character like Ella in *Ella and Penguin Stick Together*, who tries to overcome her fear of dark places. In nonfiction you may admire Clara Lemlich of *Brave Girl: Clara and the Shirtwaist Makers' Strike of 1909*, who insists on being treated fairly.

LIKEABLE

It's hard to feel compassion for a bully. Who wants to read about someone who tries to make others feel small? We root for Jacob in *Jacob's New Dress* by Sarah and Ian Hoffman. Jacob wants to wear a dress, no matter what others think. Do we cheer for his classmate who mocks and makes fun of him? No.

However, a bully with a redeeming trait can turn into a sympathetic character. Big Mean Mike, who stars in the book of the same name by Michelle Knudsen, roughly expels the sweet, fuzzy rabbits who invade his car, but when push comes to shove and his big mean friends make fun of them, he comes to the rabbits' defense, showing a soft and affectionate side.

A CHILD OR A CHILDLIKE ADULT OR ANIMAL

It is wise to make your characters children or somehow childlike because this will make them more relatable to young readers/listeners. For instance, Peter Rabbit is basically a child with fur. In *A Library Book for Bear* by Bonny Becker, Bear is a child in disguise, afraid of new experiences.

In *We Found a Hat* by Jon Klassen, the two turtles, both longing for the same thing, must work out a way to share, just as children do. In *Chicken Lily* by Lori Mortensen, a chicken stands in for every child who's shy.

IMPERFECT

We *all* have flaws. Our characters must have flaws, too. Like Peter Rabbit, haven't we disobeyed our parents? Don't most parents still love their children, no matter what? And haven't we all misbehaved so much that we've heard, "No! No! No!" like David?

Think about your imperfections. For example, when it comes to writing, I'm driven. That drive compels me to sit at my computer every day. It prods me to rarely give up on a story, and it insists I keep learning my craft. I see my drive as a strength, but maybe my husband doesn't and wishes I'd spend more time with him. Moreover, when my kids were young, they might have seen my drive as selfish, especially when I wasn't thrilled to help with their studies, drive them to soccer practice, or bake cookies for their swim meets.

Think about others' imperfections, particularly those that annoy you. My mother would hold in her anger, so I never felt sure where I stood with her. On the other hand, sometimes people's imperfections are endearing. I have a soft spot for anyone who suffers from shyness.

Often, as with my drive/selfishness, the strength and weakness are two sides of the same issue. In *A Balloon for Isabel* by Deborah Underwood, Isabel's persistence gets her into trouble with her teacher, but that quality also helps her find a solution to her problem. Whatever the specifics, the main characters in our picture books must be human, and that means they must be imperfect.

CONSISTENT AND BELIEVABLE

Your characters are not robots that have computer-driven behavior. Their actions should not be determined by plot or your whims. Suppose you've written about a shy character who stands at the back of a crowd, letting others lead the way. One day, for no apparent reason, that shy girl storms to the front of the class and leads a march, demanding chocolate cake in the cafeteria every day. This *might* work if we saw her change along the way by slowly and subtly becoming bolder and more extroverted; otherwise, it feels completely out of character. Lily in *Chicken Lily* is terrified by the idea of standing in front of the class and reciting a poem. But something else scares her more—standing up without a poem. That fear spurs her to action.

ASSERTIVE AND RESOLUTE, NOT PASSIVE

Most memorable lead characters are people of conviction who take control of their lives; they do not simply allow life to happen to them. These traits make them inspirational to readers. Even Ferdinand's act of sitting and refusing to fight was one of assertiveness and resolve because he took a stand for what mattered to him.

In *Sophie's Squash,* Sophie insists the squash she picked out at the farmers' market is her friend. She will not let her parents cook it. She holds it, bounces it, and rocks it to sleep. She covers the squash's ears so it won't hear bad things, and she defends it when kids at the library make fun of it. When her squash grows splotchy, she asks for advice from the farmer who sold it to her. Then she follows his instructions.

The narrator in *Happy Like Soccer* by Maribeth Boelts is another good example of the assertive and resolute main character. When the one soccer game her aunt could attend is rained out, Sierra takes action. She calls her soccer coach late one night to ask if they could play the next game at a park nearer to where she lives and on a day her aunt isn't working.

A PROBLEM-SOLVER

Doesn't it bother you if someone says "You should do it this way," especially when you haven't asked for advice? All day long, teachers, babysitters, parents, siblings, grandparents, relatives, or neighbors are telling children what to do.

Successful parents let children struggle to solve manageable problems. These small triumphs enable their children to confidently take on tasks that are more grown-up. When the characters in our stories solve their problems (in appropriate, childlike ways), we send an empowering message to our young listeners. In *Happy Like Soccer,* the narrator comes up with the idea of calling her coach. In *Sophie's Squash,* Sophie asks the farmer what to do and plants her squash. Although she hopes this will make her squash better, she's happily surprised when two new squashes appear in the summer.

To sum up, we want our characters in our stories to be:

1. someone the reader cares about
2. likeable
3. a child, or a childlike adult, or animal
4. an imperfect character
5. someone who behaves in consistent and believable ways
6. assertive and resolute; active, not passive
7. a problem-solver

Sound easy?

If it were, we would all write stories that editors would snap up, and each of our published books would become bestsellers. Unfortunately, creating compelling characters takes time and thought.

CREATING MEMORABLE CHARACTERS

We must *know our characters inside and out*. It's not enough to have a general image of a character when you start writing. I learned this the hard way. *Who,* I thought, *wants to spend time composing a character study? Better to just write the story.*

Wrong!

When working with my editor, Melanie Kroupa, on *Everything to Spend the Night,* she asked if I'd made a character study of the little girl. I said, "Yes," but she probably sensed the tentativeness in my voice and asked me to send it to her. I quickly wrote two or three sentences and e-mailed them to her. She called back immediately. "That's not enough."

I returned to my computer and wrote an in-depth character study that consumed several pages. Only then did I discover my character loved to play games, was full of energy, and was thrilled to be at Grandpa's house. Once I had my character firmly in my mind, rewriting was easy. I knew she would pack jacks, puzzles, and drums in her bag. She was imaginative and would bring lots of things to play queen. Although I always pack books when I go away, my character was too active for that. I was sad that the story could not end with the little girl and Grandpa reading together. However, I often autograph *Everything to Spend the Night* with "Always pack a book," and now you know why.

Completing that character study was valuable because it gave me the nudge I needed to get in the habit of doing them. So many things that first appear complicated turn out to be easy and fun. When creating a character, you get to play God. This child, bear, or bunny is entirely yours. Granted, forming well-rounded characters takes time, but it's not as much as you'd think, and it is time well spent.

Sometimes I do my character study first, but in other instances I wait until I've finished a first draft. Then I pause, fill out my character study, and revise with the character's personality and backstory firmly in my mind. Either way, the critical thing is to do a study *sometime.*

I make studies for each character in my story, but don't panic! For a minor character who speaks only a few lines, just knowing one strong personality trait is enough. But how do I make the study for my main character?

I fill in the information called for on a form I keep in my computer. It's simple, gleaned from many lists I've read in books or suggestions I've heard at conferences. Most of these lists were unduly long and too detailed for a picture-book character, so I condensed mine to five key components.

FIVE THINGS YOU NEED FOR YOUR PICTURE-BOOK CHARACTER

1. **NAME**

Names should be word pictures of the character. Michelle Knudsen named her character Big Mean Mike. Would Big Mean Joshua carry the same impact? What kind of character might you name Amanda, which comes from Latin and means "worthy of love"? Would you name a happy-go-lucky child Miriam, which has origins in Hebrew and means "sea of sorrow, or bitterness"?

What type of character might have a hard-sounding name like Curt? What personality might a boy need in order to be named Misha, with its soft sounds? Or should you defy expectations and name the gentle character Curt and the tough guy Misha? I'm working on a story about dogs. I had fun naming the dalmatian Blaze and the chihuahua Thimble.

While discussing names, here's the fastest way to get your story noticed by an editor for the *wrong* reasons: giving your characters alliterative names, like I did in one of my earlier stories. What I did not realize was that naming characters like Sammy Skunk and Billy Beaver shouts "cute" and "lack of respect for the child listener" and makes it easy for the editor to drop your story in the form-rejection-letter pile or not even bother with a response.

What is the matter with calling your characters Skunk and Beaver? In *Mañana, Iguana* my characters are named Iguana, Tortuga (Spanish for "turtle"), Culebra ("snake"), and Conejo ("rabbit"). Imagine if I'd named them Ida Iguana, Tommy Tortuga, Cathy Culebra, and Connie Conejo!

A good rule of thumb is to simply call the animals what they are (e.g., Bear, Mouse, Duck, Frog, and Mole), which Phillip C. Stead does in his book *Bear Has a Story to Tell.* Or give the animal a single human name like Lori Mortensen does in her book *Chicken Lily.* Throughout the book she just goes by Lily. Not only is she truly a chicken, but she also is *chicken*, i.e., shy, about writing and reciting a poem.

Also, try not to give characters names that might confuse the child listener. Names that are too similar like Matthew and Martin probably belong in separate stories. The name of your character will usually indicate the sex of the child, unless you are trying to keep this ambiguous. Susan and Sally are obviously girls' names. Justin and Jacob are boys' names. However, if I named a character Kirby, after my friend and Newbery Honor–winning author, Kirby Larson, it might not be so clear. She frequently gets mail addressed to Mr. Kirby Larson. Giving your character a nickname is fine, but if you want it to be easy to remember and enrich your characterization, you should give a short explanation of its origin.

2. **BIRTHDATE AND AGE**

The birthdate helps place your story in a historical period. A five-year-old child born in 1700 will be unlike a five-year-old child born in 2018. And probably named differently, too. Zebadiah is rarely the name of a child born in 2018. If you write about a child born in the mid-1700s, you can use words like *carriage*, *blacksmith*, and *hornbook*—words you wouldn't choose if your character were born today.

How old is your character, and in what ways does age influence his behavior? A two-year-old behaves unlike a four-year-old or an eight-year-old. Does your character act his age? Does he speak in baby talk? Maybe he tries to act tough like his big brother. Perhaps the other characters assume he is older or younger than he really is.

3. **APPEARANCE**

If your character is an animal, state that. It is important to know. Sometimes I keep a photograph from family snapshots or clippings from magazines and newspapers that resembles my character. Note that the illustrator may paint a character far removed from what you imagine. However, having a picture in your mind, whether or not it matches the illustrator's, makes for strong writing.

Think about whether your character spends lots of time on appearance or if such concerns are of little consequence to him. Is he generally pleased with how he looks? Is he neat or sloppy? What kind of clothes might he wear? Health might be important here, too. Maybe your character exercises a lot or gets sick often.

4. **RELATIONSHIPS**

Start first with family, especially if they are important in the story.

Who are the parents, siblings, and extended family? It's not enough to just give names here. Let the reader know about their personalities and interactions. What problems does your main character have with them? Is the family from a foreign country? If so, explain any activities or beliefs that are unique to their culture and whether they like their new home. Family income may be relevant if it affects your main character. The frequency with which he sees his parents could be a factor in their relationship. What about friends? Neighbors? Teachers? We might need to know how your main character feels about them, too.

5. **PERSONALITY**

I've saved the most important area to focus on for last. Look at picture books you love, and think about the characters. How would you define Sophie's personality in *Sophie's Squash*? What about Ralph in *Ralph Tells a Story* by Abby Hanlon? Are they similar? Differentiating between characters in published books will help you better define your own characters.

List your character's strengths and weaknesses, attitudes, fears, obsessions, special talents, and hobbies. Does your character have a favorite saying like "Go for it!" or a habit of tapping her fingers when she is bored? Try writing yourself a letter from your character about what happens in the story—it will help you hear her voice directly.

That's it! Just five simple categories to explore:

- Name
- Birthdate and age at the time of the story.
- Appearance
- Relationships with others
- Personality

Do you feel the five elements of character discussed so far are not enough for you? Maybe you've completed them and need to delve deeper into your character before you write or revise. If so, here are two elements to contemplate that are specific to the action of your story.

1. **WHAT HAS BROUGHT THE CHARACTER TO THIS POINT?**

   At the point when the story begins, what experiences and resulting traits have come to define your main character and his motives? Describe these in detail. For example, my book *Tortuga in Trouble* begins with Tortuga ready to set off with a basket of food for his *abuela*, or grandmother. I knew before the story began that he'd learned she wasn't feeling well. That's why he was going to visit her. I also knew Tortuga moved slowly and that he'd gotten burned by his friends in the past, so he was unable to trust them now. None of this needed to go into the finished version, but it enriched my connection with and understanding of Tortuga's identity at the beginning of the story.

2. **WHAT DOES THE MAIN CHARACTER WANT?**

   Does she want to conquer her fear of the dark? Does she want to learn how to ride a tricycle? If the main character is going to get what she wants, what must she overcome? Is it a bully? Is it her own shyness, or must she convince her parents that she is capable of accomplishing something?

Now that you're done, don't save your study in a file or store it in a drawer to be forgotten. Go back, and reread it. With your character firmly in mind, pause in your revising to ask: Would my character speak in that manner? Based on what you know about him, you might realize he would act differently than you initially thought.

Leave room in your writing for surprises. Characters may suddenly say or do something startling. Writers often talk about the joy of following a character's unexpected lead. Just make sure that before you finalize your story, the latest version shows your character acting appropriately and consistently with his established personality.

NO CAST OF THOUSANDS

Because picture books are short and written for children who are new to books, we write books with *just one main character*. You may wonder about the classic children's book *Owl Babies* by Martin Waddell, which features three main characters, the owlets: Sarah, Percy, and Bill. You will find exceptions to almost any statement or instruction about writing. However, each of the three owlets (substitutes for children) represents an expression of the many sides of one character. When Mother goes away, like Sarah, we're hopeful she'll return;

like Percy, we're worried something bad might happen; and like Bill, we ache with love.

If you have several characters, like I do in my series of English-Spanish books, *Mañana, Iguana; Fiesta Fiasco; Count on Culebra*; and *Tortuga in Trouble*, who get equal time in the stories, make sure they act and sound unique. I spent many hours creating each one. To summarize their longer studies, Iguana is the one who makes plans and organizes activities. She loves parties and cooking for friends. Self-centered Conejo, a trickster, will do anything to get out of work. Culebra is a tease who likes to play jokes. He's also the most cerebral. Tortuga is slow, steady, and a tad insecure, so he can be swayed by others. Establishing these characters made it easy for me to recognize when one character was speaking in the voice of another. Once you've made your studies and think your characters are distinctive, it's time to test whether each one does in fact act according to his or her personality.

TESTING FOR CHARACTER CONSISTENCY

With a highlighter, mark every dialogue and action of your main character. When you've completed that, choose a different highlighter and do the same for another character. If you have more than two characters, highlight each one's dialogue and actions with a new color. Then go through the whole manuscript, and read aloud the lines designated by one of the colors. Removing the distractions of the other characters allows you to easily see and hear whether an individual speaks or acts out of character.

A FEW FINAL WORDS

Now you know the kinds of characters we want in children's books and how to create a well-rounded one in your study. You also know how to use highlighters to test whether your character is acting and speaking consistently. Editors are looking for strong characters that will appeal to both readers and listeners. And who knows? Maybe your next character will be as memorable as Peter Rabbit.

WHAT'S NEXT?

You've created a unique and engaging character. It's time to look at structural storytelling issues—first, the all-important opening. If your story doesn't start strong, no one will ever get to read your fabulous middle and ending.

BUT . . . Before you go on

1. Make a character study for every character in your story.
2. Choose a different highlighter for each of your characters. Go through a clean copy of your manuscript, highlighting each character's dialogue and actions. Do not try to do too many characters at the same time, shifting from one color to another, because I guarantee you'll make at least one mistake.
3. Now read all the dialogue and actions designated by one of those colors. Is everything your character says consistent with her intended identity? What about her actions? If not, rewrite.
4. Did you notice any characters who appear in the beginning but not at the end or vice versa? If so, they probably aren't necessary to your story. Try deleting them or perhaps combining them with another character.
5. Look at the texts of your good and bad published books. Is a weak or inconsistent character what distinguishes the one book as "bad"?
6. Read a new picture book, maybe one mentioned in this chapter.

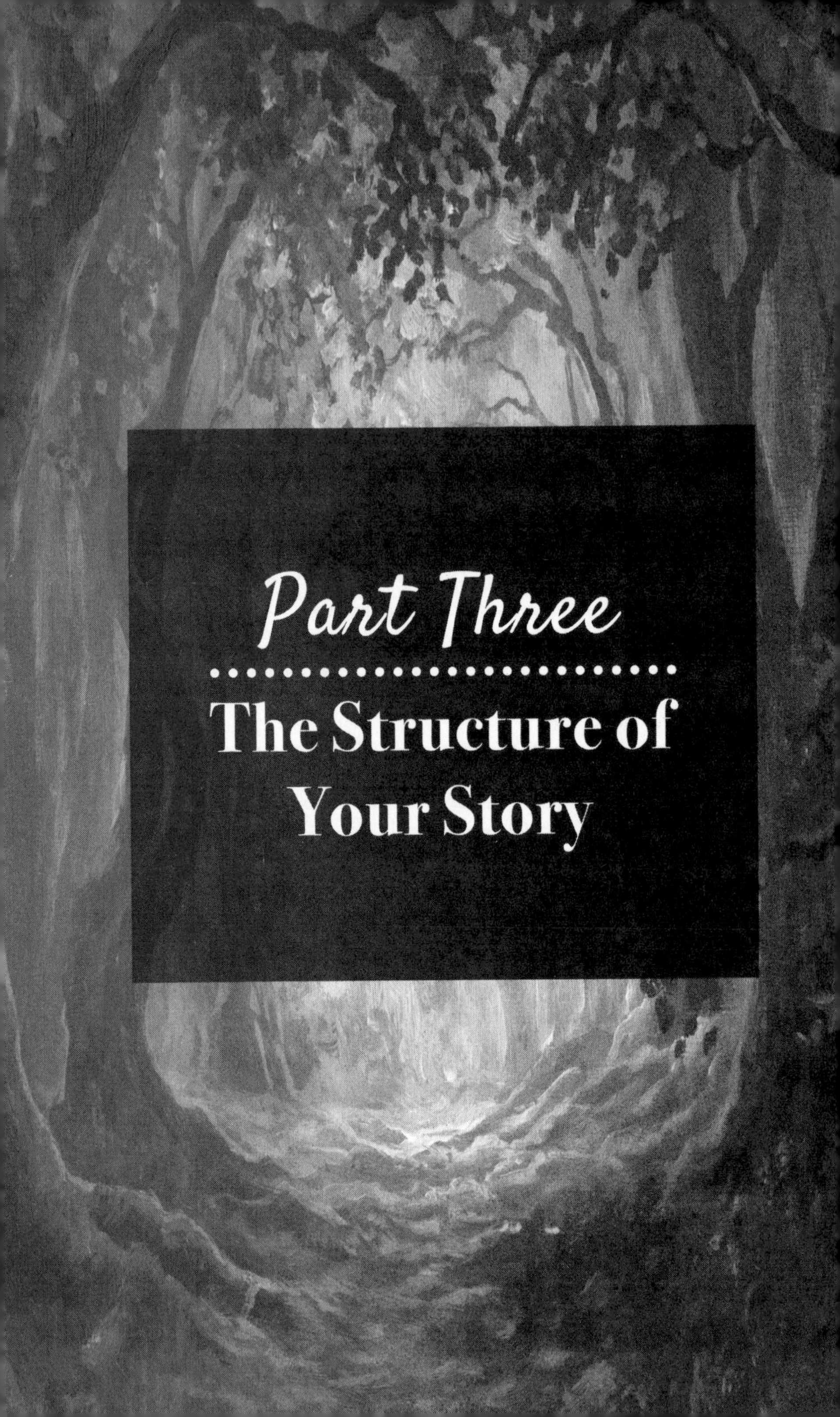

Part Three

The Structure of Your Story

7

Diving into Your Story

"The first lines of a story teach us how to read it."

—JOHN L'HEUREUX

Are you uneasy when it comes to writing your picture-book opening? Do you start as I used to, by describing your character's personality and appearance, the location, the weather, etc. before getting to the character's problem? Don't be a nervous swimmer, testing your story waters with your toe. Dive right in.

You don't have oodles of time in this busy world to grab your reader's attention, much less an editor's—the most important first reader of your manuscript. How long will an editor give you before she tosses your story into the rejection pile? Most admit that the first few paragraphs show them all they need to know about a story's potential. Picture-book writers don't have the novelist's luxury of creeping into a story. Openings have to be quick, grabbing the audience from the get-go.

A STRONG OPENING CONTAINS 6 Ws

1. WHO IS YOUR MAIN CHARACTER?

In picture books, the main character should appear onstage first. If you start with a secondary character, you'll confuse the listener. She won't know whom she should identify with. For example, if I start a story with "Sammy slammed the door in Becky's face," you would assume that Sammy is the main character, but if this is followed by Becky crying and shuffling home to tell her mom, you'd be wrong.

If it's truly Becky's story, it's better to start with "Becky stared stunned. Had Sammy really slammed the door on her? She thought Sammy was her friend." Now we know Becky is the main character.

As you can see below, a good opening doesn't describe the main character but shows him in action.

One morning Papa Pig sat reading his *Porcine Post.*

Mama Pig said, "Little Piggy and I are—"

"Have a good time," Papa Pig interrupted, not looking up from his paper.

"We will," Mama Pig answered. "Take care of —"

"—everything." said Papa Pig. "I know."

I don't tell the reader that Papa Pig is distracted and not paying attention. I show what kind of pig he is through his actions and dialogue.

In *Big Red Lollipop,* Rukhsana Khan did the same. Her main character, Rubina, shows her eagerness by rushing home to tell her *ami* (mother) about a birthday party she's eager to attend. When Ami insists Rubina should bring her little sister along, frustration and problems ensue. This beautiful, sensitive book won an SCBWI Golden Kite Award for picture-book text.

That said, you might open with a brief yet intriguing description of your character as I do here: "Bulldog loved to help, but whenever he wig-wag-waggled, look out!" Make sure you don't go on too long before plunging into action. For a fun introduction to a main character, I adore *Big Mean Mike* by Michelle Knudsen.

2. WHAT DOES YOUR CHARACTER WANT?

What is the main character's problem, goal, or conflict? The sooner a reader knows this, the sooner she'll be eager to turn the pages. Consider this possible opening: "'I'm bored, sssssssssssssso bored,' hissed Snake, 'of alwaysssss living down low on the ground.'" Fourteen words and we already know Snake would like to see the world from another perspective.

In *Flight School,* Lita Judge uses just 34 words to tell us the main character, Penguin, wants to attend flight school. Check out *The Summer Nick Taught His Cats to Read* by Curtis Manley for another tightly written opening. In the first four sentences, we learn that Nick loves spending time with his cats and has decided to teach them how to read. We can guess that this won't be an easy task, and in just 35 words, our curiosity is piqued. We want to know if he'll be successful.

Of course, some picture books don't have a character with a problem to solve. These are concept books, where the writer explores a subject. Nonetheless, the reader still needs to know right away what the book is about.

My book *If Animals Said I Love You* is an exploration of how animals might express affection. There's no story or conflict, but I wrote it intent on stretching imaginations. The opening goes like this:

> If animals said, "I love you" like we do, Gorilla would pound a loud chest, slap-slap: "I love you, my young one." Whappity whap. (23 words)

More Than Enough, A Passover Story by April Halprin Wayland has no conflict. It is a lyrical listing of what the narrator's family is grateful for. Her opening sets the tone for the entire book.

3. <u>W</u>HEN IS YOUR STORY TAKING PLACE?

Sometimes the writer will want to give the exact date and time of the story. However, that's not always necessary. In contemporary stories, the date and year need not be stated. If your story takes place in a different time, you can use character names, unusual or old-fashioned phrasing, or a unique object to indicate the period. For example, if I were writing a story that takes place in colonial times, I might open like this.

> Zachariah rushed to the woodpile. "I'll get our firewood fast!"
>
> "No," cried Father.
>
> But Zachariah scrambled up.
>
> Logs rumbled. Tumbled.
>
> Father rushed over. "How many times have I told you haste makes waste?"
>
> Zachariah tugged at his britches. All at once he brightened. "But haste is good for weeding."

The opening of *Diana's White House Garden* by Elisa Carbone is another good example of how to orient the reader temporally. The opening states that Diana lived in the White House with, among others, President Franklin Roosevelt, informing at least the adult readers of the book's timeframe.

4. <u>W</u>HERE IS YOUR STORY TAKING PLACE?

Just as the reader and listener need to be grounded in *when* the story takes place, they also should know *where* the story takes place. Is it in a city, country, or suburb? Is it set in England, Iran, or China? You don't have to set the scene with long, lovely descriptions. If I wanted to write a book about a city mouse, I wouldn't start my story by saying "Mouse lived in a big noisy city with tall apartments and office buildings and way too much traffic." I would say "Mouse waited and waited while cars, buses, and taxis sped by. Would she ever make it to school?" Notice how active the second example is, plunging into the action, letting the reader know what the problem is, and most importantly, letting the illustrator determine what the city looks like and where it's located.

Often you don't need to explicitly state the location because it is evident, as in *Ralph Tells a Story* by Abby Hanlon, which opens with Ralph's teacher making a statement about stories. Obviously then, they are in a school. If I wrote, "Timothy shuffled up to the cashier. He hoped she didn't have X-ray vision and could see the orange-juice box he'd hidden in his pocket," a reader could rightfully assume Timothy was in a grocery store.

5. WHAT IS THE STORY'S TONE?

Is your story going to be funny? Serious? Sad? How do you let the reader know what lies ahead? By careful selection of words and rhythms (we'll discuss this in depth in chapters fourteen and fifteen). Give clues for a funny story by writing playful, perhaps even made-up, words. Use upbeat rhythms in your sentences. Here's an opening that promises a lighthearted read:

> Far away on the African plain,
> under the shade of the Acacia tree,
> Ostrich Chick settles into his nest to nap, but—
> Meerkat diggity-dig-digs for seeds to eat!
> "Hush! Let Chick sleep!" barks Baboon and boppity-bops Meerkat,
> who diggity-dig-digs for seeds to eat.

Every line, excepting the penultimate one, ends in a hard beat that signals something fun. *Diggity* and *boppity* add to the happy mood.

Antoinette Portis's book *Best Frints in the Whole Universe* lets the listener know immediately that he's in for a fun story with the character names Yelfred and Omek. These names start with soft sounds and end with hard sounds. For more fun, she makes up words throughout. Here's another opening that promises a very different story than my example above:

> Once upon the prairie—the moon lit Lena's path as she shivered, trudging out her one-room sod house across prickly grass to the

dark outhouse. One hundred and fifty years later—that same moon shines on a stone and stucco house as Lena's great, great, great, great granddaughter Emily tiptoes to the bathroom. A light turns on automatically.

Each sentence is long and ends with a falling rhythm. The tone is quieter and more serious.

6. THE *WOW* MOMENT

This is where you hook the reader, like a fisherman hooks a fish, so she can't close the book until she's reached the end. It can be a word or a phrase. It can come when you meet the character or hear the problem. But it must appear early.

> Sylvia awakened to the clatter of pots and pans. "It's Sunday! Grandpa's here!" She ran to the kitchen.
>
> Mother was measuring flour into the mixing bowl. Father was squeezing oranges.
>
> "I thought Grandpa ..." Sylvia slumped. "I dreamed he didn't die."

Oh, how this tugs my heartstrings. This poor girl, convinced that her Grandpa hadn't died. How will she adapt to her new reality? I have to read on.

Here's another opening, a correspondence between two brothers—one a young man serving in WWII and the other a boy living at home.

> September 17, 1944
> Dear George,
>
> Ma and Pa and I didn't feel like doing much the day you left to join the army. Mostly we just sat around and listened to the Yankees' game on the radio. When they played "The Star Spangled Banner," Pa stood up and sang! He said we should all sing on account of you and all the others going to fight that madman Hitler. I wish I wasn't only eight years old. I want to be in the Army with you. Then Pa would sing for me, too.

I think that the *wow* moment comes when the younger brother wishes he could be in the Army so that Pa would also sing for him.

For a sillier opening with a *wow* moment, consider the passage below.

> Purrsey nuzzles Mia's leg. Purr, purr, purrrrrrrrr. "Not now, Purrsey! I have to get ready for my party." Purrsey curls around Mia's feet. Purr, purr, purrrrrrrrr. "Stop it Purrsey! I'm too busy."
>
> Purrsey slouches outside to Hen. "Every time I tell Mia I love her, she never understands."
>
> "What'd you expect?" Hen clucks. "Mia can't speak purr."

I have a *wow* moment here when Purrsey worries that Mia will never know he loves her, and if that isn't enough, I laugh out loud when Hen clucks, "What do you expect? Mia can't speak purr."

Look at the opening for *President Squid* by Aaron Reynolds. Squid is shocked by his realization that no Squid has ever been president; when he's elected, he'll be the first. A squid as president? What a *wow* moment!

Because the *wow* factor is so important, I urge you to check out the following books.

- *Sophie's Fish* by A.E. Cannon. In this opening, Sophie asks a classmate to babysit her fish, and the narrator wonders how hard that will be. We're compelled to read on and find out.
- *The Wrong Side of the Bed* by Lisa M. Bakos. Sometimes the *wow* moment isn't an overwhelming development but something small that tickles the funny bone. In this story, Lucy awakens and can find only one bunny slipper. When I saw the line that said it was going to be a one-slipper kind of day, I knew I was in the hands of an accomplished writer and that this was going to be a fun read.
- *Piggy Bunny* by Rachel Vail opens by telling us that Liam was like all other piglets. However, while every other piglet wanted to grow up to be a pig, Liam did not. He wanted to be a bunny but not just an ordinary bunny; he wanted to be the Easter Bunny. A piglet that wanted to deliver eggs and candy? *Wow!* This book I have to read.

Since the first edition of this book, I've been paying more attention to the word counts of openings. My aim is to get as many of the 6 Ws into the first 50 words of my manuscripts as possible. I'm not always successful, as you'll soon see, but it's what I strive for.

TESTING FOR A STRONG OPENING

How do you discover if your opening contains all of the 6 Ws and that they come close to the beginning? Here's a test that will give you a colorful picture of how soon your opening includes all it needs. I prefer highlighters for this, but crayons, colored pencils, or colored pens work, too. To see this test in action, here is an early draft of an opening for one of my stories.

> Bulldog hurried to his best friend's house. Poodle was making a cake. She measured cream, sugar, and eggs into the mixing bowl. Bulldog wagged his tail. "Can I help? I love to help."
>
> "That would be great," said Poodle. She added flour and handed him the mixer.
>
> Bulldog turned it on to speed number 1, WHIR! "Too Slow!" He turned it higher, 2, 3, 4, WHIRRR, WHIRRR! 5, 6, 7. "Almost done!" Bulldog turned it up to 8, 9, 10, WHIRRRR, WHIRRRR, WHIRRRRRRRRRRRRRRRRRRRR! (83 words)

Let's see how well the opening passes the color test. Start with red to mark the place that lets the reader know who the main character is. Bulldog is first onstage, so you can assume he's the main character. Next mark the words that tell what the character wants with yellow.

Bulldog states that he wants to help. Hurray! We already have a colorful opening. But I'm concerned. I know what the character wants, but I don't sense any tension. After all, Poodle basically says, "Okay, mix up my batter." Readers won't read on if the main character's desires don't lead to a problem.

Let's move on to the green highlighter. Use it to indicate the words that signal when the story is taking place. We can assume it's contemporary times because he's mixing a cake with an electric beater, so let's highlight the beater with green.

It's time to try the blue highlighter to mark where the story is happening. Right now, we're at Poodle's house. Will we stay there? There's no way to know, but still I'd give myself some blue.

Up to this point, my opening has done fairly well. But there are two more Ws and two more colors, and here's where problems crop up. The purple marker should tell us where the story's tone is established. I flunked terribly here. The language is pedestrian. There's no music. The only fun thing for kids would be the *Whirrrr* sound of the mixer. I definitely have a problem.

I'm down to the last highlighter—the most important one. Orange should show the words that make the reader want to say "Wow!" Do you get a *wow* here? Do you want to read any further?

I don't. The color test showed me I had lots of work to do. After much thought and many hours revising, here's the new opening.

> "An invitation!" Quigley ripped it open. "From Monique!"
>
> Come to a fête tonight to celebrate Blaze's new house.
>
> Quigley scampered over. "I love to help. Can I help get ready for the party?"
>
> "Merci! Thank you!" Monique handed him the beater. "Mix this batter while I curl my fur."
>
> Whirrr! "A fluffy cake needs fast mixing," Whirrrrrr, Whirrrrrrrrrrrr!
>
> Batter here! Batter there!
>
> Batter, batter everywhere! (65 words)

I've named the dogs here to add humor and help define their personalities. We still know Quigley is the main character. The element of an impending party adds tension and gives the batter disaster more impact. Quigley still wants to help, but we see much sooner that his help will be a problem. The beater continues to indicate a contemporary story, although the invitation coming in the mail instead of over the computer dates it. The story still takes place in Monique's home. The tone of the story is more obvious, and the shorter sentences speed everything up. The *Whirrrrrrrrr* remains, but I've added a rhyming couplet to lighten up the disaster. That and the main character's name make it obvious that despite the tension, this won't be a serious story. And what about *wow*? That comes in the rhyming couplet. We see trouble, and we want to read more.

I still wanted more, too—a tighter opening and more lively language—so I kept revising.

> "Woof-ooray! Woof-ooray! Monique's party today!" Quigley scampered to her house. "Can I help get ready? I love to help!"
>
> "Fantastic! Mix my cake batter light and fluffy while I curl my fur."
>
> Quigley turned on the mixer. "Fast makes fluffy."
>
> Whir! Whirrrrr! Whirrrrrrrrrrrr!
>
> Batter here!
>
> There!
>
> Everywhere! (47 words)

Don't think you're seeing my only three openings here. There were more revisions, and there still might be more. Creating fabulous openings is time-consuming but fun and challenging. Save your openings so you can compare the changes. You'll most likely be impressed by your improvements.

A FEW FINAL WORDS

Now you know the importance of a compelling opening. You know what you need to include in your opening and how to test for each element. Obviously, having all of the information as close to the beginning as possible is best (so your highlighter colors may overlap). Sometimes, though, information may be found in the illustrations and does not need to be spelled out in the text.

WHAT'S NEXT?

We haven't touched on that critical first line. That comes in chapter eight.

BUT . . . Before you go on

1. Apply the color test to your own manuscript. How successful is your opening? Can you do better? If so, revise. Sometimes you might want to do this exercise with another writer. You'll need two copies of your story so you can each mark the opening separately. Then compare the marked manuscripts. Are the colors in the same places? Perhaps your outside reader's wow-moment highlighting comes much later. Again, it's time to revise.
2. Print a clean copy of the good and bad manuscripts you typed up back in chapter one, and apply the color test to each opening. Perhaps a weak opening is the primary reason that the one manuscript is bad. Does the good manuscript have a strong opening? Comparing the color tests of your story to those of successful published books is humbling and educational. Type up the script of any new favorite picture book, and apply the color test. The more you understand about how published writers create strong openings, the more likely you'll be able to do the same with yours.

3. Read a new picture book, perhaps one mentioned in this chapter. In the bibliography, I've marked the books with especially strong openings with an *O*.

8

Baiting with a Sharp Hook

Creating a Fabulous First Line

"The first line of a poem is a hawk which won't let go of its prey."

—GABRIEL PREIL

This quote easily applies to both poems and picture books. Those who attended writing workshops with Richard Peck might have heard him say, "You're only as good as your opening line."

Here is a first line that would make me want to read more: "Finn raced to get home before his mother." Why? What was he doing away from home? What would happen if she discovered him gone? So many unanswered questions would force me to keep reading.

How about "What do pigs dream?" for an opening line? Do they dream of slops? Mud baths? Or maybe leaving the farm and living in an apartment? Lots of intriguing possibilities!

As you can see, stirring curiosity is key, which is why good first lines (such as the next one) tend to be mysterious in some way. "When the doorbell rang, Alan had no idea how his life would change." Doesn't that grab you? Who's ringing that doorbell? Is he bringing news of an accident? Has the bank foreclosed on his parents' house? Or maybe it's something happier. Perhaps Alan is getting a new puppy.

In this last example, you can see how a great first line may reel in a reader by sending his mind on an unexpected flight of fancy: "If a bakery opened on the African plains, what pastries would the animals buy?" Would a zebra buy a grass cake? Would a giraffe purchase a leafy tart? Would an elephant be tempted by dust-sprinkled cookies? I want to find out.

Pay attention to the first lines of everything you read. Does one work exceptionally well? Does another fall flat? Consider why.

Successful first lines make it feel as if those lines were so right and natural that they wrote themselves. But I suspect each author spent many hours experimenting with different ones. You will have to do the same.

What makes a great first line? In our last chapter, we discussed the importance of the *wow* moment coming early. If you can get that moment in the first line, you will hook the reader right off the bat. Joni Sensel, who writes books for older readers, suggests writers start with a bang—or with an axe. Don't be satisfied with the first line you come up with. While your first try sometimes works, more often it doesn't.

EXPERIMENTING WITH YOUR OPENING LINE

Here are nine different ways to change the focus of your opening line and create something new. To see how this works, let's look at the first line from *The Sleeping Beauty in the Wood* by Charles Perrault: "There were formerly a king and a queen, who were so sorry that they had no children, so sorry that it cannot be expressed."

INTRODUCTION OF MAIN CHARACTER

It's always preferable to bring the main character up first as I do in this sentence: "The queen bound off the last stitches of her baby blanket fearful she might never have a use for it."

TIME

The word *formerly* could refer to several months ago, several years, or even several centuries, so I'm going to make the period more specific and the language more visual and poetic: "In the time before books, a king and his queen longed for a child but in vain."

LOCATION

For an opening line focusing on the couple's surroundings, I might write "The young queen stared out her palace window at the royal garden full of the finest vegetables and the most colorful flowers but felt only sadness that though her plants thrived and multiplied, she had yet to bear a child."

MOOD

If I want to set a melancholy mood, I would focus on showing their heartache through actions rather than just by saying they were sorry, as in Perrault's line: "The king held his queen close, his whole self devoted to her comfort, but her tears continued to fall." What reader wouldn't feel compassion for the queen and her king?

OPINION

Sometimes, especially with a strong, compelling narrator, the first line can open with an opinion. Here's a negative one: "Why couldn't that queen count her blessings instead of always bemoaning her inability to have a child?" Now here's a more upbeat point of view: "How fortunate fate gave the king and queen each other to commiserate together!"

PROVOCATIVE STATEMENT

A provocative statement is an opinion specifically meant to elicit a reaction from the listener and reader, one so strong that they can't stop reading. Maybe this would work: "Aren't you tired of people who luxuriate in their misery?" This next possible opening sentence is also provocative: "Children are such a bother; the king and queen should be relieved not to have one."

MIDDLE OF THE ACTION

One of the best ways to get the readers and listeners of our stories involved is to cut out introductory and backstory material. Instead, start by thrusting the reader into a moment that changes or defines the characters and advances the story: "'Every day I pray for a child,' the queen told her husband, 'so why doesn't God hear me?'" One might also try capturing the same moment from the husband's point of view: "'I, too, want a child,' said the king, 'but perhaps it's not meant to be.'" Both of these sentences plunge us into the drama of the story.

CONFLICT

Just as it's good to start a story in the middle of the action, it's even better to immediately show the conflict. For example, a rewrite of *The Sleeping Beauty in the Wood* might begin with this line: "'You don't want a child as much as I do,' complained the queen." If the writer chose to give the king the opening line, we might see something like "'Can't you think of anything other than a baby?' asked the king."

SCRAPBOOK

This could also be a newspaper article, a journal entry, or a letter. For the wife's scrapbook, I might have listed possible baby names and then angrily crossed them out or I might have drawings of baby clothes. The scrapbook is a great way to show backstory.

A newspaper article might open with a headline such as "Hopes Dashed!" The first line of a a journal entry might be: "October 1—Another childless day." A letter might begin thusly: "Dear Husband, I met with the doctor today, and he gave me hope that we may yet have a child."

And there you have it—nine different ways to focus your first line. Check out the following books for some of my favorite opening lines, and compare how each one promises a different reading experience:

- *Happy Like Soccer* by Maribeth Boelts
- *Noah Webster & His Words* by Jeri Chase Ferris
- *The Boss Baby* by Marla Frazee
- *Lovabye Dragon* by Barbara Joosse

A FEW FINAL WORDS

Careful consideration *and* risk-taking will open new directions for your writing. Play around with possible approaches for your first line, just as you did while experimenting with different storytelling voices. It won't be wasted time.

WHAT'S NEXT?

In the following chapter, we'll examine basic plotting.

BUT . . . Before you go on

1. Look at your first line. Is it the best it can be? Experiment, altering it according to the nine different focuses outlined in this chapter.
   a. Main character introduction
   b. Time

c. Location
d. Mood
e. Opinion
f. Provocative statement
g. Middle of the action
h. Conflict
i. Scrapbook

Are you still having trouble revising your opening to your complete satisfaction? Perhaps you are like Blaise Pascal, who said, "That last thing one discovers in writing a book is what to put first." If this is you, don't be discouraged. Set your opening aside, and continue with the exercises in this book. Then come back to your opening with a fresh attitude.

2. Look at the first lines in the good and bad published books you selected. Do they grab you or not? Why?
3. Some writers find making up first lines a great story-sparker exercise. Free-associate for a few minutes, and jot down some intriguing ones. Then pick a favorite, and write a story.
4. Read a new picture book, perhaps one mentioned in this chapter.

9 Basic Plotting

"Tragedy is when I cut my finger.
Comedy is when you fall into an open sewer and die."

—MEL BROOKS

Since the first edition of this book, I've discovered *Seven Basic Plots: Why We Tell Stories* by Christopher Booker, which has helped me examine plots in a new way. It will help you, too, when considering what kind of a story you are telling. Let's see how the seven plots relate to picture books.

OVERCOMING THE MONSTER

Booker gives as an example of this form, which you see in many classic adult stories. It often involves a knight fighting dragons and monsters and being rewarded with gold or the hand of a beautiful maiden. But monsters don't need to be dragons. They appear in James Bond and Sherlock Holmes mysteries as criminals. In war stories, they're the enemy; in westerns, they're the thief or murderer.

Picture books' monsters need only be creatures that appear monstrous to children. Consider *Where the Wild Things Are* by Maurice Sendak. The angry feelings and behaviors residing in Max are his monsters. He overcomes them by sailing off to where wild things live. He tames them and his own impulses and returns home, not to the hand of a princess but to his supper, warm and waiting for him.

Ella and Penguin Stick Together by Megan Maynor is also an example of this basic plot. To see Ella's glow-in-the-dark stickers, Ella and Penguin must overcome the monstrous dark and their fears of what resides there. They try several ways of seeing the stickers in partial dark and fail. Only when they agree to hold hand and flipper do they conquer their fears. Their reward is the stickers' beauty.

RAGS TO RICHES

This type of story revolves around someone impoverished and possibly mocked by society who overcomes these obstacles and dramatically improves her situation. We see this story play out in the lives of historical figures such as Abraham Lincoln. For a nonfiction picture book in this category, check out *Brave Girl: Clara and the Shirtwaist Makers' Strike of 1909* by Michelle Markel to learn about a poor immigrant girl who empowered herself and her fellow employees by leading a strike that ended up improving their working conditions.

Noah Webster and His Words by Jeri Chase Ferris is another true-life story in the same vein. Here a young man who was destined to be a farmer overcame his father's objections and attended school. He went on to become a teacher and wrote the first dictionary of American English.

One might even make an argument that *Winnie: The True Story of the Bear Who Inspired Winnie-the-Pooh* by Sally M. Walker fits into the rags-to-riches category. An unknown bear cub whose mother was shot was adopted by a veterinarian during World War I. He later became the inspiration for one of the greatest series in children's literature.

For a fictional book, look no further than *Ralph Tells a Story* by Abby Hanlon. Ralph suffers from a poverty of story ideas. All his classmates are busy writing, but he can't think of anything. He struggles and struggles until finally, with encouragement from his classmates, he trusts his own experiences and realizes that he, too, is full of stories.

THE QUEST

The quest can be for something as grand as a pot of gold at the end of the rainbow, the secret of immortality, or the discovery of a new planet. It may also be seemingly small and insignificant, except to the main character. Look at Jacob, who only wants to wear a dress, in *Jacob's New Dress* by Sarah and Ian Hoffman. In *There's a Bear on My Chair* by Ross Collins, Mouse is determined to get the bear to leave his chair. In *Clark the Shark Takes Heart* by Bruce Hale, Clark has set his heart on winning Anna Angelfish's affection, but everything he does to impress her fails until he learns big gestures aren't always the best way to express one's love.

VOYAGE AND RETURN

In this plot, the hero or heroine leaves familiar surroundings and travels to a place that is different and often threatening but returns home changed. For example, Dorothy is carried off by a tornado to a dangerous new land in *The Wonderful Wizard of Oz* by L. Frank Baum, and she returns to Kansas by the end of the book. The clown in *The Farmer and the Clown* by Marla Frazee falls from his circus train into a new, strange place that looks very much like Dorothy's Kansas. He is befriended by a farmer, but eventually returns to his circus family. Both Dorothy and the clown have had experiences that gave them a new appreciation for home and family. In *Time for (Earth) School, Dewey Dew* by Leslie Staub, Dewey Dew travels to Earth for his first day of school. Nervous and afraid, wishing he could stay home, he connects with schoolmates and although he returns home with his mother, he looks forward to going to school again.

COMEDY

The history of comedy traditionally focused on misgivings and misunderstandings in love. For a picture-book romance, read *Otter and Odder: A Love Story* by James Howe. Much to his consternation, Otter falls in love with his potential dinner, a fish named Myrtle. Other water creatures attempt to discourage him, but because it's a comedy and a love story, everything works out for Otter and Myrtle.

Today's comedies for children occur most often when characters are not fully aware of the truth of some situation and/or the personal truths of themselves or others. *Sophie's Fish*, written by A.E. Cannon, is a great example of a story where the main character is not aware of what's going on. He's been asked by a classmate to take care of her fish for a few days. His imagination runs wild as he thinks about what that will entail. Finally, he realizes that it will probably be okay. Then he meets the fish, and all bets are off.

TRAGEDY

In Booker's analysis of the tragedy plot form, a main character succumbs to his weaker, malevolent impulses. This usually leads to dangerous and nightmarish incidents that culminate in that character's death. Look back in history, and you'll find many examples of the tragedy plot in children's stories. Consider *The Dreadful Story of Pauline and the Matches* by Heinrich Hoffmann. It's available online at germanstories.vcu.edu/struwwel/pauline_e.html. Pauline has been repeatedly warned about playing with matches but pays no mind and dies a horrible, fiery death.

For a modern tragedy written for the picture-book audience, check out *This Is Not My Hat* by Jon Klassen. A small fish has stolen a hat from a big fish. The small fish knows it's wrong but rationalizes that the big fish won't miss it and that it fits him better. Guess what? The big fish does miss his hat and goes searching for it. Although not stated or shown, he probably eats the small fish (since that's what big fish do in nature). In many ways, this feels like a modern Aesop's fable with the moral (don't steal) left unspoken. Because it's about a fish who dies for his crime, we aren't nearly as upset as we would be if it were a human who stole something and was murdered. Also, seeing a fish swimming through the water without losing the hat is so impossible that it's laughable, taking the edge off this tragedy.

As picture-book writers, we don't shy away from tragic stories, but unlike Klassen's tale, we try to leave our young readers and listeners with some hope. Just look at *The Tree in the Courtyard: Looking Through Anne Frank's Window* by Jeff Gottesfeld. The murder of Anne Frank, her family, and millions of Jews during World War II is a horrific tragedy, but because this is told from the viewpoint of the tree, there's some emotional distance. In the end, the tree eventually dies, but cuttings from that tree have been planted around the world and continue to grow and thrive.

REBIRTH

To understand traditional stories of rebirth, you need only look at the classic children's stories "Sleeping Beauty" and "Snow White." In each, the main character falls under the spell of a dark power but is restored (by a kiss from a handsome prince) to her true self by the end. Rebirth tales have evolved over the years to include stories where a main character awakes (not literally) to see the world in a new way, like the monster in *The Monster Who Lost His Mean* by Tiffany Strelitz Haber. The monster has lost the *m* in its name and has become an onster, so he can't do anything mean. Though he tries to be bad, he always ends up doing nice things. He realizes that while he's lost his monster friends, he's gained new ones and likes being an onster better.

We mentioned *The Farmer and the Clown* earlier as a voyage-and-return plot for the clown. For the farmer, it's a story of rebirth. He's a lonely, standoffish man who has little experience interacting with others. The clown's accidental arrival forces him to relate and try to wipe the frown off the clown's face. He dances, plays games, makes faces, and even learns new tricks from his guest. When the clown is reunited with his family, we ache for the farmer because he has come alive to the joys of connecting with others. We are relieved when, on the last page, we see that he will have someone with whom to share in this rebirth.

A FEW FINAL WORDS

Now that we've looked at different plot possibilities, how might you apply this knowledge to your writing? If your story is missing something and you don't know what, think back to these basic plots and see where yours might fit. If it doesn't fit, why not? Maybe if you revise with these plots in mind, you can strengthen your story. These plots have evolved over the years because they work—each in its own satisfying way. See if your plot can be satisfying, too.

WHAT'S NEXT?

In the following chapter, we'll go over the three-act structure and discuss ways to firm up the sagging middle of a story.

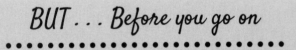

BUT . . . Before you go on

1. Look at your manuscript. Does it fit into any of these basic plots?
2. Look at the good and bad published books you selected. What is the plot form of each?
3. Find examples in your own reading of these different kinds of plots.
4. Read a new picture book, perhaps one mentioned in this chapter.

10

More on Plotting

The Three-Act Structure

"A plot is what happens when there is a problem that needs solving."

—JEAN KARL

You've just learned seven basic plots and seen how they may be implemented in published picture books. Now let's examine how to build those different plots with the three-act structure. All too frequently I have a great idea for an opening. It's catchy, the character is appealing, and the problem is engaging. I've cut away the setup and started in the middle of the action. Often, I know how my book is going to end. And my ending is tight, surprising, and satisfying. The problem is I don't know how to get to my ending in a way that isn't:

1. too thin to fill up my book
2. predictable and obvious from the get-go
3. so boring I yawn while I'm writing it
4. lacking in tension and incentives for the reader to turn the page

When books fail, the author is usually driving along a word highway without a map to the destination. Don't get lost in your story. This chapter is about how to drive your story forward. But a word of caution: No single map can get *every* story to its destination.

Each story reaches its end, sometimes traveling down similar roads as other stories but often demanding its own path. As much as we'd love a simple formula to plug every story into, not having one makes writing more challenging. In the movie *A League of Their Own*, Tom Hanks said, "It's supposed to be hard. If it wasn't hard, everyone would do it. The hard is what makes it great." It also makes every workday more stimulating. What fun would it be to write the same thing over and over again?

Nevertheless, understanding and putting into practice basic plot structure will strengthen your writing and minimize the frustration of each story journey. Plot structure did not develop overnight. It evolved over centuries of storytelling. Not every story must be written within this framework, but most authors find it to be the most dramatic way of writing.

THREE-ACT STRUCTURE

Even though we are writing books (and short ones at that), we adapt the theater's three-act structure so each story contains a beginning, middle, and end. John Gardner states it this way: "In nearly all good fiction, the basic—all but inescapable—plot form is: A central character wants something, goes after it despite opposition (perhaps including his own doubts), and so arrives at a win, lose, or draw." How are these three acts constructed in our picture books?

The opening is the first act. The characters and problem are introduced along with an inciting incident that moves the reader from the first to the second act. In picture books, this first act needs to happen within the first half page of your typed manuscript. In the second act, the main character takes action, more action, and even more action to solve her problem. This act most often culminates in a low moment when all feels lost.

Then it's time to move to our final, short third act, which contains the problem's resolution, or the ending. Once the problem introduced at the beginning is solved, the story is over, finished—except perhaps for quickly tying up loose ends. The solution to the problem usually occurs on pages twenty-eight to twenty-nine or thirty to thirty-one of a published picture book. The tying together of any dangling threads falls on page thirty-two.

Acts in picture books, unlike acts in a play, are not equal in length. A graph of picture-book plot structure might look like this:

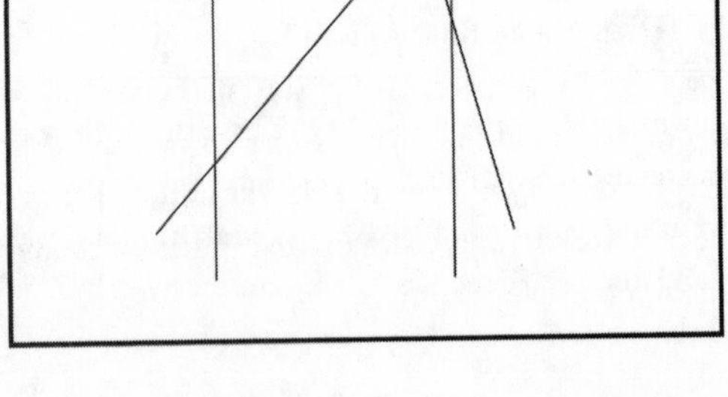

The left-hand vertical line indicates the end of the first act. The other vertical line indicates the end of the second act. The graph here shows the relative briefness of the first and third acts. This three-act structure is equally valid for nonfiction, whether it be narrative nonfiction about history or science or concept books. The first act introduces the subject. The second act explores the subject. In the final act, the writer reaches a conclusion.

The second act is the one that most often needs work. Many manuscripts fail in the middle of the book. To fully understand how this three-act structure works, let's go back to the story I mentioned earlier about Bulldog, whom I eventually named Quigley.

In Act I, Quigley wanders to Monique's house, where she's mixing a cake. He offers to help. End of Act I. In Act II, he does help.

In Act III, together they eat the cake—the end. Does this work? No! Why not? Quigley wants to help and does. There's no tension. It's too easy. The only actions consist of helping make the cake and eating the cake. Nothing interferes with his goal.

This story is seriously lacking a strong second act. But it's also missing something else—conflict. There are four kinds.

CONFLICT WITH ONESELF

In this type of conflict, the main character needs to overcome some struggle or deficiency within herself, such as fear of the dark, difficulty sharing toys, or jealousy over a new baby. For example, Ralph in *Ralph Tells a Story* by Abby Hanlon must conquer his insecurities to learn that stories are everywhere. Lily in *Chicken Lily* by Lori Mortensen must overcome her shyness so she can recite her poem at the school assembly. For a nonfiction picture book featuring this type of conflict, look at Doreen Rappaport's *Helen's Big World: The Life of Helen Keller.* The story shows how Keller managed to lead a productive life in spite of her blindness and deafness.

CONFLICT WITH OTHERS

Sometimes your main character will butt heads with another character. Perhaps your character doesn't want to clean his room, but Mother insists. Perhaps two siblings want to read the same book. For instance, in *Jacob's New Dress* by Sarah and Ian Hoffman, Jacob's father is hesitant to let him wear a dress to school and his classmate Christopher is downright mean about it.

Mouse is in conflict with Bear, who won't get out of his chair, in *There's a Bear on My Chair* by Ross Collins.

Piglet in *Piggy Bunny* by Rachel Vail wants to be a bunny who hops, has long ears, and delivers Easter eggs, but his family insists that's impossible.

CONFLICT WITH SOCIETY

In this type of conflict, your character has issues with a group in the community. Stories of this sort might have your character convincing the government that a stoplight is needed at her school crossing, trying to halt construction of a freeway being built through her backyard, or insisting the city enforce leash laws so that a big dog wouldn't attack her. One may find an example of this conflict type in *Hillary Rodham Clinton: Some Girls Are Born to Lead* by Michelle Markel. The book shows how throughout her life, Clinton came into conflict with a society that didn't believe women should be political. *The Case for Loving: The Fight for Interracial Marriage* by Selina Alko relates the story of Richard Loving and Mildred Jeter, who were not permitted by Virginia state law to marry. For a fiction example, check out *Mostly Monsterly* by Tammi Sauer. Bernadette looks and acts like a monster, but sometimes she does nice things that conflict with society's perception of how a monster must behave.

CONFLICT WITH NATURE

Here the character is not battling himself, a person/persons, or society but nature. Perhaps a swimmer struggles against strong tides, or a child shovels snow but the storm keeps dropping more. Maybe a tornado rips through town. *Little Dog Lost: The True Story of a Brave Dog Named Baltic* by Mônica Carnesi, recounts the tale of a dog trapped on a sheet of ice drifting down a river. Firemen failed to help, and the winds and river carried the dog out to sea as the harsh winter weather threatened to kill him. Another good nonfiction example is *The Kite That Bridged Two Nations: Homan Walsh and the First Niagara Suspension Bridge* by Alexis O'Neill. Homan had to deal with his father's opposition to his actions and with biting winds and snow. For a fictional conflict, I love *Stormy Night* by Salina Yoon. In this story, a young bear helps his stuffed bunny and his parents feel safe and loved in spite of the thunder and lightning raging outside.

PUTTING CONFLICT INTO PRACTICE

In my story of Quigley, I am going to add more dog friends and put him into conflict with each one.

I'm also going to use some other techniques like those noted below.

UP THE STAKES

In addition to employing one of the aforementioned conflict types, you may need to work to convince the reader that the characters have something to lose, should they fail in their endeavors. Suppose I add a goal to Quigley's story—a party to celebrate Blaze's finally finishing painting his house. Now this is a more important cake because it is meant to commend a special event.

A goal was added to good effect in *Chicken Lily* by Lori Mortensen. A chick named Lily is fearful of many things. When she hears that she has to participate in a poetry jam at school and recite an original poem, she does everything she can to get out of it, but to no avail. She has to write a poem by the deadline. But there's still something missing in my story.

TENSION

No tension means bored readers and, worse yet, a rejection from an editor. How can I add tension? Let's suppose that Quigley's personality is overly enthusiastic and when he tries to help, that leads to problems. Great! Now I'll change the second act to have Quigley take the mixer from Monique and turn the speed up to the max, and *voilà!* The batter goes everywhere. Now we have a problem.

But what's going to happen next? Will he and Monique laugh about the mess, clean it up together, and make a new cake? Not if we want a compelling story. Suppose Quigley rushes to clean it up and offers to make a new cake. Alas, when he takes the beater out, he drops it on the floor, and now he's made another mess.

Unfortunately, these mistakes are too similar, which will make the illustrator's job difficult. It might be better if after the mixer accident, Monique angrily sends Quigley away. Quigley slumps to Blaze's house, where Blaze is rushing to finish painting it. Quigley offers to help. Blaze hands him a bucket of black paint and a brush and asks him to paint the door. Quigley not only paints the door but decides to paint the white walls with black spots so the house will look like Blaze, a dalmatian. Blaze will not be happy, and Quigley will leave looking defeated. Do we feel enough of Quigley's discouragement yet? I think not. So far, we have only two incidents.

THE RHYTHM OF THREES

This rhythm of threes is all around us: three strikes and you're out; Father, Son, and Holy Ghost; the Three Bears; the Three Little Pigs; the Three Stooges; tic-tac-toe. You can add others. It's part of our history and our culture. Why? Because it's satisfying. Three failures up the stakes so the reader worries more about the outcome and cares more for the main character.

Let's add another complicating action to our developing story. Let's have Quigley bump into his friend Thimble (a chihuahua). She's rushing about and asks Quigley to put her dress in the washing machine. Quigley agrees and, in his enthusiasm to get it really clean, adds lots of soap. The bubbles overflow through the doors and windows and cover the yard. Now Quigley is devastated. He's convinced everyone is furious and hates him.

What happened here? We gave the reader more time to get to know Quigley and feel his increasing distress. You'll find that the rhythm of threes works to intensify the tension and our feelings for the main characters in picture books. This happens in *The Christmas Boot* by Lisa Wheeler. The main character, Hannah Greyweather (how about that for a great last name?), finds a boot and makes three wishes—one for the boots, another for warm mittens, and then a final one for a big fancy house.

Jacob's New Dress by Sarah and Ian Hoffman also has a rhythm of threes. Jacob wants to wear a dress to school but can't (because of individual and societal objections), so he puts on a dress from the dress-up corner (and gets teased). Then he tries to make a dress (he calls it my "'like-a-dress'") out of a towel (and his classmate pulls it off). Finally, he sews a real dress. By this time, we're feeling his pain. We worry what will happen, and we cheer when he finally stands up for himself.

CAUSE-AND-EFFECT ACTION

Many of the actions in my story are incidental. They could happen in any order. Quigley could just as easily have helped Thimble first. He also could have painted Blaze's house last. The action we want in our stories is action that leads directly to a reaction that in turn leads to another action. This is where many manuscripts fall flat.

Confession: I forgot this point. I submitted this manuscript about Quigley to several publishers. In retrospect, this probably did not improve my reputation with editors, but it did give me emotional distance from my manuscript. After several rejections, I looked at it again.

No wonder no one was interested. I loved each of the actions I'd included, but I needed to make sure each action led to the next. Now when Quigley leaves Monique's house after the batter disaster, he determines that mixing too fast was what got him into trouble. He vows to go slow next time.

When Blaze asks for help with the painting, Quigley says, "I have to go slow." Blaze encourages him to do just that because then the door will be beautiful and he does want a beautiful house. Quigley paints the door slowly, but he remembers Blaze mentioning "a beautiful house" and has an idea for how to make the house beautiful: He'll give it spots just like those on Blaze's fur. Oops! *Trouble!* Blaze is furious. In the aftermath, Quigley realizes that he should have done exactly what Blaze told him to, i.e. paint the door. Nothing else!

Quigley bumps into Thimble, a high-strung chihuahua who has a habit of speaking quickly and repeating the last three words of every sentence. When she asks Quigley, "Could you put this dress in the washing machine and add soap, soap, soap?" he's happy to oblige, doing exactly what she said, with predictably disastrous results. I hope you noticed that we've still kept our rhythm of threes but added cause-and-effect action. Quigley learns a lesson from each mistake and applies this new knowledge in the very next scene, which directly leads to another disaster.

In *Imogene's Last Stand* by Candace Fleming, Imogene's love of history leads her to clean up and reopen the Historical Society Museum. If she hadn't cleaned up the museum, she wouldn't have been upset to learn it was going to be torn down. If she hadn't been so upset, she wouldn't have gone to the mayor to try to dissuade him. If he hadn't refused to budge on the issue, she wouldn't have felt compelled to spread the word to all the townspeople. If the townspeople hadn't turned a deaf ear, she wouldn't have gone back to the museum, thrown herself on the bed, and—seen something that just *might* save the museum.

ESCALATING ACTION

Notice with Quigley that I didn't write the biggest, most exciting action first. In a humorous book, don't place your funniest incident first either. Stories need to build from smaller to larger, or from slightly laughable to ridiculous—cake batter in the kitchen, then spots all over the outside of a new house, and finally, bubbles saturating Thimble's house and beyond. Big, bigger, biggest! If any of these had been reversed, the story wouldn't have been nearly as satisfying.

It's Raining Bats and Frogs by Rebecca Colby is another story with plenty of fun escalating action. Rain is pouring down on the Witch Parade, so the main character, a witch named Delia, waves her wand and uses magic to make it literally rain cats and dogs. That presents problems, so she changes it to hats and clogs and then bats and frogs. Each new "rainfall" leads to more hilarious complications. This book is also an example of the rhythm of threes—three different attempts to make the parade a success. After the bats and frogs, Delia is at her lowest. At the end of my story's second act, Quigley slumps home, flops onto his bed, sure that his friends hate him and want nothing to do with him. He couldn't feel worse. All seems lost, but is it?

The third act is the place where resolution and redemption are possible. In my story's third act, Quigley's friends barge into his house. Instead of being angry, they're grateful. While tasting the batter, Monique realized she'd forgotten sugar. That first cake would have tasted terrible. And Blaze? He decided it's cool to have a house that looks like him, so he painted even more spots. But how can Thimble be happy about all those bubbles? Easy. Her house has never been so clean. All's well that ends well.

DETERMINING YOUR PLOT'S STRENGTH

Print out a hard copy of your manuscript. Then, with a colored marker, highlight when the story problem catapults the reader into the second act. Afterwards, with the same color, highlight where the character solves that problem. The part in between is the second act.

On separate sticky notes, write down each moment the character actively attempts to solve the problem. Are there at least three actions? If not, add more. If you have more than three, perhaps some can be deleted.

Then spread out the action notes on your desk or table to verify that each action leads directly to the next. Whenever this is the case, draw an arrow on another note that leads from one to the other and place it in between them. If they don't link directly, rewrite so they do or simply shift the order of your actions around.

Lastly, use your notes to consider whether your book builds to an exciting climax. If the most dramatic action comes first, rework and reshuffle. Pretend you're playing cards, and deal yourself one story hand. The scenes aren't intensifying? Shuffle them around again, and try another ordering of the same events. This test shows exactly where your plotting is strong and where it needs extra work.

Once in a while, after testing a manuscript where I've used the rhythm of threes, cause and effect, and escalating action, something is still missing. Raymond Chandler said, "When the plot flags, bring in a man with a gun." Fortunately, we children writers have less violent methods to up the ante in our books.

RHYTHM OF SEVENS

Instead of trying to solve a problem three times, consider trying seven times. In the same way that the rhythm of threes is all around us, we also have the rhythm of sevens in our days of the week and in "Snow White" (the Seven Dwarfs). It's familiar and comfortable and forces the reader to wonder when the character will solve his problem. For my story, I didn't consider giving Quigley seven attempts to help his friends or adding enough characters to total seven because my manuscript was already nearly 500 words. However, in a recent book by Candace Fleming called *Oh, No!*, there are seven characters. Frog falls into a hole, followed by Mouse, SlowLoris, Sun Bear, Monkey. Tiger comes along and is about to eat them all, but Elephant saves them. Perhaps some more characters and complications are just what your story needs to soar.

SUSPENSE

Do you still feel like something's missing in your story? Every picture book needs suspense. I'm not referring here to the suspense one feels when reading a mystery and wondering if the murderer will be caught. In picture books, suspense is more akin to worrying if the main character can solve the problem. Without that worry, the story is too flat, too predictable.

The suspense in my story about Quigley stems from the question: Will he ever be able to help without causing trouble? In *When Blue Met Egg* by Lindsay

Ward, Blue is a bird who finds something strange in her nest and assumes it's an egg. We worry if and when she'll discover it's nothing but a snowball. In the lyrical *Old Robert and the Sea-Silly Cats* by Barbara Joosse, we wonder if Old Robert will ever open his heart and conquer his fear of sailing at night. Play around with your story to see how you might heighten the suspense so neither the reader nor the listener knows until the very end what the outcome will be.

A FEW FINAL WORDS

The three-act structure is critical to everything you write. The rhythm of threes is important in creating tension, just as cause-and-effect and escalating action build toward your character's lowest moment, when all feels lost. Keeping the three-act structure and basic plotting concepts in mind will help you effectively arrive at the end of each new story.

WHAT'S NEXT?

Picture books are short and focused, but fortunately there are numerous techniques one may use to organize and hold a story together. In chapter eleven we're going to learn all about those techniques.

BUT . . . Before you go on

1. Test your story in the manner outlined in this chapter. Does your middle need to be expanded? If each action doesn't lead to the next, reshuffle your sticky notes. Perhaps you'll want to add some more actions and delete others. Rewrite if necessary.
2. Study the two published picture books you typed up in manuscript format. Mark their three acts, and examine how well they follow the techniques discussed in this chapter.
3. A great way to learn about plotting is by rewriting a fairy tale or popular story, like "Goldilocks and the Three Bears" or "Cinderella," by changing the characters or the setting but sticking close

to the action. This way, you'll experience how an enduring tale is plotted. Then you can apply it to your own writing.

4. Paying special attention to its plotting, read a new picture book, perhaps one mentioned in this chapter.

11

Holding Your Story Together

"The sinister thing about writing is that it starts off seeming so easy and ends up being so hard."

—L. RUST HILLS

If only this quote weren't true. But it is. Be that as it may, we picture-book writers are lucky. We have more techniques to help hold our stories together.

JOURNEY

We discussed the voyage-and-return plot in chapter nine. But the character doesn't need to return for the ending to be satisfying. Quigley's story could be a journey if I changed the setup. Perhaps his friend Blaze has moved away, and Quigley wants to see him and his new house. Then he would set off and have adventures related to this journey. Two recent books, Lindsay Mattick's *Finding Winnie: The True Story of the World's Most Famous Bear* and *Winnie: The True Story of the Bear Who Inspired Winnie-the-Pooh* by Sally M. Walker, are journey stories of the same bear's travels from Winnipeg, Canada, to a World War I training camp, then across the ocean to England, where he eventually ended up in the London Zoo. Read both of these exceptional books to compare how similar stories can be told differently. *Last Stop on Market Street* by Matt de la Peña is a lovely fictional story about a bus trip that a little boy, CJ, and his grandmother take from church to a soup kitchen. Its 2016 Newbery Medal and Caldecott Honor Award were well-deserved. It's a touching and timely book.

CIRCULAR FORM

The circular form isn't limited to a voyage and return; a story can begin with a certain phrase and end with that same phrase or a slight rewording of the initial phrase. In my last opening of the Quigley story, I had Quigley woof, "Woof-ooray! Woof-ooray!" when he's excited about the party and then exclaim the same at the end when he realizes his friends aren't mad. Lisa M. Bakos uses a longer phrase in *The Wrong Side of the Bed*. Her main character wakes up on the wrong side of the bed and throughout the day has problems. The next day, again, she wakes up on the wrong side of the bed, but this time she reacts differently to change the outcome.

COMPARISON

As the name implies, this form compares one thing to another. With my Quigley story, I could move back and forth between all the characters, showing what each one was doing to get ready for the party. That might be a bit much. Just focusing on two characters might be a better approach. I could show Blaze rushing to finish painting his house and Quigley getting ready for the party. Obviously, this would change the story's direction, but if you come away with anything in this newest edition, hopefully it's that experimenting is critical to creating unique stories. Kate Messner compares beautifully in *Over and Under the Snow*. The young narrator is skiing and takes note of what happens above and beneath the snow.

ALPHABET

This is often used by nonfiction writers to organize their information. Alphabet books are popular with teachers because they reinforce a basic skill that students are learning. I love this form. My book *Eight Hands Round: A Patchwork Alphabet* introduces a different patchwork-design name for each letter. A more recently published example is Esther Hershenhorn's book *S Is for Story: A Writer's Alphabet*. The ABCs start with *alphabet* and then proceed to *book, character, drafts, edit*, and so on. It's packed with writing tips and information for students and professional writers. Another example of an alphabet book is *A is for Activist* by Innosanto Nagara—a board book that has warmed the hearts of progressives.

The books mentioned above are in the more traditional form, which involves listing letters, but when you're writing today, it's not enough to just list "*A* is for *apple*," "*B* is for *banana*," etc. Publishers want alphabet books to tell a story. In my book *Everything to Spend the Night*, a young girl packs her suitcase with all she needs for an overnight at Grandpa's house, only to discover she's forgotten the most important item.

A note of warning: An alphabet book needs *every* letter of the alphabet. You can't cheat by using a hard *C* sound for *K*, but you can be creative with your letters. In *Everything to Spend the Night,* I managed to slip the letter *X* into the dialogue as she begs Grandpa, "Just one more game? I brought my jacks. Toss the Xs. Cat, stay back." Sneaky? Definitely!

How might I adapt this approach to Quigley's story? Here I might have Quigley collecting an alphabet of gifts for Blaze's new house. First an alarm clock, then a fancy bowl, a set of coasters, a dining table, and so on. Be sure to check out *Z Is for Moose* by Kelly Bingham and *Alpha Oops!: The Day Z Went First* by Alethea Kontis, two books that play with the order of letters.

COUNTING

Teachers also seek out counting books, but as with alphabet books, they, too, must tell a story. Rethinking the Quigley story, let's say he decides to bring one television, two chairs, three plates, and so on to Blaze's housewarming party. You get the idea, but I'm not terribly excited about taking the story in this direction. That's probably because both of my suggestions for Quigley's alphabet and counting stories lack tension or a problem—something I'd have to work on before submitting the manuscript to a publisher. *Counting Crows* by Kathi Appelt and *Count the Monkeys* by Mac Barnett are notable for their creative integration of numbers.

REPETITIVE PHRASE

Kids love hearing repetitive phrases. They anticipate them and say them along with the adult. They feel like they're "reading." But too often, beginning writers overuse these phrases. When you're starting out, a good rule of thumb is *less is better.* Or you might consider varying the phrase slightly so it isn't predictable.

The repetitive phrase should be lively, fun, and novel. A phrase that's repeated can add rhythm and poetry to a story. It can also be used to indicate passage of time for younger readers who don't understand the concepts of tomorrow, next week, or next year. Could I use a repetitive phrase with my Quigley story? Absolutely. Whenever Quigley gets excited about helping his friends, I could have him "wig-wag-waggle," signaling to the reader something bad is about to happen.

Many books employ this technique to great effect. For example, H. Joseph Hopkins, who wrote the beautiful nonfiction book *The Tree Lady: The True Story of How One Tree-Loving Woman Changed a City Forever*, holds his story together with a simple declarative statement that he repeats with slight variations throughout the text. In April Halprin Wayland's *More Than Enough: A Passover Story*, the Hebrew word *dayenu* is repeated over in the course of the book.

In my books *If Animals Kissed Good Night* and *If Animals Said I Love You*, both concept books without a conflict or problem, I used recurring characters to hold the story together. In the kissing book, those characters were a mama sloth and cub, who, being slow, kept kissing all night long. In the loving book, those repetitive characters were a mama gorilla and her infant. The title of each of the books is also repeated periodically.

DAYS OF THE WEEK

This is a fine way to organize your story, but beware: If you aren't going to mention every day of the week, don't mention any. When you state a specific day, you set the reader up to expect the rest of them. Books including days of the week are popular with teachers because they reinforce the learning that goes on in preschool and kindergarten. If I were going to use days of the week with Quigley, perhaps I'd make the party a week away and for each day, highlight activities in which the friends engage.

My book *Mañana, Iguana,* which adds a Spanish twist to the classic story *The Little Red Hen*, uses this technique. Iguana is planning a party, and every day (the story starts on a Monday) she asks her friends for help. They make excuses until Saturday, the day of the party, when they're eager to participate. Iguana says, "NO!" and they slink away to watch the fun from afar. Feeling badly over their lack of help, they decide they must do something. On Sunday, Iguana awakens to a big surprise, and everyone is happy. Of course, I've already written that story, so for Quigley's book, if I do days of the week, I'd better come up with something different. For other books in this vein, have a look at *Monday Is One Day* by Arthur A. Levine, where working parents and children mark the days of the week with special moments. *Perfect Square* by Michael Hall, where each day the square's shape is modified into something new, is another creative work that includes the days of the week.

MONTHS OF THE YEAR

I'm not sure months of the year would work for Quigley's story as it is now plotted. Perhaps the story would turn into Blaze's story about the process of building his house, or I could make it Quigley's story if I had Blaze move away. Over the course of a year, Quigley might remember all the things they had done together during each month. Both *Hap-pea All Year* by Keith Baker and *Winterberries and Apple Blossoms: Reflections and Flavors of a Mennonite Year* by Nan Forler use months of the year as an organization tool.

SEASONS

This would be easier than months of the year. However, I realize I'd have to change my story from being about how enthusiasm can get in the way of helpfulness to something about the stages of Blaze's building his house. In my nonfiction book *The Seasons Sewn: A Year in Patchwork,* it was natural to organize the patchwork patterns by season since people lived according to the changing seasons in pioneer times. Other examples of the seasons' approach include Joyce Sidman's beautifully poetic *Red Sings from Treetops: A Year in Colors* and *All Around the Seasons* by Barney Saltzberg.

STORY WITHIN A STORY

It is common for adults to tell children stories. Suppose we bring in Quigley's dad and start the story with Quigley slumping home after his disastrous attempts to help. His dad sits down with him and tells him about the kind of trouble he used to get into as a pup, and together they figure out a way to make things right again. I'm not liking this though because I don't like parents in my stories.

A classic example of a story within a story is the sensitive and tender book I mentioned earlier, *Finding Winnie: The True Story of the World's Most Famous Bear* by Lindsay Mattick. A boy asks his mother to tell him a story, so she relates how a veterinarian bought a bear cub and took him along to England. They have fun adventures along the way and become attached, but it soon becomes apparent there's no place for a bear on the battlefields of World War I, so he goes to live in a zoo. The mother goes on to explain how this bear became a character in children's books. What makes the book work so well is that the author brings the two stories (the one of her telling the story to her son and the actual story of the bear) together at the end. It's a must-read example of this form.

QUESTION AND ANSWER

What if we used this technique with Quigley's story? It might read like this: "What will Quigley do to help get ready for the party? He'll rush over to Monique's house and oh, splatter batter all over the walls. What will Quigley do then? He will slump outside, feeling down in the dumps."

Not a Box by Antoinette Portis is one book that successfully uses the question-and-answer format. It was such a hit she followed this up with the similarly organized *Not a Stick. Creature Features* by Steve Jenkins and Robin Page also uses the question-and-answer format. The narrator asks animals questions like, "Why don't you have any feathers?" The Egyptian vulture answers, and then the narrator asks a different animal a separate question, eventually totaling twenty-five different questions and answers.

CUMULATIVE ACTION

In these stories, events pile up and frequently repeat, as in the classic nursery rhyme "The House that Jack Built."

> This is the house that Jack built.
>
> This is the malt
> That lay in the house that Jack built.
>
> This is the rat,
> That ate the malt
> That lay in the house that Jack built.
>
> This is the cat,
> That killed the rat,
> That ate the malt
> That lay in the house that Jack built.
>
> This is the dog,
> That worried the cat,

That killed the rat,
That ate the malt
That lay in the house that Jack built.

On it frolics for many stanzas. If I applied this kind of rhyme to Quigley's story, I might start with the following.

This is the cake Quigley tried to bake.
This is the horrible mess he made,
Trying to bake a cake for his friend.
This is the way he scrubbed up the batter,
After the horrible mess he made,
Trying to bake a cake for his friend.

Who Woke the Baby? by Jane Clarke is a wonderful take on the cumulative-action approach. This method is not easy to master, which is why I so love *The Wrong Side of the Bed* by Lisa M. Bakos.

COMBINING TECHNIQUES

Feel free to use more than one of these techniques to strengthen your story's midsection. In *Manaña, Iguana,* I used the three-act structure, cause and effect, and escalating action, having Iguana grow increasingly frustrated that her friends won't help her prepare for the spring fiesta. For good measure I added several repetitive phrases, "*Mañana, Iguana,*" "*Yo no!*" and "And she did." Last but not least, the story unfolded across a week.

A FEW FINAL WORDS

After you write your story with a three-act structure, using the rhythm of threes, cause and effect, and escalating action, experiment with the techniques in this chapter to add depth and structure to your stories. Sounds simple, right? Of course not. When you're alone with your story, it's tough.

Unfortunately, you'll need to use different techniques to reach the destination of everything you write. No one formula works for each story. That's the challenge of writing, *and* that's also what keeps writing stimulating. When you're working on a story and it is not moving forward or maybe has come to a dead stop, see if one of these techniques might strengthen it.

WHAT'S NEXT?

We've made it through the middle of picture books. Now it's time to make sure your ending is as satisfying as your beginning and your middle.

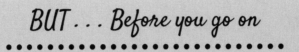

BUT . . . Before you go on

1. Check your manuscript to see if you use one of these techniques. Some stories incorporate several into their text. Play around with adding one or two or changing the techniques to improve your story.
2. Reread the published good and bad texts you chose to see what techniques, if any, the authors used in their respective midsections.
3. Read a new picture book, perhaps one mentioned in this chapter.

12

Does Your Story Have a Satisfying Ending?

"A book should end with the unexpected expected."

—JANE YOLEN

A book without a strong ending feels like dinner without dessert, a party dress paired with running shoes, or a baseball game called off on account of rain. In the same way chocolate cake can leave one feeling full and satisfied, so too can a great ending leave one pleased and content. Chocolate cake is so tasty you want more, so you continue to indulge. Likewise, a good picture-book ending compels a reader to go back and read the story again and again. That taste of chocolate and those final words linger long afterward.

On the other hand, a weak ending leaves an unpleasant taste in one's mouth. Far too many books start out with great promise but fall flat. It's too bad that the third act in any book, play, or movie has such power to make us either love, be ambivalent, or even loathe what came before.

Katherine Anne Porter said, "If I didn't know the ending of a story, I wouldn't begin. I always write my last lines, my last paragraph, my last page first. . . ." Other writers don't have any idea where the story will take them and insist on being surprised by what comes out of their mind and ends up on the page. Regardless of when you write your ending, labor long and hard to avoid leaving your readers and listeners with a *blah* feeling. Here are some points to consider in evaluating your ending.

THE ENDING MUST BE UNPREDICTABLE

It needs to originate from the story yet still be surprising. Who wants to read any further in a mystery if we know immediately that the butler killed the master of the house? Who wants to continue reading a picture book if we are certain how the bully will get his comeuppance? Naturally we want to assume the bully will be brought down, but we don't want to know *how* until the end.

THE ENDING MUST SOLVE THE ORIGINAL PROBLEM

Sometimes writers start out with one problem, introduce another problem along the way, and then solve only that second problem. Suppose the main character is trying to decide what kind of birthday present to buy his mom. On the way to the store, he gets distracted by friends playing a game of baseball, stops to play, and must endure torments by his teammates for missing an easy catch. He forgets about his mom's gift and is now focused on how to deal with the teasing and how to improve his game. Even if the writer does go back to the first problem, there are cases where the secondary story line and conflict have no relation to it. We talked earlier about the importance of focusing a story. This helps create a satisfying ending.

EVERYTHING YOU'VE WRITTEN RELATES TO THE ENDING

If it doesn't, delete. Get rid of anything that doesn't advance your story line. In the above example, I'd have to get rid of the baseball game. Sometimes this will mean saying goodbye to your favorite words or lines. Be brutal. If it's too painful, create a file of phrases you would love to use in a poem or another story.

THE MAIN CHARACTER SOLVES THE PROBLEM

If a wise, well-meaning adult steps in to show the way, get rid of that adult. We should aim to empower children, but the ending is where writers often forget to do that. A child, like the one in our example, is bothered by the teasing he gets from his teammates. He tries several ways to stop it. They all fail, so Father steps in. No! Our main character must determine his own satisfying solution.

THE MAIN CHARACTER EVOLVES

Malcolm Cowley said, "Any fiction should be a story. In any story, there are three elements: persons, a situation, and the fact that in the end something has changed. If nothing has changed, it isn't a story." Each character in our picture books must learn something new about herself or her outlook on the world or overcome something that kept her from acting.

In a few stories, a character struggles to change or take some action but cannot. Think about a child whose beloved puppy dies. Not understanding the concept of death, she calls and calls for him, to no avail. Maybe, she worries, he might be trapped in a tight place, so she goes searching, with no success. She puts out food, hoping he'll return to eat. Notice the rhythm of threes here. Eventually, she realizes her puppy will never return. She accepts the finality of his absence. That acceptance is change.

LUCKY COINCIDENCES DON'T INFLUENCE THE OUTCOME

A child is invited to a birthday party that includes swimming in a lake. He can't swim and doesn't want his friends to know. He begs Dad to let him stay home, but Dad says if he doesn't attend the party, the birthday boy will be disappointed.

He sobs and feigns a stomachache. Nothing works, so he leaves for the birthday party. All of a sudden (many editors say that *all of a sudden* should be banned in every story), he trips over a log and breaks his leg. An ambulance is summoned to take him to the hospital.

Lucky him! He didn't have to go to the party. His friends won't learn about his fear of the water. It's a happy ending for him, except for that scary time in the hospital, but is it satisfying? Not at all. However, it would be satisfying if he could admit to his friends he can't swim and if instead of laughing, they offered to teach him.

NO EXTRA CHARACTERS AID IN THE RESOLUTION

Suppose a cheetah is about to attack a zebra. The cheetah drools. He opens his jaws. The zebra is sure she's a goner. But just in time (*just in time* should also be eliminated from stories), a hyena howls and chases off the cheetah. The zebra hurries away. *No! No! No!*

What if the zebra had a plan? Perhaps she could wait until the cheetah is eye to eye with her, spin around, and kick him. The cheetah would be stunned, giving the zebra time to escape, all because of her courage and smart thinking. Bravo! We can cheer for her.

ALL CHARACTERS PLAY AN IMPORTANT PART

In picture books, unlike other books, we don't want characters to appear briefly, only to disappear forever. Listeners will wonder what happened to the barking dog. They will anticipate that the big brother who went to school will come home again. And they will worry if Mama Bear, who fed her cub breakfast, isn't around for lunch. If characters disappear, never to return, they probably can be cut. Notice I said *probably.* The exception to this sometimes appears in folktales, where the main character is given powers along the way to aid her on her quest. However, if those gifts are not part of the solution, the characters who gave them must go.

THE ENDING COMES AT THE END

This might appear to be obvious, but surprisingly it isn't. In picture books, the solution to the primary problem usually falls on pages twenty-eight and twenty-nine, or better yet, pages thirty and thirty-one of the published book. But some writers solve the presenting problem in the middle and then go on and on. Want to see an example of this? Look at my book *Count on Culebra.* The primary problem was that Iguana stubbed her toe on a stone and hence, couldn't make her *dulces* (candy). The snake, Culebra, insisted he was a doctor and could cure her. To summarize, he tied a bunch of objects to her tail, and when she walked, the noise distracted her so much she forgot her pain and could make her candy. That should have been the end. However, I went on for eighty-one more words. I added another story element, the animals cooperating to make the *dulces.* Unnecessary! And as if that wasn't enough, I had everyone congratulate Dr. Culebra. Those extra words distracted from the humor and the accomplishment of the cure. That book never sold as well as the other books in the series. I still love this story but suspect that letting my ending go on too long might explain the lower sales.

I've shared this example from my work, not only to illustrate this problem of not knowing when to stop but to help you realize that even published writers sometimes don't tell their stories in the best possible way. However, professional writers learn from their mistakes. I promise you that with every story I write, I am now alert to this issue. As Igor Stravinsky said, "Too many pieces

… finish too long after the end." When the problem is solved, your story is over, except for one quick last bit.

NO LOOSE ENDS

Picture books have space on page thirty-two for dealing with unresolved issues. It's a page with room for a half-spread illustration (an illustration that doesn't cross over onto the next page). Unless the book is forty pages or more, page thirty-two is perfect for a quick, sharp, often humorous line.

In my book *Little Monkey Says Good Night,* Little Monkey has romped through the circus saying good night to everyone. He should be done, but he insists he has one more to say. On page thirty-two, we see him tucked into bed and hear him say, "Good night, me." In *Chicken Lily* by Lori Mortensen, the story begins with a statement about how despite her talent, she is scared to recite a poem at the school's poetry jam. By the end, Lily conquers her fear of public speaking, but the final image reveals that she has another fear to face—riding her bike without training wheels. In *The Wrong Side of the Bed*, Lisa M. Bakos also does a fine job of tying up loose ends. At the beginning, the main character wakes to find she has only one bunny slipper. Her day goes downhill from there. The next day, she wakes to the same problem—a missing bunny slipper. Is her day going to be the same? No. She puts on galoshes, and the final line indicates that was the perfect choice for the day it turned out to be.

Because of the last line's importance, don't be lazy. Work hard shaping this final bit of your story. Your ending should resolve all story lines and answer all story questions. While writers may leave things up in the air in books for adults and older children, our young listeners don't want anything left untold.

Picture books are not series books in the traditional sense, even though we often have several books written about popular characters, like Olivia and Rotten Ralph. My If Animals books may be a series, but each one stands alone. They don't follow an unfinished thread from one book to another. Each picture book stands on its own merit.

If a book is successful and an editor wants another, wonderful! That's like getting two scoops of ice cream instead of one. But don't start a series by leaving loose ends. Start a series by writing a runaway, best-selling book.

NO EXPLICIT MORAL OR MESSAGE

Sam Goldwyn said, "If you want to send a message, use Western Union." Although he was talking to screenwriters, his advice applies to picture-book authors. Our stories are to entertain, to carry reader and listener to another place, another life, another world. If the writer wants to teach a lesson, she should write a nonfiction book or perhaps a book for the religious market. Children have minds, just like adults. They will get the message without the author pounding them over the head with it.

Aesop got away with tacking morals onto his stories' endings, but we don't do that anymore ... unless we're writing a new take on one of Aesop's fables, as Arnold Lobel did in his Caldecott Medal winning book *Fables.* Today we write differently. Think of the bad taste in one's mouth if, in my *Count on Culebra*, in addition to the long ending, I had written a line about how, even if a friend isn't a real doctor, he might know about healing a bad toe. *Yipes!* My sales might have plummeted even further. Your listener will get that lesson without it being explicitly stated. Respect your audience.

HAVE A HOPEFUL, IF NOT HAPPY, ENDING

We touched on this when discussing Booker's classic tragedy plots in chapter nine. This necessary element of hope is distinctive to picture books and most writing for children. Unlike adult books, where horrific things happen and authors share their depressing views of life, we children's authors try to write in an upbeat manner. There's too much war and death, too much hunger and cruelty, too many dangers to which children are vulnerable. We owe it to today's children to not add to their anxieties. This doesn't mean that you can't write about war or death, hunger or global warming, but when you write about it, find something to give the listener a smidgen of hope.

EXAMPLES OF STRONG PICTURE-BOOK ENDINGS

Time for (Earth) School, Dewey Dew by Leslie Staub has a wonderful ending. It is a humorous story in which a creature from a faraway planet is terrified to attend his new school on Earth. There are fun made-up words for *ankles, feet, middle*, and *okay.* Dewey Dew faces the usual nervousness of starting school and meeting new kids who are different from him, but when one fellow classmate reaches out in friendship, a beautiful thing happens (in both the words and illustrations), and Dewey Dew knows that everything will be fine. So comforting and satisfying! In *Sophie's Fish* by A.E. Cannon, another book with a strong ending, a boy is asked by his classmate to babysit her fish, Yo-Yo. The boy has never taken care of a fish and tries to imagine what it will entail. The more he thinks about it, the scarier his fantasies become and the more nervous he gets. He is about to call Sophie and refuse, when she rings his doorbell. She gives him such simple instructions that he decides this won't be difficult. Not so difficult, that is, until on page thirty-two, he meets Sophie's fish.

My Favorite Pets: by Gus W. for Ms. Smolinski's Class by Jeanne Birdsall has two fun, very brief endings. The first is the ending of Gus's report, and the tie-up includes his teacher's grade and written comments. In *The Summer Nick Taught His Cats to Read* by Curtis Manley, Nick struggles to teach his cats to read. After trying for a long time, he succeeds. At the end, he's thinking that now maybe he'd like to teach them to talk! His stubborn cat answers as only a cat can.

I love the punch-line ending of *There's a Bear on My Chair* by Ross Collins. The mouse tries many times to get the bear out of his chair but finally gives up. The bear is then done with the chair (as children typically are when others lose interest) and heads back home, where a surprise is waiting. In *Bike on, Bear!* by Cynthea Liu, Bear can do many wonderful things, just not ride a bike. The book shows his struggles and eventual success. Everyone cheers. Now Bear can do almost everything. But on the last page, as successful as he was in riding a bike, yet another skill requires his attention.

A FEW FINAL WORDS

I could write an entire book on strong endings, and maybe someday I will. They are your last opportunity to impress your audience and are the difference between someone shutting your book with satisfaction or disappointment. Spend as much time as necessary to create your ending.

WHAT'S NEXT?

Give yourself a pat on the back. You've finished every section on story structure. It's time to discuss language and how to write in a lively, compelling manner.

BUT . . . Before you go on

1. Highlight the place in your story where the characters solve the problem. If it's too early, delete or tighten what follows.
2. How many of the following characteristics are in your ending? Put a star beside each that you successfully included in your ending.

   a. The ending must be unpredictable
   b. The ending must solve the original problem
   c. Everything you've written relates to the ending
   d. The main character solves the problem
   e. The main character evolves
   f. Lucky coincidences don't influence the outcome
   g. No extra characters aid in the resolution
   h. All characters play an important part
   i. The ending comes at the end
   j. No loose ends
   k. No explicit moral or message
   l. If not happy, is hopeful

3. Are you satisfied with your ending, or do you need to revise?
4. Look at the endings of your good and bad published books. Do they work? Why?
5. Read a new picture book, perhaps one mentioned in this chapter. In the bibliography, I have indicated books with strong endings with an *E*.

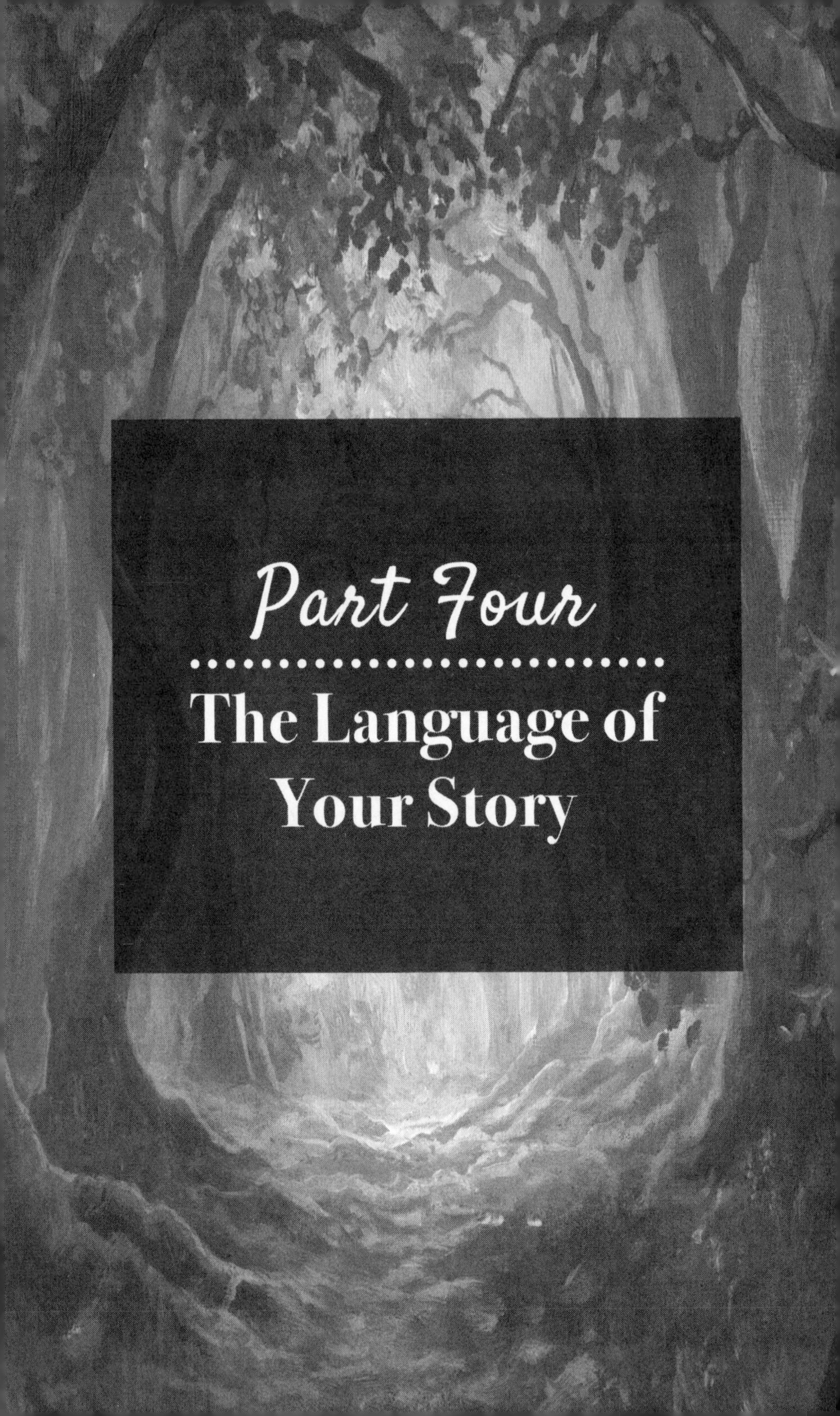

Part Four

The Language of Your Story

13

The Two Ss of Strong Writing

"Effective writing depends on showing through action, dialogue, or detail."

—OLGA LITOWINSKY

Isn't it a relief to be done with picture-book form? Now we'll turn to the Two *Ss* of strong writing, which are essential regardless of your audience's age. Let's delve into the first *S*.

SCENES

Nancy Lamb, in *The Writer's Guide to Crafting Stories for Children,* says, "Think of … scenes … as stepping stones that steer you down the path of your plot." Too often authors don't write the most important scenes. It's much easier to write "The two friends made up" than to write the dialogue that allows readers to observe their emotional transition from hostility to understanding. Skipping an important scene is not only lazy writing; it's poor writing. Scenes are critical, permitting readers and listeners to experience events with the characters, watching the story unfold along with them. But to write a scene, you must know what a scene is.

My favorite definition comes from Jack Bickham in his book *Scene and Structure.* He says scene is "a segment of story action, written moment-by-moment, without summary, presented onstage in the story 'now.' It is *not* something that goes on inside a character's head; it is physical. It could be put on the theater stage and acted out."

In the Bickham quote, *action* means something is happening that you can see. A character punching another character is action. A character crying is action, and a character storming out of a room is more action. Because action is illustratable and contemplation isn't, picture-book writers must put as much action as possible into their manuscripts. If a scene is written "moment-by-moment, without summary," that means we see it exactly as it happens. It is not a condensation of an event. A scene is physical in that outsiders can observe it.

WHY WRITE IN SCENES?

Scenes are the best way to communicate conflict and tension. The scene is the primary device for making readers and listeners respond to your story in the manner you desire. A scene allows them to play out in their minds what is taking place on the page, making them participants in your book. The vaguer you are, the more you summarize and push your audience away from the character. You are permitting them to imagine what the scene might have been, and that can be very different from knowing what actually happened.

WHEN SHOULD YOU WRITE IN SCENES?

A scene must do one of two things: advance the plot or reveal something new about your characters. If a scene in your picture book doesn't advance your story, write it as a narrative summary. For example, if the route your character takes to the soccer game isn't relevant, you can simply write "when he arrived at the stadium." If your writing doesn't let the reader discover some unknown facet of your character, you can summarize this, too, but be sure that your choice of scene or summary is correct. Don't write a summary just because constructing a scene is more challenging.

HOW DO YOU WRITE A SCENE?

If scenes were easy, everyone would write them. The best way to ensure that your audience experiences a scene is for you to put yourself in it. This isn't as difficult as it sounds. Be an actor. Pretend you're the character. Slip out of your skin, and put on your character's. By this point, you've already created your character study. You know your character so well that you don't have to wonder what she might say; it's already on the tip of your tongue. Now pace the room like your character might, or fidget nervously in your chair. Speak in whispers; speak in shouts. Don't be embarrassed or self-conscious. Unlike an actor onstage, no one can see you. Each time you perform and revise, you refine and improve your performance.

Years ago, when someone in my critique group said, "You're not in the scene," I was terrified. At first, I thought I *never* could be in the scene, but with time and practice, I was surprised at how effortless it became. Soon it was second nature to me.

Try this simple exercise if you're afraid you can't become your character. Pretend you're a child experiencing your first Christmas tree. Your eyes widen at the sparkling lights. You scramble close on your hands and knees. So many bright baubles. You reach for one, but your parents shout "No!" You can't believe they won't let you hold these new toys, so you grab one. Your father wrenches it out of your fist. You cry! Compare this to how you look at the tree as an adult. You ooohhhh. You aaaahhhh. But you know better than to touch those decorations. You know how fragile they are and how much they cost.

Let's be a child again but older, going to school for the first time. You cling to your mother's hand. The classroom is huge, with so many tables. One has puzzles, one has clay, and one has snacks—graham crackers. You hate those crackers. And who is this strange lady who bends down and greets you by name? So many other kids here. And you don't know any of them. You squeeze Mom's hand tighter. You bury your head in her dress and cry.

Your mother, on the other hand, sees all the activities spread out and thinks what fun you'll have. And all the potential friends for her child. Why is he crying? What's scary about this exciting new adventure?

Now make believe you are the child's grandparent. Wow! All those low nursery-school chairs. If you sit down, how will you get up again? And what about those children racing around? You step back, afraid one might knock you down.

Try pretending you're the class's pet rabbit who's awakened by the sudden activity in the room. What's all this squealing? And now someone's poking a finger into your crate. You hover in the corner.

Next, imagine you're in a hurry and can't find your car keys. Pretend you're sitting courtside at a Lakers' game. Pretend you're trying to fly a kite, learn how to knit, or high-jump. Pretend; pretend; pretend using all of your senses. The more you do, the less effort it will take to get into your character's skin and make scenes come alive for your listeners. I know authors who have helped their writing by taking an acting class. You might want to try it.

Still having trouble writing your scene? You might be writing too quickly. Writing a scene involves slowing down and paying attention to each line. Pause to see what else might be happening around your character. Take as much time as you need to play with different possibilities for dialogue and action until you're sure you're writing what actually occurred. Here are some sample words and phrases that warn you're not writing a scene:

- *Whenever* I go swimming
- *Each time* Mom yells at me
- *Every time* Jimmy chases me
- *Every day* at school
- *Year after year,* the increasing snowfall

These indicate several scenes are clumped together. Sometimes you want that, but watch out. These clumpings aren't scenes, and most should really be played out individually.

EVERY SCENE HAS A DIFFERENT INTERNAL RHYTHM

In the same way that life has different rhythms, scenes present different rhythms. We don't go along with the same emotional and psychological energy every hour of every day. Each twenty-four-hour period offers a unique pattern of high and low points. In strong, successful writing, the listener and reader should not only know intellectually what is happening but also *feel it physically and emotionally.*

Imagine you are on an African safari. The guide stops for you to take pictures of a lion. You admire his golden fur, fluffy mane, and sleek muscles. Although his eyes are alert, he seems to be relaxing, enjoying the sun. You put down your camera and enjoy the warmth of the sun and the smell of the African savanna. Thoughts ramble through your mind. What a fabulous trip this has been! You remember the last time you saw a lion in the zoo, separated by a deep moat. You were with your children, and they loved growling at the lion in his enclosure. You laughed at their game and their interpretations of the lion's roaring responses. Then that lion stands, roars, and races towards your vehicle. The guide grabs his gun. Your body tenses. Your mind spins! Would he really attack? Why did you come here? Your breathing quickens. Your heart pounds. You're on high alert.

Notice what happened. In the beginning, you were relaxed. Your mind had time to contemplate and linger. The sentences were longer to match that lazy mood. However, when the lion attacks, everything changes. The sentences grow shorter, tighter—no time for metaphor or simile. Your writing must echo the energy in the actions of each scene. We'll discuss how to do this in more detail in chapters fourteen and fifteen.

QUIZ TIME

Before we move on, let's make sure you understand the difference between a scene and a narrative summary. Write *S* if it's a scene and *N* if it's a narrative summary.

1. There was a riot at the concert.
2. Jon jumped up. "Let's get out of here."

   "Beat you to the car," Matt said, sticking his foot out and tripping Jon. "Sorry!" he smirked.

   Jon rubbed his knee. "I'll show him." He pushed himself to stand. "Ow!" He couldn't believe the pain. He hobbled, cursing under his breath. "I hate, hate, hate Matt."
3. "I just want you to love me again," she said between sobs. "That's all I want. Just like you used to."
4. She was devastated when her dog died.
5. He pretended not to hear.
6. Cat twitched her tail. She waited. Waited.

   Mouse peered out of her hole. He looked left, right. He stepped outside.

   Cat pounced.
7. Peter gripped Father's hand. "Can we buy ice cream at the store?"

   "Not today," he said.

   Peter dropped Father's hand. He flung himself onto the floor and sobbed. "You always say that. Why are you so mean?"
8. Lena was scared and begged to go home.

Answers: 1. N 2. S 3. S 4. N 5. N 6. S 7. S 8. N

From these examples, you might assume that scenes are always longer than narrative sections. That's not always true. For example, if you wrote, "Finn was really scared," you'd be writing a narrative summary. But if you wrote, "'I'm scared,' said Finn," although you'd be using the same number of words, being able to hear Finn's dialogue means that we're experiencing it with him. If you got all of the examples right, you're on your way to understanding that oft-repeated phrase heard in conferences and classes that is our second S.

SHOW; DON'T TELL

This phrase admonishes you to write a scene rather than a summary statement. However, "show; don't tell" applies not only to scenes but also to descriptive phrases. For example, the statement "Our dog was happy to see me" is a telling statement. "Our dog yipped and yapped and leaped up" is specific and therefore shows. It allows the reader to conclude on her own that the dog was happy.

This is not insignificant. Imagine the sentence "Joanne was depressed." Now pretend we can't use the word *depressed.* Describe the action that would make the reader realize she was depressed. Here are five possibilities:

1. Joanne sat in a corner, her head in her hands.
2. Joanne stared at the open book, but her mind raced with suicidal thoughts.
3. Joanne threw herself on her bed. "Why can't everyone leave me alone?"
4. Joanne stared at her plate of pasta. Picking up her fork felt like too much effort.
5. Joanne wiped away the tears spilling down her cheeks. More tears flowed. Would they ever cease?

In number one, Joanne isolates herself from others. In number two, she tries to distract herself, to no avail. In number three, she lashes out at others. In number four, she can't even eat. Lastly, in number five she tries to stop her tears, fails, and fears her depression might last forever. Each response indicates a different kind of character or a different point in her journey.

When you tell, the reader must imagine what your character might do. Showing instead of telling makes *you, the writer,* define your character and paint a full picture for the reader and listeners of what's going on. It breathes life into the scene. Every reader brings her own set of experiences and feelings to a book. If you tell instead of show, you give the reader too much power in creating your character.

"Show; don't tell" also concerns the details you choose for your story.

Too many details will bog down the reader and diminish your story's momentum, but a specially placed vivid detail can be all the reader needs to be in a scene. Make sure the details in a picture-book description are ones a child would relate to.

For example, "The stadium was huge" is a telling statement. Huge to whom? A mouse would find any stadium huge, even if it had only one chair. Be specific. "The stadium seated 70,000 patrons" is a clear explanation for an adult but not so meaningful to young listeners. "From our high seats in the stadium the players on the field looked smaller than mice" is much easier for a child to visualize.

To make sure you understand this concept of "show; don't tell," play around with transforming the following telling statements into showing statements.

1. Thea was happy.
2. There was an atmosphere of expectation and excitement.
3. The hole looked tiny.
4. There were many wildebeests and zebras.
5. I was hungry.
6. Her mind ran wild with possibilities.
7. He was terrified about the upcoming trip.
8. Shots were fired, and people rushed helter-skelter.
9. Owen was scared.
10. Ship passengers were awed by their first sight of the Statue of Liberty.
11. He was worried the police officer would stop him.

So you know you're on the right track, here are possible answers to compare with your own.

1. Thea giggled.
2. People clapped and stomped. Susan nudged her date. "I can't wait for the show to start."
3. The hole was smaller than my pinkie nail.
4. As far as the eye could see, wildebeests and zebras roamed the plains.
5. My stomach growled. I rushed to the refrigerator, frantic for something, anything to put into my empty stomach.
6. Should she call him? Would he think she was being too forward? Or would he be happy to hear her voice? Maybe she should wait for an hour not to appear too eager. She wouldn't want to scare him away.
7. "Paul! You're not packed yet! What are you thinking?"

   He looked down. "I-I-I," he stammered. "Do I *have* to go?"
8. Pop! Pop! Guns! Someone pushed Bonnie. She stumbled. "Out of my way!" Bonnie tried to see ahead, but people swirled around her. Where was the

exit? Why hadn't she looked earlier? She turned and knocked a child down. She offered her hand to help him, but he jumped up and raced away.

9. Owen opened his mouth to scream. No sound came out.
10. People clambered to the deck. They pointed. They laughed. "We made it!" A man hugged his wife. "We're really, truly here."
11. Maybe he should cross the street, Matt worried, but the police officer might wonder why. And he couldn't cross in the middle of the block. Jaywalking wasn't legal. But a ticket for jaywalking wouldn't be as bad as a ticket for the packet of white powder in his pocket.

How did you do here? Do you feel comfortable with the difference between showing and telling? Do you feel secure about writing scenes instead of summaries?

A FEW FINAL WORDS

You probably have noticed that writing in scenes and showing instead of telling usually requires more words. Don't worry if writing in the two *S*s initially adds extra words to your picture-book manuscript. Your story can be revised and tightened up. As I noted in the post-quiz discussion, showing doesn't necessarily increase your word count. "Rabbit was scared" can be shown with "Rabbit hopped away." No additional words are necessary to present a vivid image.

WHAT'S NEXT?

We've covered two of the big general issues in writing. In chapter fourteen we're going to get more specific about language and consider the advantages of poetic storytelling.

BUT . . . Before you go on

1. Look over your manuscript, and circle places where you're writing narrative summary rather than an unfolding scene. Also, circle any places where you tell instead of show.

Do you have lots? Good! That means you recognize where you need to revise. You're well on the road to getting out of lazy writing habits.

2. If you don't have many circles, let another writer go over your manuscript to make sure you spotted them all. In the beginning, it's often easier to pick these out from someone else's manuscript. The more you practice, the better you'll get at finding them in your stories.
3. Now go back to all of those circles, and write scenes rather than summaries; show rather than tell.
4. Check your typed published-book texts. Did the one you don't like do more telling than showing?
5. Read a new picture book.

14

Rhyme Time

"There is no better feeling to me than writing. I love to make a picture come to life and dance under my pen."

—LOLITA PRINCE

The above quote comes from a homeless woman who is active in the Los Angeles Downtown Women's Center's writing workshop. When Lolita said, "I love to make a picture come to life and dance under my pen," she expressed as good a definition of poetry as I know. Poets use words—only words—to create pictures for the reader. The dancing under the pen relates to the music of those words. A successful poem not only brings up a visual image of the subject, but through word choice, sounds, rhythm, and rhyme, it creates a physical reaction to enhance and reinforce the image.

Children love poetry. They love the music of it. They love anticipating rhyming words and saying them along with adults. This is the beginning of their reading. Studies show that children who hear poetry from a young age become proficient readers earlier than those not exposed to poems.

If this is true, why do editors frequently groan when they read picture-book manuscripts that incorporate rhyme? Why do they throw up their hands and beg, "Please! No more rhymed picture books!" The answer is simple. Most writers have failed to master the elements of good poetry. Yet writers persist. When they think of stories for children, they think of rhyme. It's lively, and fun, so they give it a try.

You wouldn't trust a doctor to perform your surgery if he hadn't first studied medicine. You wouldn't let a pilot fly your plane if she hadn't taken flying lessons. And you wouldn't hire a teacher if he hadn't gone to college. But too many writers think they can write a rhymed picture book without any knowledge of poetry.

This chapter will help you determine your ability to write in rhyme and whether you first need to educate yourself about poetry.

We're at that part of the book I warned you metrophobes (those who fear poetry) about earlier. Don't panic. Take a deep breath. Now take another. I was a nervous wreck when I walked into my first poetry-writing class, but studying poetry is the best thing I did to strengthen my ability to write publishable picture books.

It's time to take a dip in the rhymed, metrical poetry pool. I guarantee that by reading the next two chapters and taking practice swims, you and poetry will eventually get along fine. Let's get our feet wet with four elements of good poetry—brevity, focus, consistent rhyme, and consistent rhythm. The first two elements have already been discussed in relation to picture books. To understand these concepts in relation to poetry, let's look at that well-known nursery rhyme "To Bed!" by the prolific Mother Goose. Using this familiar work will help you spot errors more easily than you would in your poetic endeavors.

BREVITY

When I was in high school and assigned to write papers of a certain length, I often padded my work. After all, I had to make the assigned word count. Writing picture books, whether in prose or poetry, forced me and will force you to unlearn padding techniques. Picture books are short. Poems are short, too. Let's look at our example below.

> Come let's to bed,
> Says Sleepy-head;
> Sit up a while, says Slow;
> Put on the pan,
> Says Greedy Nan,
> Let's sup before we go.

Mother Goose used only twenty-four words to tell us about bedtime for these three distinct personalities. Many writers get started writing a poem or a rhyming picture book and can't stop. Students have shown me poems that go on for thousands of words. What a lot of work for nothing! Why nothing?

Remember we're writing for children with short attention spans; they can't sit still for long. *War and Peace* would never appeal to a five-year-old or even a ten-year-old. They simply can't focus on such a long but fabulous book. So why do rhyming writers go on too long?

FOCUS

Sadly, too many writers lose their focus. Focus is staying on message, not going off on tangents. It's following the poem or story road to the end without detours or side trips.

Writers lose focus in two ways. The first: They don't have a focus to start with. They're not sure what they're writing about and maybe don't realize they need to know. As discussed in chapter two, you, the writer, must think about what you're trying to say. You don't need to state it in your writing, but you need to know what it is. Otherwise, your writing will be like that house without a frame and collapse into a pile of "So what?" or end up a mere incident instead of a story.

Our poem "To Bed!" may be about three different characters, but it's all focused on their going to bed. There's nothing about what brought them to that moment or what they will do afterward.

The second: In poetry, writers lose focus because they're having too much fun with rhyme and forget about the story, as I did here.

Come let's to bed,
Says Sleepy-head.
It's been a day
Of too much play.
We climbed a wall.
We tossed a ball.
We had a race—
A game of chase.
Slow takes a seat.
I'm feeling beat,
She yawns. She sighs.
She rubs her eyes.
I'm starved, Nan said.
Let's bake some bread,
A cherry pie,
Oh me, oh my,
And pizza, too.
I'll also brew
A pot of tea,

But just for me,
And then I'll make
A layer cake
And one cream puff.
Still not enough!

This began as a story about three characters in specific relation to bedtime. Then I had so much fun explaining what caused Sleepy-head to be tired and demonstrating Slow's personality through her actions. Being a fan of food, I imagined what Greedy Nan would eat. Couplets are addictive and easy to create. Once in the flow, I added too many details that distract from the rhyme's purpose. It was a lark to write, but the focus changed too much.

There's nothing like opening a rhyming dictionary and finding a word that takes you off in new directions, but stop and ask yourself: What's the point? If the story is about these three characters at bedtime, details about their day, their food, and what Slow does when tired aren't relevant.

RHYME

As we've seen from the above example, rhyming, or the repetition of sounds, can be fun. Unfortunately, many newcomers who try to write a rhyming picture book don't understand that rhyming must be *consistent*. Let's look again at "To Bed!"

Come let's to bed, (a)
Says Sleepy-head; (a.1)
Sit up a while, says Slow; (b)
Put on the pan, (c)
Says Greedy Nan, (c.1)
Let's sup before we go. (b.1)

Those letters at the end of each line let you know which lines rhyme. See how we have a repetition of sound at the end of the lines in an aabccb pattern? There are three sets of rhyming lines, but each of these rhymes differently. If there is a number after the letter, as in line two, that means the ending word beside it rhymes with an ending word from a preceding line but is not the same word. If this poem had a seventh line that read, "They'll share; I know," the appropriate designation would be *b.2*. Unfortunately, trying to maintain consistent rhyme patterns leads beginning writers to make unwise word choices such as using words that rhyme but don't add to the overall meaning, or forced rhyme, as in the following example.

Come let's to bed,	(a)
Says Sleepy-head;	(a.1)
Sit up a while, says Slow;	(b)
Put on the pan,	(c)
Says Greedy Nan,	(c.1)
Let's sup before we go.	(b.1)
I'll mix and make	(d)
A yummy cake.	(d.1)
It won't take long; I know.	(b.2)

"I know" is only there so I can rhyme with "slow" and "go." If you're going to write a picture book in rhyme, *every word* must advance your story.

Rhyming leads to another problem. It can make your picture-book poem too predictable. You don't want your reader to be able to guess every rhyming word. This most often happens when each line is a complete sentence, as in the following:

Come let's to bed.
Lay down your head.
Sit up a while, says Slow.
I'm Greedy Nan.
Put on a pan.
Let's sup before we go.

Create some spill-over lines (sentences that don't end when the line does), so your rhyming will not be so predictable. This original poem, like many Mother Goose poems, breaks in obvious places, so its rhyme words are fairly obvious.

Here's an example from one of my poems to demonstrate how spill-over lines add freshness. This poem is titled "Spider to Owl" and is written as a one-way conversation.

Owl, can't you watch
the direction you're going?
Your wing ripped my web!

You have no way of knowing
the rebuilding it takes.
I don't have your talons,
or sharp curvy claws.
I have to rely on
my skills as a lacey,
white tablecloth spinner
to tempt in the bugs
I crave for my dinner.
Hear me, I beg you,
night's quiet flier!
Please do your soaring
a little bit higher.

Notice how some of the rhyming words fall in the middle of a sentence. Beginning writers striving for a perfect rhyme scheme often use unnatural sentence inversions, as in the following.

Don't beat your drum.
To bed, now come.
But I'm not tired, says Sue.
    I want to eat
    some cake, yum-sweet.
I'll share a piece with you.

If line two were written in modern diction, it would be: "Now come to bed." For line five to sound more like everyday speech, the adjective would need to come before the noun: "some yum-sweet cake."

In our rhyming picture books, we want the writing to sound as natural as normal conversation. While poets may have gotten away with sentence inversions years ago, don't let your poem today sound stilted and old-fashioned. If you are tempted to use forced rhyme or sentence inversions to keep your rhyme consistent, resist the temptation!

On the other hand, too many writers are unwilling to spend the time to establish and maintain rhyme patterns. They may be unaware of the importance of consistency, so they break the rhyme pattern, as in the example below.

Come let's to bed,
    Says Sleepy-head;

Sit up a while, says Slow;
    Put on the pan,
    Says Greedy Nan
Let's sup before we go.
    A great idea!
    And we can read
A silly comic book.

These last three lines are jarring because the listener has accepted the pattern set up in the first six lines of a, a1, b, c, c1, b1, not only in his ears, but in his body. He expects this pattern to continue, in the same way we expect the sun to rise in the east and set in the west. Imagine what would happen if the sun suddenly rose in the north and set in the south! We would be thrown off-balance big-time. To a lesser degree, we were thrown off-balance by the last stanza added to the Mother Goose poem.

You may rightfully wonder if there are times when it's okay to break the rhyme pattern. The answer is "Yes." But *only* break the rhyme scheme to echo a change in the action of your poem. For instance, if the action in your poem is slowing down, you might insert an extra line to echo that slower movement. If the action in your poem speeds up, you might even delete a line, thereby bringing the rhymes closer together. Often writers change the rhyme scheme at the end of a poem (or a rhyming picture book) to signal the finish. Perhaps they write a nice rhyming couplet, thereby breaking the abcb pattern established throughout the piece.

It isn't only a lack of brevity, focus, and rhyme that makes editors groan over poem picture-book manuscripts. Rhythm, too, is a key element of successful poem picture books. It's also the element writers have the most trouble understanding. It's time to take a deep breath and remind yourself that you can do this. If I could learn this, believe me, you can, too.

RHYTHM

As with rhyme, the key is consistency. Don't be fooled into thinking that if you can count syllables, you have mastered rhythm. Rhythm is *not* syllable count; it's counting stresses and rhythmical feet. Rhythm is a pattern of stressed and unstressed syllables. Look at our example poem, where I have placed slanted lines above the words to indicate which beats are stressed.

. / . /
Come let's to bed,
. / . /
Says Sleepy-head;
. /. / . /
Sit up a while, says Slow;
. / . /
Put on the pan,
. / . /
Says Greedy Nan,
. / . / . /
Let's sup before we go.

In this poem, we have a soft beat followed by a stress, . /, otherwise known as an iambic rhythm. The soft beat and stress together form one metrical foot. In the lines above, the first, second, fourth, and fifth consist of two iambic metrical feet. The third and sixth lines have three iambic feet. While every line does not have an equal number of feet, the overall poem has a repeated pattern of two feet, two feet, three feet. When writing a story in rhyme, you must create a consistent pattern in your number of feet, or else you will jar the reader, as would the following poem.

It's time we go to bed,
Yawns Sleepy-head.
Sit up a while, says Slow.
I'd rather cook a treat. Get out the pan,
Says hungry Greedy Nan.
Let's eat and watch a scary video.

In this example, I kept the same iambic rhythm but paid no attention to how many feet in each line. Again, let me emphasize that poetry written in a lock-step rhythm often needs to be broken but *only* if it echoes a change in the story's action. I did this in my book *Everything to Spend the Night*. The poem is iambic and has four metrical feet per line until the moment below.

/ . / . / . / . . / . / . /. /
Time for bed? But I'm not sleepy. A l l l l r i i i i i i ght, I'll put my pj's on.
. / . / . / . . /
Oh, no! Where are they? What can I do?

. / . / . / . /

Yours fit me, Grandpa! I love you.

The little girl denies she's sleepy in a line that is out of sync with the established pattern, indicating, not only in words but in the music (or lack of music), that a change is coming. The next line may have four rhythmic feet again, but the iambic rhythm is broken. The last line returns to the book's characteristic iambic tetrameter (four feet) because everything is finally okay.

Here's what happens when the writer uses no rhythmic pattern at all (different rhythms *and* a different number of metrical feet) but sticks to a consistent rhyme scheme:

Shouldn't we maybe think about bed?
    Yawns a very sleepy head.
I'd rather stay up and finish this book, says Slow.
    First, I'll bake a cake in this pan,
Says a famished-for-sweets Nan.
You can each have a piece before we go.

I have to cover my ears reading this aloud. Can you hear how no rhythm translates to no poem?

Sometimes new writers use old-fashioned language to make the rhythmic pattern consistent:

'Tis time for bed,
Says Sleepy-head.

Don't do this! Your poem will be outdated before your editor reads the second line.

If you still want to write your picture book using rhythm and rhyme, you must become familiar and comfortable with the following four basic rhythms.

IAMB

We saw an example of this in "To Bed!" Each iambic foot starts with a soft beat and is followed by a hard beat. A good way to remember this is by thinking of the nonsensical sounds *da DUM*. An iambic foot is designated by . /, a period and a slash, and it is considered an upbeat—rising and happy—rhythm. Examples include *beneath, before, betwixt, between, the bat, the ball*, and *a score.*

An iambic sentence might be *It's time to buy a loaf of bread.* Iambic meter is the most commonly used rhythm, probably because it echoes one's heartbeat.

ANAPEST

Each anapestic foot starts with two soft beats and ends with a hard beat. Its nonsensical sounds would be *da da DUM,* designated with . . /, or two periods and a slash. You'll find it in the words *underscore, interlock,* and *disagree* and in phrases such as *at the lake, in the sand, a shy dog.* This is an even happier, more upbeat rising rhythm than iambic. Using anapest signals to the reader that you are writing something humorous. In my book *'Twas the Late Night of Christmas,* a new take on Clement Clarke Moore's "A Visit from St. Nicholas" ("The Night Before Christmas"), I copied his almost-perfect anapestic rhythm. Here's my opening line: "'Twas the late night of Christmas, when all through the house, everyone was exhausted, even the mouse."

TROCHEE

Each trochaic foot starts with a hard beat and is followed by a soft beat. Its nonsensical sounds would be *DUM da,* designated first by a slash and then a period (/ .). It's found in the words *diving, quickly, under,* and *nation* and in phrases such as *eat this, read slow,* and *go in*. Here's a trochaic sentence: *Don't you drink that water.* The trochee tends to be used in sadder, perhaps more serious, poems.

DACTYL

Each dactylic foot starts with one hard beat and is followed by two soft beats. Its nonsense sounds are *DUM da da,* designated with a slash and two periods (/ . .). You can find it in the words *stealthily, natural,* and *airiness* or in phrases such as *apples and, under the,* and *beating him.* A dactylic sentence might read *Munching fresh grass, the small snail overwhelmed by its tastiness waved his thin feelers with gratitude.* This downbeat, heavy rhythm is most often found in poems that deal with serious matters.

BECOMING COMFORTABLE WITH THE RHYTHMS

Now you have had a quick overview of the four basic rhythms. That wasn't so bad, was it? If you want to write rhymed picture books, you must be able to differentiate between the rhythms and create them consistently. I would suggest clapping or drumming each one out and then memorizing poems in each of the rhythms. Recite them until you feel comfortable with each one. To help you do this, here are four of my poems about rhinoceroses, each written in strict meter.

IAMB

Old Rhino's frame
is built too thin.
It's way too small
for fitting in
the folds and wrinkles
of his skin.

ANAPEST

See young Rhino. His skin, how it sags,
hangs in wrinkles, and folds!
So no matter his age,
You'd assume that he's old.

TROCHEE

Rhino's wrinkles hang so loosely,
like a sweater, big and baggy.
He should wear a skin more fitting,
not so oversized and saggy.

DACTYL

Poor old Rhinoceros
tired of rain's pitter and pattering,
drenched from drops' splattering,
took off to search for a

place more hospitable.
Staggering, swaggering,
Wandering far and meandering,
finding a dry spot eventually,
just as the rain began tapering.

Please note all of these poems are written in mostly strict meter and therefore may feel stilted, but they work for the purpose of helping you learn rhythm. When you feel comfortable with these four basic rhythms, feel free to combine them so you don't sound like Dr. Seuss, who sticks to a tight rhythm. In *If Animals Said I Love You*, I combined the upbeat iambic and anapestic rhythms so my poem didn't feel sing-songy, as you can see in this couplet:

. / . . / . . / . . /
Gorilla would say it and pat-pat her lap.
. . / . / . . / . . /
Let me hold you close in my hairy arm wrap

To feel comfortable with these different rhythms, read poetry. Determine the predominant rhythm, and mark the stresses. It's imperative for rhythm to feel as comfortable as an old sock. If you're not sure where the stress comes in a specific word, look it up in a dictionary.

However, stress may fall differently depending on the word's placement in the sentence. For example, the word *honey* is a trochaic word, with the stress on the first syllable. But if the words preceding and following it create the phrase *taste honey now*, the stress would be on *taste* and *now*, with no stress on *honey* at all. And if I wrote, "Taste the honey now," the stresses would appear over *taste* and *hon* and *now*. What words are stressed is determined by each one's relationship to others in the line. So how do you know which words or syllables are stressed?

Read them aloud as if they were normal sentences, not poetry. That way you're more likely to hear where the real stresses fall. Another approach is to ask someone else to read your lines and pay close attention to where they put the stresses.

QUIZ TIME

Let's see how well you identify the rhythm in these lines.

1. Peter Rabbit picked a peck of pickled peppers.
2. Horse dashes down the meadow lane.
3. Look at the cavalry.
4. In the field I saw cats and a dog.
5. Dressing up in fancy sweaters
6. I'm tumbling, rolling down the hill.
7. Water spilling, rushing, splashing, down the streambed, never resting.
8. Hear me shout! Hear me roar!
9. Take in the beautiful scenery!
10. I long to write a book.
11. Is it true you're the one who insisted on baking a cake?
12. Nothing is better than broccoli.

ANSWERS: 1. trochee 2. iamb 3. dactyl 4. anapest 5. trochee 6. iamb 7. trochee 8. anapest 9. dactyl 10. iamb 11. anapest 12. dactyl

A FEW FINAL WORDS

Perhaps you did well on this quiz and feel comfortable using rhythm and rhyme. If you've decided you would like your story to be a poem, your newfound knowledge of the form should protect you from its potential pitfalls. On the other hand, if you have decided a poem picture book is not for you, then there is always prose.

WHAT'S NEXT?

Choosing to write prose does not give you license to abandon poetry. A picture book does not need to be a poem, but it must be written poetically, and we'll talk about that in chapter fifteen.

BUT . . . Before you go on

1. If you've written your picture book in rhyme and want to keep it that way, go back over it line by line to be sure you haven't made any of the errors that drive editors to pull out their hair.

2. If you think poetry will be your thing but you want to read more, check out the bibliography section for a list of my favorite books on poetry writing. Also, read some of the works of poetry listed in the bibliography.
3. Read some poem picture books. They're the ones marked with a * in the bibliography.
4. If you've decided to forgo poetry, rewrite your story in prose and go on to the next chapter.

15

Making Music with Your Prose

"Every word only has to be perfect."

—URSULA NORDSTROM

If you've decided not to write a poem picture book, you may think you can skip this chapter and avoid all contact with poetry. Don't! Unless you want to risk having your manuscript rejected by an editor. Theodor Geisel, more famously known as Dr. Seuss, said, "Write a verse a day, not to send to publishers, but to throw in wastebaskets. It will help your prose. It will give you swing. Shorten paragraphs and sentences; then shorten words. … Use verbs. Let the kids fill in the adjectives. …" Poems are our shortest and tightest form of writing. Every word counts.

Every word must also count in picture books. Each word needs to be the best one for advancing the story and echoing the action in the story. You can have a fantastic plot, but it will fall flat if the language is flat. Remember Mark Twain's statement, "The difference between the right word and the almost-right word is the difference between lightning and a lightning bug." This is probably the most important chapter for helping you create a saleable manuscript.

RHYTHM

In our last chapter, we talked about the rhythm of words. Some words ended with a stress, while others ended with a soft beat. The meters that ended with a stressed beat were called iambs or anapests or upbeat rhythms. The meters that ended with a unstressed syllable were called trochees or dactyls or falling rhythms.

When you write prose, you should still be aware of these rhythms, but you don't need to write your entire story in one of them. Certain sections will call for different rhythms. Here is a line from my manuscript about World War II: "Sellers joked about how embarrassing it would be if we died during training instead of a real battle. Not funny!" Notice the falling-rhythm words: "Sellers," "during," "training," "battle," and "funny." The line would sound quite different if I substituted upbeat rhythms instead: "Sellers made a joke about what if we died here today instead of in combat. I didn't laugh." Of course, it says the same thing but somehow feels lighter. Not so heavy and serious.

Suppose one is writing about the death of a dog like this: "When Dad told me the news, how I sobbed and I cried! Then I flung myself down on the bed." This poor character is devastated, but her words, written mostly in the upbeat anapestic rhythm, make it hard for me to believe her pain. It's much sadder when it's written with more falling rhythms: "When Father told me the news, I burrowed under my blanket, sobbing, crying." Similarly, in *Me and Momma and Big John* by Mara Rockliff, when the narrator, a young boy, sees the stone his mama has been carving for the Cathedral of Saint John the Divine in New York City, his disappointment is echoed in sentences with falling rhythms.

Let's look at another upbeat rhythm. In this line from a manuscript of mine, Purrsey the cat is talking to Hen, who wonders how Purrsey will lay an egg: "'Eggxactly like you.' Purrsey gathers hay and makes a nest. He sits and dreams of bringing Mia his very own eggsquisite egg." One of my favorite parts of writing is inventing new words. I had great fun naming my cat and combining words to create something unique that fit into the story.

Sentence length is an important part of rhythm. Here's an example from the same manuscript: "Purrsey dashes out. He squirms under a bush. Mia mustn't find him!" The sentences are short and tight, reflecting Purrsey's tense state of mind. You wouldn't feel as much tension if I had written the same scene as one long sentence: "Pursey dashes out and squirms under a bush, all the while worrying that Mia might find him." To gain a better sense of how powerful short sentences and fragments can be, read *The Kite that Bridged Two Nations* by Alexis O'Neill. Pay close attention to the scene where the kite string breaks.

In a story of a young girl who is sad about her grandfather's death, I wrote: "Sylvia shuffled into the kitchen and climbed up on the stool. Each Sunday with Grandpa, she had laid the empty pods in a path across the sink. This Sunday she dropped them, one by one, into a paper bag." But suppose I had written the passage with shorter sentences: "Sylvia shuffled into the kitchen. She climbed onto the stool. She remembered how she and Grandpa shelled peas. He would drop them in the bowl. She would lay the pods in a path on the counter. Today, she dropped them in the trash." The long sentences in the first example are more contemplative and capture her serious mood. Short sentences focus attention on her actions and detract from the intended slow, emotional pace.

Long and short sentences can also be combined to great effect. Here's an example from another of my manuscripts: "When the rain kept pouring, Lena's house leaked so badly, everyone squeezed under the table to stay dry. And they had an unexpected visitor! A snake squirmed through the damp dirt roof. It fell onto the floor! Her sister and brothers screamed, but Lena scooped the snake up with the end of the broom and flung it outside." As you can see, short sentences are useful for moments when you want to generate excitement. While thinking about the rhythm of words and sentences, you may want to contemplate another aspect of words: phonetics.

PHONETICS

To become familiar with the sounds of every letter of the alphabet, hold your hand close to your mouth, not touching your lips. Say the sounds of each letter, paying attention to the shape of your mouth and the strength or weakness of the different breaths on your hand. When I say the *a* sound in *sat*, I feel little breath on my hand. My mouth stays open. When I say *a* as in *day*, my lower lip rises, creating a bigger air puff on my hand.

Do this for the entire alphabet to get a sense of those letter sounds that create the biggest puffs on your hand. The bigger the puffs, the harder and stronger the sounds. The shorter puffs are softer and weaker. Here's a chart to help you remember:

Low-Range Vowel Sounds

oo	moon
o	phone
aw	taught
oi	toy
ow	bough
ah	star

Middle-Range Vowel Sounds

u	fun
u	burn
a	bat

e	ten
i	sift

High-Range Vowel Sounds

i	night
a	stay
ee	bee

Hard-Sound Consonants

b, d, k, p, q, t, and hard c

Softer, Liquid Consonant Sounds

l, m, n, and r

How do these sounds apply to your story? The various types and combinations of sounds generate different kinds of energy on the page. Some sounds are ideal for communicating intense emotions and/or fast-paced situations. One of my manuscripts is about a cat who is upset and disappointed that he has failed. He complains thusly, "Oh, fleas, ticks, and mites!" Lots of hard consonants and long vowels! The upset would not be as strong if the cat said, "Oh, veterinarians, fur balls, and vaccinations!" These are still things that cats don't like, but the shorter vowel sounds and softer consonants weaken the intended emotional intensity of the phrase.

Consider these two sentences from a different manuscript: "A shooting star soared across the dome of sky. She squealed with delight." In the first sentence, we have a predominance of low-energy vowels and many soft consonants. The second sentence reinforces the subdued excitement of that quietly remarkable moment. If I'd paid no attention to my word sounds, I might have written: "A shooting star zipped across the black night sky. She laughed." The second example reverses those sounds, and you can judge for yourself which is more successful. Read picture books, noting how authors use phonetics and rhythm to echo the action and mood of the story.

QUIZ TIME

Let's take a break and test how well you understand phonetics and rhythm and how to use them in your story.

1. When writing about a police officer chasing a criminal, what kind of sentences, long or short, might you use?
2. You're writing a quiet before-nap-story. What specific rhythm should you avoid?
3. Your character lies down in a grassy meadow to contemplate the meaning of life. Would you write long or short sentences?
4. A humorous story about a cat and mouse would use what kind of rhythms?
5. In a scene with a boy dashing home to tell his mom he made the softball team, what word sounds, high and hard, or low and soft, would you want to use?
6. Your main character is at a county fair, overwhelmed by the rides, booths, and noise. What kind of sentences, long or short, would reflect her feelings?
7. What kind of sentences (long or short), rhythm (upbeat or falling), and word sounds (low and soft or high and hard) would you write in a story about a boy whose beloved cat died?
8. What kind of sentences, long or short, would best express the action of a story where a warthog is frantically trying to escape the clutches of a cheetah?
9. In the above example, which of these two words might you use, *dart* or *run*?
10. Long-awaited good news has finally arrived. You've sold your first manuscript. What kind of sentences, long or short, would demonstrate the moment's excitement?
11. Your story takes place in a quiet meditation room. What word sounds, low and soft or high and hard, might you use? Give a few examples of some words that might fit.
12. When a series of large, powerful waves crash violently upon the shore, what consonant and vowel sounds, low and soft or high and hard, might you use?

ANSWERS: 1. short sentences 2. the lively, upbeat anapest 3. long sentences 4. iamb and anapest—the upbeat rhythms 5. hard sounds and high vowels 6. short sentences 7. long sentences, falling rhythms and low, soft sounds 8. short sentences 9. *dart* 10. short sentences 11. low vowels and soft sounds like *flow, linger, ramble* 12. harder consonants and higher vowels

ALLITERATION

Being a prose writer doesn't mean that you can't use poetic tools; they belong to all writers. One of these tools is alliteration, the repetition of words' initial consonant sounds in a succession, e.g., the phrase *racing rushing river.* Using too many, too close together can turn a sentence into a tongue twister and a nightmare for your reader. Our words need to roll off the reader's tongue. Notice there's still alliteration in this: "The storm caused the river to race, splashing and rushing around rocks and boulders." Judiciously incorporating alliteration into longer sentences is gentler on the tongue and ears. Depending on what you are writing, you might want to put your alliterative words closer together. At other times you might drop in only at intervals to be subtler.

Here's a partial sentence from one of my manuscripts: "She dipped the ladle in a pail for a drink of water." If I hadn't used the alliteration of multiple *d* words, it might read like this: "She scooped the water out of the pail into her mug." Both of these sentences say basically the same thing, but the first sentence is more musical. In my book *Little Monkey Says Good Night*, I chose three *b* names for the clowns so that Little Monkey could say, "Good night, Bozo. Good night, Buttons. Good night, Bumbles."

ASSONANCE

This is the repetition of vowel sounds in succession as in "Cat bats man's hand." Can you can pick up the medium-range *a* sounds here? You also can make the sounds subtler and still achieve a similar impact on the reader: "The cat batted his paw, striking the man's hand and leaving a scratch." In my same book about Little Monkey, I used the assonance of the long vowel in these two sentences: "Horse rears high. Little Monkey slides." Without that assonance, it might read: "Horse rears high. Little Monkey tumbles." The first example is much more fun to read.

CONSONANCE

This poetic tool repeats the same middle and end sounds, as in *time, rhyme, chime*, and the same beginning and ending consonants in a word sequence, as in *tick tock.* Again, in prose it's acceptable to spread out those words in a sentence: "He heard the clock tick and then tock." Here are two sentences from *Count on Culebra*: "**CLINK, CLANK, CLANG** thumped the rolling pin and kettles. **KLATTER, KLITTER, KLING** bumped the skillets, pots and pans." Here you can see the beginning and ending consonants are the same for the first two words in each sentence. Later in the book, I combine all of the sound effects so that, in addition, the last words in lines one and three and in lines two and four have the same middle and end sounds. They're written here exactly as in the book, bold and capitalized to emphasize the noisiness:

> **CLINK, CLANK, CLANG,**
> **KLATTER, KLITTER, KLING,**
> **PLINK, PLANK, PLANG,**
> **BATTER, BITTER, BLING.**

For a book overflowing with consonance, read *Nanette's Baguette* by the prolific Mo Willems.

ONOMATOPOEIA

This poetic device involves words imitating sounds as in *beep, whoosh, meow,* and *smash*. Kids and adults love onomatopoeic words. Because I tend to write for younger children, I use them lots. They're easy and fun, and the reader can naturally add her own stress and dramatic flair. *Little Monkey Says Good Night* is chock-full of onomatopoeic words: *boing, swish, clunk, bump, wheee, thump, rat-a-tat, ring-a-ding, toot-a-toot-toot, crash*, and *swoosh*. In a more recent book, Karen B. Winnick uses many onomatopoeic words to sweet effect in her book *Good Night, Baby Animals You've Had a Busy Day.* In *Jingle Dancer,* Cynthia Leitich Smith uses them twice on the very first page.

QUIZ TIME

What poetic tools are being used below? Alliteration, assonance, consonance, or onomatopoeia?

1. bend, bond
2. swim, sway
3. bow wow
4. big boots
5. beating the cream
6. moo
7. seeing the key

8. cat, cut

ANSWERS: 1. alliteration and consonance 2. alliteration 3. onomatopoeia 4. alliteration 5. assonance 6. onomatopoeia 7. assonance 8. alliteration and consonance

METAPHOR

There are three more poetic tools that have nothing to do with word sounds and repetition, and one of these is metaphor. Simply put, a metaphor is when a writer says one thing is actually something else. Taken literally, metaphors often read as lies, but they are intended to figuratively communicate some emotional truth through implied comparison of seemingly unlike things. Observe my use of metaphor in the following haiku.

> Silently stalking,
> the dark night comes ... a Cyclops
> staring one moon eye.

SIMILE

Similes directly compare one thing to another by using the words *like* or *as*. Can you find the similes I included in this poem?

> Watch out, Rat!
> High over trees and chimneys,
> hidden in fog,
> Owl slips,
> through the deep night dark—
> swooping silent as a whisper,
> hazy as a shadow
> hungry as can be.
> Watch out, Rat!

As with metaphor, write in simile to give the reader a strong visual image with emotional impact instead of a plain description. An added benefit is that using figurative language allows you to say a lot in very few words. Consider "hazy as a shadow." How might I describe Owl without a simile? I could write,

"The dark night made it hard to delineate Owl's outline or to make out the majestic bird's individual feathers." Notice how pedestrian that description is.

Remember that whether you're creating a simile or a metaphor, you must be careful not to write clichés. *Two peas in a pod* and *big as a bus* have been done to death. If you're unsure whether you've written a cliché in your first draft, check out www.englishclub.com/vocabulary/figures-similes-list.htm.

You might be wondering how one creates unique, arresting, tone-perfect metaphors and similes. This method works for me: Suppose my object is an orange. I number one to ten on a piece of paper or on my computer and free-associate until I have ten possibilities, e.g., "round as the moon," "orange as a carrot," "juice sweet as summer," "rind like a treasure chest holding precious juice," "rind rough and pocked like my grandmother's skin," and so on. When experimenting, I consider my subject from different angles. For example, I can make lists related to its shape, color, smell, taste, texture, or how it grows. If I like one of them, I'm done. If I don't like any of them, I number from eleven to twenty. I continue on until I finally create one that feels right.

Do I hear a moan? Are you overwhelmed at how long this could take? Writing is time consuming, but the time spent is worthwhile. Remember we're not cranking out stories; we're creating compelling early-book experiences for our listeners.

PERSONIFICATION

Personification is a literary device that gives human characteristics to something that is not human, as I do in this short poem.

> Where night fades to blue
> and tiptoes away,
> stars turn off their twinkles,
> lay down their heads,
> and drift through the sky
> asleep in cloud beds.

Night can't literally tiptoe away, but I chose that word because it's a quiet action. Stars can't turn off their twinkles the way we turn off a light, and stars have neither beds nor heads to lay down.

QUIZ TIME

Let's see how well you understand metaphor, simile, and personification.

1. Books are trains that carry us to faraway lands.
2. I tried to pass the test, but failure held on tight and wouldn't let go.
3. Alan raced as fast as a gazelle.
4. The owl's hoots soothe like a lullaby.
5. Last night, Jimmy was a pig at dinner.
6. The photograph taunted her with memories of happier days, gone forever.

ANSWERS: 1. metaphor 2. personification 3. simile 4. simile 5. metaphor 6. personification

A FEW FINAL WORDS

If you didn't do as well as you would have liked on the quizzes in this chapter, study some of the poets listed in the bibliography. The list isn't exclusively children's poets. The more poets you read, no matter what genre or age they write for, the more poetic your writing will become. Almost all of the picture books listed in the bibliography are there because not only do they tell a good story but the author writes lyrically. My favorites are marked with an *L*. I urge you to read each one, looking for examples of the different poetic devices I discussed. And if you want a children's book that has examples of all of them, read the 2014 Caldecott winner, *Locomotive* by Brian Floca. The illustrations deserve the accolades they've received, but the writing is equally stunning. This book is long for a picture book but perfect for its target audience of lower- and middle-elementary children.

WHAT'S NEXT?

We've been talking about language in the last two chapters, but now we'll turn to the last point to consider—word count. Get ready to make some serious cuts to your manuscript.

BUT . . . Before you go on

1. Go over your manuscript. Did you use any of these poetic techniques? If not, can you improve your manuscript by doing so?
2. Check your two typed published books to see how the authors use the tools discussed here.
3. Read a new picture book, perhaps one mentioned in this chapter.

16

The Importance of Word Count

"In composing, as a general rule, run your pen through every other word you have written; you have no idea what vigor it will give to your style."

—SYDNEY SMITH

Beginning picture-book writers rarely comprehend how few words are necessary to reach their young audience. Who would believe, for example, that the classic *Goodnight Moon* by Margaret Wise Brown needed only 130 words to tell the comforting story of a bunny bidding good night to his room and its contents?

If Animals Said I Love You uses a mere 225 words to demonstrate how ten different kinds of animals might express their affection. Rarely do I see a student manuscript that couldn't be improved by serious cutting. Don't be like the speaker who, finally given the podium, has so much fun in front of the audience that he doesn't know when to stop. To be a concise picture-book writer, you must have the following attributes.

AN UNDERSTANDING OF THE ILLUSTRATOR'S JOB

The illustrator's pictures are the descriptions of our words. Pictures will show what the character looks like, the color of her skin, the ribbon in her hair, and her missing tooth. They will show the breed of dog, style of house, and kinds of trees in the woods. Trust the creativity of the artist.

Linda Zuckerman, a former editor who is now an author, often shares this story at conferences. She asks the writers in the audience to imagine what a mousery—a place where mice live—might look like. Some people suggest a Victorian dollhouse. Others say an old trunk or perhaps a hatbox. Then Linda holds up *The Mousery* by Charlotte Pomerantz. The mousery illustrator Kurt Cyrus created was an old abandoned car. Throughout my career, I've been stunned by the imaginations of illustrators.

Writers don't have to write directions for what each picture should be. Nearly all instructions to illustrators on unpublished manuscripts I've read are unnecessary and probably something of an insult to an artist. Chances are they will be ignored anyway. Whenever the talented artist Marla Frazee gets a manuscript from an editor to consider illustrating, she first takes a thick black marker and crosses out the writer's suggestions.

When artists aren't encumbered with our suggestions, they can be creative and add that crucial separate story that is so important to our youngest readers. In my book *Hello Toes! Hello Feet!*, illustrator Nadine Bernard Westcott added a dog that I never mentioned in the text. She also added a baby brother. These new characters allowed for more interesting and active illustrations and gave the main girl others to interact with.

Ironically, while we must write with a visual image in our minds of how our story may look, we must eventually let go of that image. When we send our sons and daughters to school, we essentially allow teachers, friends, the crosswalk guard, and the whole wide world to influence our children and help shape them into adults. We trust all will be well. In much the same way, we need to trust that our illustrators will help each story grow into the best version of itself.

None of my books came out the way I imagined they would. Every one of them came out *better*! So delete descriptions and instructions, and your illustrator will love you. You may rightfully argue that in some stories, especially humorous ones, the words contradict what's happening in the pictures. If that's going on in your manuscript, there are several ways to submit it to a publishing house:

1. In your cover letter, explain that contrast, and submit your manuscript in two forms—one with just the straight story and the other with your illustration suggestions.
2. Submit just one manuscript, but keep all illustration suggestions in the margins so they don't disturb you editor's progress through your story.
3. Submit your manuscript, but put illustration suggestions in parentheses and in a light gray font so the editor knows they are not part of the text.

RESPECT FOR CHILDREN'S INTELLIGENCE

Don't make the mistake of explaining everything in excruciating detail for your young listeners. There's no need to include an explicit moral or lesson for this audience. I can't repeat this enough. Please, writers, give children credit for their cognitive abilities. While kids' world experiences can't begin to compare to adults' in number, they still have eyes and ears and brains for figuring things out. A child may take longer to verbalize a book's theme, but that doesn't mean that deep inside he doesn't understand the theme on some level. Get rid of sentences that sound like overt moralizing. Here are a few examples: "Owen learned to always ask before taking a piece of cake"; "Ellie realized the best way to do well in school is to listen to the teacher"; "Thea now knows she should always look both ways before crossing the street."

CONSIDERATION AND SYMPATHY FOR YOUR READER AND LISTENER

Remember that children with short attention spans are listening to our stories. Have compassion for the adults reading aloud to them. Children respond best to books that are appropriate for their respective developmental stages.

These days doctors and reading specialists are encouraging parents and childcare workers to read to children as soon as they are born. But not *Crime and Punishment*! Babies should start out with board books. Their bright, simple illustrations are easy for young eyes to focus on. These books require few, if any, words, and their brevity accommodates a child's wiggles and squirms and his inability to concentrate for an extended period. Children under eighteen months discover their world through their senses, so it's natural for them to stuff books in their mouths. Normal, thin paper pages are simply objects to tear and crumple. Board books, which are made of sturdy materials, take this into account.

Babies and toddlers love the feel and texture of books, which makes *Pat the Bunny* by Dorothy Kunhardt and other touch-and-feel books popular. Board books for children this age usually contain eight double-sided cardboards, or sixteen pages, including the front and back covers. Additional pages can be added if needed.

The illustrations are simple, typically rendered with few details in bright colors, and the text is short, with no more than a line or two per page.

Sometimes these books are wordless or have just one word per page. A board book about Bunny might be as simple as the following.

Bunny hops to the garden.
Hop! Hop! Hop!
Bunny chomps a carrot.
Chomp! Chomp! Chomp!
Bunny chews a radish.
Chew! Chew! Chew!
Bunny nibbles a strawberry.
Nibble! Nibble! Nibble!
Bunny pats his stomach.
Pat! Pat! Pat!
Bunny is full.
Bunny is sleepy, too.
Hop! Hop! Hop!
Bunny hops home.
Bunny lies down.
Zzzzzzzzz, zzzzzzzz, zzzzzzzzzzzzz

The story might not be the most exciting, but it's short—just 55 words.

Here are some titles and word counts of a few of my favorite published board books:

- *Peek-a Boo!* by Nina Laden, 17 words
- *My Little Cities: Paris* by Jennifer Adams, 33 words
- *Tiny Town* by Suzy Ultman, 38 words
- *Smile, Pout-Pout Fish* by Deborah Diesen, 52 words
- *Little Bitty Friends* by Elizabeth McPike, 95 words
- *Happy Hippo, Angry Duck: A Book of Moods* by Sandra Boynton, 143 words
- *Cuddly Cow* by Axel Scheffler, 146 words

Board books frequently rhyme because babies may not yet recognize words but love the music that rhyme makes. They also make use of onomatopoeic sounds like *woof, cheep,* and *who-oo* that babies can imitate. In addition, some of these books are part toy. *Pat the Bunny* is a classic of this type. *Peek-a Boo!* by Nina Laden is in part a game where children can guess what's peeking through the die-cut windows. Most often, board books are created by an author-illustrator.

Publishers today have begun reprinting popular picture books in board-book format, and as someone who has benefitted enormously from that trend with *If Animals Kissed Good Night*, I'm thrilled for the success so many board books are enjoying. However, board books adapted from the longer format are normally not for the youngest set. It's rare for a child under eighteen months to sit still for an entire read of most of these. A child nearing two might show the required patience for longer board books, and parents surely appreciate that publishers finally recognize children of one or two don't suddenly know how to treat books with the care and respect they deserve. Check out Alice Schertle's *Little Blue Truck* for an example of a well-designed picture-to-board book.

Picture books for older toddlers and preschoolers can be longer because they've been learning to sit still for increasing amounts of time. Many of these books show a separate story in the illustrations so our listeners who are pre-readers can "read the pictures." These books need a simple story line. When I say simple, I don't mean simplistic. I mean the story must be focused without too many issues or characters.

Following up with the bunny we used as an example earlier, I might now put her in a new situation, like going to the first day of preschool, picking out a birthday present for Mother, or learning how to swim.

In these, as in board books, repetition and rhyme allow the listener to anticipate what's coming, and after several readings, she might even say some of the words in advance. This age group of children likes stories pertaining to the world around them, and they would rather hear familiar stories more than once than listen to a new long story. That's why the books listed below will still be short.

- *I Love Bugs!* by Emma Dodd, 104 words
- *My Bus* by Byron Barton, 134 words
- *I Used to Be a Fish* by Tom Sullivan, 183 words
- *Z Is for Moose* by Kelly Bingham, 190 words
- *We Found a Hat* by Jon Klassen, 215 words
- *Hello Toes! Hello Feet!* by Ann Whitford Paul, 217 words
- *Nellie Belle* by Mem Fox, 222 words
- *If Animals Said I Love You* by Ann Whitford Paul, 225 words
- *Make Way for Readers* by Judy Sierra, 248 words
- *Suppose You Meet a Dinosaur: A First Book of Manners* by Judy Sierra, 263 words
- *Little Monkey Says Good Night* by Ann Whitford Paul, 271 words

- *Baby Bear Sees Blue* by Ashley Wolff, 281 words
- *The Black Rabbit* by Philippa Leathers, 302 words
- *Weeds Find a Way* by Cindy Jenson-Elliott, 314 words
- *City Dog, Country Frog* by Mo Willems, 330 words
- *My Favorite Pets: by Gus W. for Ms. Smolinski's Class* by Jeanne Birdsall, 368 words
- *Seven Hungry Babies* by Candace Fleming, 387 words
- *It's Raining Bats & Frogs* by Rebecca Colby, 440 words
- *Panda-Monium!* by Cynthia Platt, 452 words
- *Ella and Penguin Stick Together* by Megan Maynor, 454 words
- *Sleep Like a Tiger* by Mary Logue, 480 words
- *Bike On, Bear!* by Cynthea Liu, 515 words
- *The Wrong Side of the Bed* by Lisa M. Bakos, 557 words
- *A Balloon for Isabel* by Deborah Underwood, 576 words
- *Samantha on a Roll* by Linda Ashman, 582 words

Years ago, when I was writing for this age group, my antennae used to perk up at around 700 words. Now editors want even shorter manuscripts, so at 500 words, I look for ways to cut. If the topic is more advanced, I realize I'm writing for an older audience and revise, expanding my story into a picture storybook for elementary-age students.

Once children are in kindergarten and elementary school and practicing their sitting and listening skills, stories can be longer and more complicated. Here are some sample books (along with their word counts) that would be appropriate for an elementary-age child:

- *Mañana, Iguana* by Ann Whitford Paul, 675 words
- *Old Robert and the Sea-Silly Cats* by Barbara Joosse, 710 words
- *A Library Book for Bear* by Bonny Becker, 781 words
- *A Hat for Mrs. Goldman: A Story About Knitting and Love* by Michelle Edwards, 788 words
- *School's First Day of School* by Adam Rex, 829 words
- *Me and Momma and Big John* by Mara Rockliff, 873 words
- *Balderdash! John Newbery and the Boisterous Birth of Children's Books* by Michelle Markel, 886 words
- *Ada Twist, Scientist* by Andrea Beaty, 915 words
- *Noah Webster & His Words* by Jeri Chase Ferris, 1417 words

- *The Great Moon Hoax* by Stephen Krensky, 1438 words

Going back to our story about the bunny. ... Now with an older child's wider experience of the world, I might make my bunny an astronaut, exploring faraway planets. Maybe I'd make it into a series so kids could learn more about the planets.

Don't take my word about subject matter and word count in picture books. Read to children, and find out for yourself about their attention spans. Volunteer at your library, public school, or neighborhood daycare center. Observe how long children of different ages sit still and listen. See when they start fidgeting or talking to the person next to them. Then type up those stories that held the kids' interest. Don't groan.

Typing manuscripts is the best practice for knowing in your head and in your fingers how long stories should be. My computer is filled with texts of published picture books. If you're like me, you'll be surprised by how few words are needed to tell a story.

I'll bet your manuscript (especially if you are just starting to write) is still longer than it should be. We've already discussed deleting descriptions and morals. Read on for more suggestions about how to reduce your word count.

CUT ADJECTIVES AND ADVERBS

Cross off words like *gorgeous* or *handsome* in your manuscript. Let your illustrator create the character. Delete adverbs, and substitute more specific verbs; this will help your story spring to life. Not long ago, in rereading a manuscript of mine, I discovered that I kept repeating the verb *run.* Sometimes I varied it a bit by saying "runs ahead fast," "runs quickly," or "takes his time running," but over and over again, there was that dull word *run.* I cut out all those adverbs and replaced each verb with a more specific one. "Runs ahead fast" became "dashes," "runs quickly" became "bolts," and "takes his time running" became "jogs." A good thesaurus reminds writers of the depth and breadth of the English language. The *right* word exists for every moment in our stories, and we owe it to our audience not to settle for less.

USE ACTIVE VERBS

Owen read a book is more active than *The book was read by Owen.* In the first sentence, the noun *Owen* is doing the reading. In the second sentence, *book* isn't performing the action. Not only is the first sentence more active; it also uses fewer words. Every time we change a passive verb to an active verb, we're cutting words. Hooray! Of course, sometimes the passive form of the verb is needed, but be sure it's truly necessary.

CUT WORDS

Look out for *really, nearly, almost*, and *seems*. "She was really sad," can be stronger without "really." "The tree stood nearly ten feet tall," could be written more specifically, "the tree stood nine and a half feet tall." "He almost got a perfect score on his spelling test," would be more exact, if written, "He missed only one answer." Stand behind what you write. You've done your research. You know what's true. Don't hide under these hem-and-haw words. What you say is either true or false. There's no middle road.

GET RID OF WASTED WORDS

You say, "I don't write wasted words."

Phooey! We all write wasted words. Remember those term papers? How many times did you go over the word limit? I'll bet it happened rarely, so you padded numerous reports. You made longer sentences and explained concepts several times.

Now you're writing picture books and are faced with the opposite situation—too many words! Wasted words are those that don't advance your story. If your main character is a bunny in search of his mother, do we need to know his thoughts about his best friend, too? No matter how beautifully that section is written, it needs to go in the wastebasket.

Ann Hoppe said, "The words must be chipped away and chipped away so that only the essential few needed to carry the narrative forward and give it its unique flavor remain. The writer's job is to pare a story or experience down until the essence remains, spare and shining."

JETTISON THE *JUSTS*

Consider the following sentence: "Maybe you could just wait for me at the bookstore." Get rid of *just*: *Maybe you could wait for me by the bookstore.* Granted, times will come in your writing when you want to add emphasis with *just*, but it tends to be a word that is thrown in thoughtlessly. Most *justs* can be jettisoned.

THERE WERE; IT IS; IT WAS; IT ISN'T

These words and words like them can easily be cut. When you see *There were,* as in "There were seven cats stretched out on the bed," rewrite it as "Seven cats stretched out on the bed." The words *it was* are a signal to combine that sentence with the one preceding it, as in "Tade found his soccer ball. It was under a bush." Tighter writing would be "Tade found his soccer ball under a bush."

SEE, HEAR, WATCH, AND *LOOK*

Check your manuscript to determine if these words are necessary. When a story is being told from Hazel's point of view, don't write "I saw my father standing by the picnic table." She's obviously the one seeing him because Hazel is telling us the story. It's more succinct and makes more sense to write "Father was standing by the picnic table." You might want to leave in *she saw* for emphasis sometimes, but often this phrase and similar ones can be discarded.

DO YOU NEED BOTH AN ATTRIBUTION AND AN ACTION?

Examine the following passage: "'Go away!' Ronnie said. He pointed at the door. 'Go now!'" This could be written with only the attribution of who's speaking: "'Go away!' Ronnie said. 'Go now!'" Or alternatively, with only the action: "'Go away!' Ronnie pointed to the door. 'Go now!'"

WHICH IS A WITCH

Certain words raise my dander. *Which* is one of them. Writing "She found the soap which was in the drawer" is unnecessary. A smoother sentence would be "She found the soap in the drawer."

DON'T BE AN OWL—GET RID OF WHO-OOS

Who is another word that grinds my gears. "Jamie, who was racing to the ball, knew she had an easy shot to the goal." A tighter and more exciting way to write it would be "Racing to the ball, Jamie knew she had an easy shot."

THWACK *THAT*

I frequently overuse the word *that*. Consider how "I wonder if she knows that she has poppy seeds in her teeth" can easily be written "I wonder if she knows she has poppy seeds in her teeth."

DON'T DOUBLE-DIP

Assuming a verb is strong, we don't need to add an adverb saying the same thing.

In "Jon sobbed loudly," we know sobbing is loud without the adverb.

TWO IS NOT BETTER THAN ONE

Sentences like the following come from the writer thinking more is better and having trouble deciding which words to use. One could say "Lena was proud of the delicious, yummy, ever-so-tasty cake she'd baked," but here's the shorter version: "Lena was proud of the delicious cake she'd baked." In this sentence, the writer used several verbs: "Hazel laughed and giggled and twirled a happy jig." All those verbs show joy, but because a visual is good, I'd rewrite it as: "Hazel twirled a happy jig."

CHARACTERS DON'T PEE IN STORIES

We don't need every detail of their lives. When you're cutting, look for those spots where you've written more activities than are necessary. Consider the following passage: "Eddie walked to the dining room. He pulled out his chair. He sat down. He picked up his fork. He started to eat his supper." Those sentences could be trimmed to just four words: "Eddie ate his supper." At dramatic moments in your story, you may want to slow things down and include all the activities a character engages in, but usually they can be reduced to a single action.

CUT OUT PURPLE PROSE

Don't write *Remembering their time together filled her with joy sweeter than chocolate cake, sweeter than the sun's warmth on her face, sweeter than a baby's first smile, sweeter than honey from the hive, and much, much sweeter than her first kiss.*

We mistakenly think the more we say and the greater we exaggerate, the more likely we are to make our point. Instead our point gets buried in a landfill of words. The reader may say to herself "That's ridiculous!" and close the book. Settle on one description, and make it a plausible one.

DON'T SHOW *AND* TELL

Doing this often comes from a writer's insecurity. He wonders whether the reader and listener will get what he's saying, so he says it twice: "She was so happy. She threw her arms around him." Delete the telling statement, "She was so happy." "She threw her arms around him" shows happiness.

A FEW FINAL WORDS

Mary Calhoun said, "Writing a picture-book story involves all the focusing and intensity and control of writing a poem." Achieve that focus by deleting anything that doesn't advance your story. Tighten up your writing, and make sure it's geared toward your specific audience.

WHAT'S NEXT?

You're finished with plotting. You know how to make your words lyrical and how to make your manuscript as tight as it can be. What more could be left? The next two chapters are about the last step—checking for important page turns and making a dummy of your story—so get ready to leave your computer again to do some cutting and pasting.

BUT . . . Before you go on

1. Time to cut excess words from your manuscript. Be cold and ruthless. Try deleting half of the words. You may put some back, but I guarantee you'll be surprised by how many words you don't need.
2. Check out your good and bad picture-book manuscripts. Is wordiness one of the reasons one book didn't work for you?
3. Read one of the books mentioned in this chapter.

Part Five

Tying Together Loose Ends

17

Page Turns

"What happens next?"

—EVERYONE THROUGHOUT EVERY CENTURY

One reason I was thrilled to update *Writing Picture Books* is that I neglected to put enough emphasis on the importance of page turns in the original edition.

Those lucky people who write novels don't need to pay close attention to each word in their manuscripts. A weak word, like a tiny minnow, can get lost in the rushing stream of sentences. They have pages and pages of writing before they reach the end of a chapter and need a hook that compels the audience to keep reading.

The picture-book writer's job is more challenging. We must focus on each word *and* create chapter hooks on every page, hence the term *page turns*. In our short books, these may come every sentence, every few sentences, or every few paragraphs, but they must always come on the odd-numbered pages of our published books.

HOW DO WE CREATE STRONG PAGE TURNS?

To keep readers turning the pages of your book, you must write a story filled with action, tension, and conflict. Page turns are that point in your story where your readers ask "What happens next?" If a character is about to open a door, what happens next? What's behind that door? If a warthog is being stalked by a lion, what happens next? Will he become the lion's supper? If a character doesn't want to wear a monster costume for Halloween, what happens next? What will he finally wear? When a reader has a question, she must turn the page to find the answer.

Great page turns that create tension come when the result of an action is in doubt. If "Billy stomped next door to demand Owen return his superglue," will Owen slam the door in his face? Will he confess that he used up all the glue? And if so, how will Billy react? The reader wants to know.

Another story technique is to leave your main character in a state of severe frustration: "Ellie hated her picture so much she scribbled all over it." Don't you feel her disappointment? Don't you wonder if she'll ever draw a picture that will please her?

Let's look at some recently published books with strong page turns. In *Sophie's Squash* by Pat Zietlow Miller, Sophie has planted the squash and snow has fallen, and we keep reading because we wonder if that squash will survive the winter. In *Big Mean Mike* by Michelle Knudsen, we turn the pages to see how and where the bunnies will appear next time. *Oh, No!* by Candace Fleming is a charming story told as only she can, in her lyrical, musical prose. We read on to find out if anyone will help Frog get out of a deep hole. Mouse and other creatures try to assist, and we're forced to turn the pages to find out if they will be successful.

Perhaps you have a tremendous plot with lots of action, tension, and conflict. If so, maybe it's time to work on implementing some other techniques to pique the reader's interest.

ADD AN ALPHABET OR COUNTING ELEMENT

Both approaches have built-in page turns. If Ant eats an apple, you must turn the page to see what Baboon and Camel eat. If one squirrel and then two robins come to a picnic, you turn the page to find out what three, four, and five creatures will join the feast. I used the alphabet to strengthen my page turns in *Everything to Spend the Night*.

BREAK UP A SENTENCE

"When Warthog arrived at the ball [page turn], she wore a leafy gown." I did this in *If Animals Kissed Good Night*. The full text of the first page is "If animals kissed like we kiss good night," so in mid-sentence, the reader must turn the page to finish it. Laura Numeroff does this successfully throughout her always popular If You Give a … series.

BREAK UP WORDS

Weigh the effect of breaking the following sentence thusly: "Jon went to the play [page turn] yard to climb the jungle gym." The reader might imagine Jon is going to the theater, only to discover, after turning the page, he's in a schoolyard. If you do this enough in your story, the reader will know not to trust first assumptions and will be intrigued to turn yet another page.

ASK A QUESTION

Another way to keep your reader hooked is to end a page with a question: "Will Jimmy make it to school before the bell rings? [page turn] He would have, but an elephant blocked his way and showered him with a wet-washing spray." To see more of this technique in action, check out *Sophie's Fish* by A.E. Cannon; it's chock-full of question page turns.

ELLIPSES

Now observe the delayed gratification a writer can create with a purposefully placed ellipsis: "'Momma's going to give you ...[page turn] a squish, squashy hug.'" Both *Hush Little Monster* by Denis Markell and *They All Saw a Cat* by Brendan Wenzel use this approach to motivate readers to forge ahead.

DASHES

You can also use dashes to entice the audience: "Billy did not want to go to the dentist—[page turn] so he hid in the closet." In *Time for (Earth) School, Dewey Dew,* Leslie Staub employs the dash technique in her first sentence; later she uses ellipses.

WORDS THAT IMPLY CONTINUATION

Breaking a sentence after a word that suggests more is to come can work to build excitement as well: "All was well until [page turn] Piggy, fresh out of her mud bath, went into the farmer's house to show how clean she was."

REPETITIVE PHRASES

If you want to build anticipation and spur a page turn, try repeating a particular phrase throughout your book. A lot of great songs have refrains that hook listeners, and people are willing to listen to the verses (even when they aren't as engaging) if a song has an irresistible refrain. Your story can operate similarly.

"Peter, time to put on your shoes."
"Not yet!" *[page turn]*
And then later: "Peter, time for your bath."
"Not yet!" *[page turn]*

Although Margery Cuyler's *That's Good! That's Bad!* was published back in 1993, it remains in print and is worth studying, not only for its fantastic page turns but its playful language. Recently she followed it up with *That's Good! That's Bad! on Santa's Journey.*

IS YOUR BOOK A PAGE-TURNER?

I print out a hard copy of my manuscript and make stars in each spot I think is a possible page turn. You could, I suppose, make stars on your computer screen, but I'm old-fashioned and the act of doing it by pencil reinforces either the presence or absence of page turns. Seeing lots of stars makes me happy, but if there aren't enough, I check to see if I can use some of the aforementioned techniques to add more.

An important note—your page turns may not turn out to be the actual page turns in the published book. The editor and illustrator may have different ideas, but you still must make sure you have them. The final decision regarding where they go will not be yours, but if you always consider them in your writing, they might end up falling exactly where you imagined.

A FEW FINAL WORDS

We've discussed lots of ways to create page turns, but let me emphasize again: A story with lots of drama, tension, and conflict will always spur readers to turn your pages.

If you're successful, you probably have fourteen page turns, but don't punish yourself if you don't have dramatic ones on every odd-numbered page. Many picture books don't have them on every one, but be aware of their importance, and create as many as you can.

WHAT'S NEXT?

In the next chapter, we'll look at an even better way to test for page turns—making a dummy.

BUT . . . Before you go on

1. Study the page turns in your good and bad picture books.
2. Examine your story's manuscript, and star each possible page turn.
3. Look at the texts of your published picture books with special consideration to their page turns.
4. Read a new picture book, perhaps one mentioned in this chapter.

18

Cut and Paste

Making a Mock-up Book

"Putting together the … book dummy is a necessary process—it is the foundation for your book and lies at the heart of good bookmaking."

—URI SHULEVITZ

You've written your story. You've revised the opening until it's tight and engaging. You've experimented with different ways to tell your story and chosen the best one. Your characters are strong, unique, and believable; your plot is a page-turner, and the ending resolves the main conflict. You've tied things together so that your audience will be satisfied and will want to read or hear the book again. Your manuscript, whether written in poetry or prose, is poetic. You've worked to use the right words, and you've cut out unnecessary ones. You should be finished, but. …

You're not done yet! You need to make a dummy. A dummy is a layout of your text onto thirty-two pages. It's helpful in determining if the structure of your story fits the picture-book format.

"But I'm not an illustrator," you plead. "I write the words. Illustrators may find making a dummy a positive exercise, but it's a waste of time for me."

Trust me on the helpfulness of dummies. For years I tried to get away with not doing them. Making check marks or stars on the hard copy of my manuscript was surely enough to show me where the page turns came and if I had enough illustration possibilities. *Wrong*! I am one of the converted—a born-again dummy maker. I never send out a manuscript without first doing a dummy—a visual and tactile way of evaluating my story.

Most of us who write for children are kids at heart. Creating a dummy takes you away from your computer and gives your back and neck a break.

Cutting and pasting allows you to use different hand and arm muscles, so it can be a nice change of pace.

We think of a dummy as the last stage of the revision process, but it may expose less obvious problems and lead to more revisions and more dummies. None of my dummies are for my editor to see. Some writers sketch out a simple, rough dummy early in the writing process, sometimes even before a word is written. They do this storyboard on a single sheet of paper, dividing it into separate pages and spreads as I have done below:

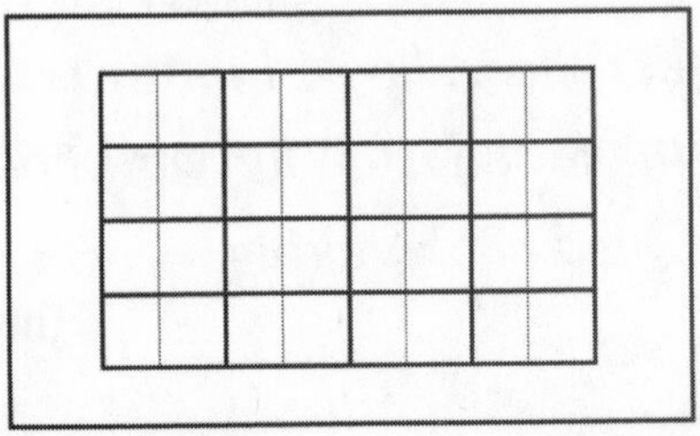

A spread is two facing pages that end up with an illustration that fills and spans both of those pages. You can purchase these forms in most art stores. The writer then uses single words or brief phrases to indicate action, page turns, etc. This initial dummy/storyboard does not include the story text. Its purpose is to give a general overview of the story's spacing.

The dummy we're going to make next is closer to a finished book with numbered pages you can turn. Print a hard copy of your story, and then grab some blank paper, lift-off tape, and scissors.

THE DUMMY FORM

Staple sixteen pieces of 8½" × 11" (22cm × 28cm) paper together along the left side. Picture-book manuscripts rarely have enough text to fill full pieces of paper, so save a tree and use only eight sheets of 8½" × 11" (22cm × 28cm) paper. Cut them in half, either vertically (portrait) or horizontally (landscape). You will then have pieces measuring either 5½" × 8½" (14cm × 22cm) or 11" × 4¼" (28cm × 11cm). Depending on what side you staple it, your dummy may be long or tall. Choose what shape you want your dummy to be, depending on the amount of text and the line lengths. If your text lines are short, you can have a taller dummy. If they are long, you should make a longer dummy.

If you have a particularly brief text, use just four pages of paper; cut them into quarters, and staple them together.

Number your pages from one to thirty-two. The first is page one. Turn the page, and put a two on the back of page one. Number three will go on the right-hand page. Continue in this manner until you reach the back page, which should be thirty-two.

CUTTING AND PASTING

Now you're ready to cut and paste sections of your manuscript onto the pages. To do that, you need to consider how many pages will be taken up by front matter. This can include four different items.

1. **HALF-TITLE PAGE:** This usually appears on page one and traditionally is the title with only a small illustration.
2. **FULL-TITLE PAGE:** This usually appears on pages two and three and includes the title and the writer's, illustrator's, and publisher's names.
3. **COPYRIGHT INFORMATION:** This usually appears on page four.
4. **DEDICATIONS:** They usually appear on page five, directly preceding your story's opening page.

Notice, the repetition of the phrase *usually appears*. These days publishers display a wide range of creativity in laying out front matter. You should browse through picture books to see the variety of ways front-matter information may be presented, but for right now you can familiarize yourself with the approaches listed below.

- Page one of *Me and Momma and Big John* by Mara Rockliff has a half title on page one, and the story opens with a double-spread on pages two and three. The copyright and dedications appear at the end of the book.
- *School's First Day of School* by Adam Rex is a forty-page picture book. Because the endpapers are part of those forty pages, the front matter begins on page four with the dedication and copyright info, and then the half title is on page five. The story begins on pages six and seven.
- *Old Robert and the Sea-Silly Cats* by Barbara Joosse is another forty-page book and begins completely differently. The first sentence is on page one. Pages two and three are a full-title page, and the dedication and copyright info appear on page forty.
- *Bike On, Bear!* by Cynthea Liu has a half title with no illustration on page one. Page two is dedication and copyright info, and page three is another half title, this time with an illustration. The story begins on page four.

- *Mousequerade Ball: A Counting Tale* by Lori Mortensen has a half title on page one, copyright info on page two, and dedications on page three. The story begins on page four.
- *Dot.* by Randi Zuckerberg begins with a half title on page one, copyright info on page two, and dedications on page three, but page four is blank—no picture, no text. The story begins on page five.

When you cut and paste your manuscript, plan where that information will go. Usually I start pasting my story on page six. If I find I need more story pages, I tighten my front matter. Don't use ordinary tape. You need a lift-off tape—Scotch brand calls it "removable tape"—so you can shift text from one page to another without creating tears. I'm a creature of habit and prefer tape, but non-permanent glue sticks and sprays work as well.

BREAKING UP THE TEXT

Always cut whenever one of the following story elements changes.

1. **LOCATION:** Your character leaves the house, enters a store, or goes to a friend's house. The different setting calls for a different picture, which means it's time to move on to the next page.
2. **CHARACTERS:** A new character is introduced, or a character disappears. Mother comes home from work, the tooth fairy sneaks into the bedroom, or the cat hides, but the result is the same: The picture must change.
3. **ACTIONS:** Two characters are fighting. Someone breaks up the fight, and then the characters start working together. Each of these would signal the need for a different illustration.

Note that on odd pages it is not enough to have simple changes in the story. There should be developments dramatic enough to compel your reader to turn the page. Try to leave your character in peril on the odd-numbered pages.

Using your lift-off tape, paste your text onto the pages of your dummy. An important benefit of making a dummy is that it shows whether you have those necessary page turns we discussed in the previous chapter. You'll need to do some experimentation and realigning to decide where your text works best.

Once your dummy is as complete as you can make it, read it aloud with pen or pencil in hand. The act of reading and turning the pages, as your reader will, allows you to see the story in a new way. Then make the necessary changes to your dummy.

I'm always surprised to find changes need to be made because I wait to dummy my manuscript until I think my story is ready to send off. Invariably, though, I discover places for revision I hadn't noticed before. Pay special attention to the following questions when evaluating your dummied manuscript.

CAN YOUR STORY FIT INTO THIRTY-TWO PAGES?

Perhaps your story is quite short and would work better as a board book. But maybe your story needs forty pages. Beware if you are a first-time writer with a manuscript that needs more than the traditional thirty-two pages. Publishing a new writer's book is an expensive gamble for the publishing house. Any additional pages might cause an editor to think twice about buying your story.

DOES YOUR STORY HAVE ENOUGH ILLUSTRATIONS?

The minimum number of pictures is thirteen double-spreads and one single-spread. Thoughts cannot be easily illustrated. The days of characters with thought bubbles over their heads have passed. Nevertheless, dialogue is often printed comic-book style in those kinds of bubbles. Some dialogue can be illustrated. "I'm leaving right now" indicates action and could be illustrated with Rabbit leaving her den. "I'm not sure what to do" would be more difficult. Negative statements, such as "He didn't jump" or "She didn't read her book," would require great creativity on the illustrator's part. Look at *My Favorite Pets: by Gus W. for Ms. Smolinski's Class* to see how Harry Bliss deals with the negative statements Jeanne Birdsall wrote.

DOES YOUR TEXT SUGGEST A VARIETY OF ILLUSTRATIONS?

Does your story take place entirely in one room? While Margaret Wise Brown got away with that in *Goodnight Moon*, give your illustrator a break and vary the illustration possibilities. Give your listener a break, too, so she won't be looking at the same pictures over and over again.

DOES THE READER KNOW YOUR BOOK'S PREMISE WITHIN THE FIRST THREE PAGES?

After the front matter, no more than three pages should be required to give your reader a good idea of your story's subject matter. Really, though, allowing three pages is being generous. All that opening material we discussed in chapter seven should be on the first page.

DOES YOUR STORY HAVE PAGE TURNS?

Not every page needs a cliff-hanger, but something should be left unanswered or unfinished so the reader wants to proceed.

IS THE ACTION SPREAD OVER THIRTY-TWO PAGES?

Or is it clumped together at the beginning or the end? Are big chunks of text on some pages and little slivers on others? Ask yourself whether all that text is important and if some can be deleted.

ARE THERE SPOTS WITH UNNECESSARY WORDS?

Scrutinize any clumps of dialogue and description. Can they be condensed? Can they be eliminated? Seeing one's text on the page reveals new possibilities for edits.

DOES YOUR CLIMAX HAPPEN IN THE STORY'S FINAL PAGES?

Ideally, your climax will occur near page thirty or thirty-one. If it happens on pages sixteen and seventeen, you have a problem and need to cut much of what comes afterwards. On the other hand, you might consider adding more action to your story's middle section.

DO YOU TIE UP LOOSE ENDS NICELY?

You have until the last page to accomplish this. We discussed this in detail in chapter twelve, which focused on endings. With your dummy, you'll see how well you've handled this element of your story.

IS YOUR STORYTELLING CONCISE, POETIC, AND DRAMATIC?

To answer this question, read your dummy one last time for an overview of how your plot and language work together.

COLOR-TESTING THE DUMMY

After you've made your dummy, get out your highlighters. Use the green highlighter for the *wow* moment, that initial intriguing development that compels the reader to proceed. You did this before when we worked on openings, but it's important to repeat here. Turning the pages can sometimes show you the *wow* moment isn't that much of a *wow*.

Next use a blue highlighter to show where the problem of the story is revealed. If this wasn't within the first three pages of text, text juggling and cutting are in order. Using that same blue highlighter, mark the place where the problem is solved. If it comes before pages twenty-eight and twenty-nine, revise to bring it closer to the end of your text. Circle dramatic moments in red. Are there enough? Where did they occur? If they're all close together or too far apart, can they be moved, expanded, or shortened? Then with an ordinary pen or pencil, go through your dummy story again and star places where some question or drama creates a page turn. Remember: These should come on every odd-numbered page. And last of all, the dummy will show if there's a satisfying wrap-up moment on page thirty-two. If you have that, draw yourself a smiley face.

Here's a sample page of one of my dummies, with corrections and changes for you to see.

Pretty sloppy, isn't it?

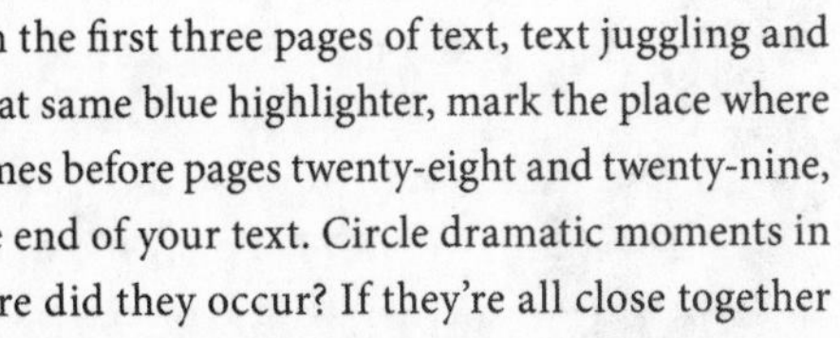
At that moment, Mother arrived.

"Your son is trying to take my cow," the tailor said.

"It's our cow!" Zachariah pointed. "See the black spot over her eye."

"Oh, dear," said Mother. "Many cows have black spots over their eyes. That's why I always check her earmark."

Zachariah's cheeks grew warm. Every time he tried to help, he caused trouble.

He shuffled behind Mother to find their own cow.

A FEW FINAL WORDS

Your dummy doesn't have to be neat and pretty. It's only for you. Don't send it to an editor, but don't trash it. Save each dummy. Later, you can compare it to the published book. The layout may be the same or wildly different. That doesn't matter. Just make sure your story fits the picture-book format. Don't be a dummy—make a dummy!

WHAT'S NEXT?

In chapter nineteen, we'll look at the absolute last writing task: creating a title.

BUT . . . Before you go on

1. Print your manuscript, and dummy it up. Now color-test your dummy.

   Evaluate how well your story works, and play around with the positioning of text. Revise if necessary.
2. Make dummies of the good and bad published books you selected. Using your highlighter, evaluate each story's strengths and weaknesses. Don't stop with these two texts. Whenever you find a new book you love, type it up and print it out. Then make a dummy, study it, and write notes on the pages. Doing so will teach you much about creating a publishable manuscript.
3. Read a new picture book, perhaps one mentioned in this chapter.

19

Grabbing the Reader with a Great Title

"Many a book is chosen by a reader because the title seemed promising."

—BARBARA SEULING

Your picture book is written. You've revised until it's as close to perfect as possible. You've spent weeks, months, possibly even years getting your manuscript to this point. Surely now you are done, finished!

But no! You must create a title. Perhaps you already have one. Maybe it came first and inspired your story. You still like that title, but is it the best it can be?

Boring titles can result in your book collecting dust on shelves in stores and libraries or in turning off that all-important editor. The title is the first thing the agent, editor, librarian, or buyer sees. Carol Mann called it "a ten-second advertisement." With so many new books published each year, that advertisement better be, as Mary Poppins and Bert might sing, supercalifragilisticexpialidocious.

How hard can coming up with a title be? you think. *Titles are short. They should be easy.*

Not so. The editor Richard Jackson said, "Next to finding a jacket artist, I think titling is the hardest thing to do in children's books." Editor Reka Simonsen said, "Titles can be a nightmare." While writing this chapter, I combed the picture books on my shelves. Here are eleven titles that jumped out and shouted, "Read me!"

1. *Best Frints in the Whole Universe* by Antoinette Portis: The word *frints* for *friends* telegraphs a humorous book.
2. *School's First Day of School* by Adam Rex: Readers know this isn't going to be the usual first-day-of-school story.

3. *A Fine Dessert: Four Centuries, Four Families, One Delicious Treat* by Emily Jenkins: This title grabs anyone who loves desserts. Notice how musical the title is with the alliteration of the letter *f*, the repetition of the word *four*, and the wonderful rhythm, whose many stresses are marked below.

   . / . / / / . . / / . . / . / . /

   A Fine Dessert: Four Centuries, Four Families, One Delicious Treat
4. *Chicken Lily* by Lori Mortensen: This is familiar, reminding us of the old tale of Chicken Little but with a twist.
5. *Would You Rather Be a Princess or a Dragon?* by Barney Saltzberg: I'm a sucker for question titles, and the choice between such opposites as a princess and a dragon compels me to read the story.
6. *Little Dog Lost: The True Story of a Brave Dog Named Baltic* by Mônica Carnesi: Wow! A lost dog? Dog lovers will have to pick up this book to see if anyone finds him.
7. *The Yuckiest, Stinkiest, Best Valentine Ever* by Brenda A. Ferber: "Yucky" and "stinky" are funny in this context, but "best" makes the title intriguing. How can a valentine be all three?
8. *I Dissent: Ruth Bader Ginsburg Makes Her Mark* by Debbie Levy: The firmness expressed in that main title makes me want to find out what she dissents from.
9. *Balderdash!: John Newbery and the Boisterous Birth of Children's Books* by Michelle Markel: Love the *b* words here. Such fun!
10. *Penguin and Pinecone: A Friendship Story* by Salina Yoon: The *p* alliteration and such an odd pairing make me curious about the book.
11. *The Summer Nick Taught His Cats to Read* by Curtis Manley: Taught his *cats* to read? Who wouldn't want to see how that worked out?

Do you want to create a title as enticing as these? Then let's experiment with our old friend "The Ant and the Dove" and vary its title according to each of the following attributes.

BRIEF

Not every title can be brief. However, realize you don't have space on your cover for a long, involved title. My first book about patchwork was submitted with the title *Anvil, Buggy Wheel, Churn Dash* and the subtitle *A Patchwork ABC*. The art was done, and the book was about to be printed when my editor called to say the marketing department needed to shorten the title so it would fit in their catalog's index. They came up with *Eight Hands Round.* Besides being the name of one of the patterns in the book, it also conjured up an image of women working together around a quilting frame. I happily accepted the editor's suggestion.

Recently at an American Library Association meeting, I wandered the aisles looking at picture books and was surprised by how brief most of their titles were. Some of my favorite brief titles include *Yard Sale* (Eve Bunting), *Swamp Song* (Helen Ketteman), and *Found* (Salina Yoon). My one-word title for Aesop's fable would be "Help!" This would express how both characters find themselves in desperate situations.

CATCHY

Random House Dictionary defines *catchy* as "pleasing and easily remembered." *Pleasing* certainly relates to the poetry or musical language of titles like *Alpha Oops!* (Alethea Kontis), *Counting Crows* (Kathi Appelt), and *The Yuckiest, Stinkiest, Best Valentine Ever* (Brenda A. Ferber). Alliterative titles can be catchy, so for our fable we might try "Double Danger." "Rescuing Ant, Rescuing Dove" makes good use of repetition, but unfortunately, it gives away the ending.

UNIQUE

Titles are not copyrighted. While nothing can stop you from choosing a book title that's the same as another work's, why would you? For a middle-grade historical-fiction story I've been working on, my initial title was *A Time to Heal.* However, when I checked Amazon, I found too many similar titles. I changed it to *Bucket of Trouble.* No other book came close.

Research Amazon or *Books in Print*, published by R.R. Bowker (available at your library), before you settle on a title. Make sure there aren't hundreds of others like or close to yours. *Doggone Dogs!* (Karen Beaumont), and *Otter and Odder* (James Howe) are fine examples of appealing unique titles. "Wild Water and Birdcatcher" would not be a great title for Aesop's fable, but at least it's unique.

STRAIGHTFORWARD

Don't be too fancy with your title. You may like the way certain words sound together, but if they don't reflect what happens in the book, they must go. This happened to me with a manuscript about life on the prairie in the mid-1800s versus life today. I chose the title *Griddle Cakes and Frosted Flakes*. I loved the sound of it. The old-fashioned words versus contemporary words indicated the form of the book. I thought I had a winner.

The members of my writing group disagreed. They said it sounded like a breakfast cookbook! *Duh!* Why hadn't I realized that? The title now, after lots of experimentation, is *Twice Upon the Prairie*, which is a twist on the familiar "Once upon a time" and accurately describes the book. I hope an editor will agree. *Brave Girl* (Michelle Markel), *Happy Like Soccer* (Maribeth Boelts), and *The Leprechaun Under the Bed* (Teresa Bateman) are all straightforward titles I love. Our fable's straightforward title might be "Two Friends' Adventures."

EXPRESSES THE BOOK'S MOOD

Is your book going to be funny or serious, silly or sad? You must get that across in your title. Readers want to know what kind of a story journey they're embarking on. *I Don't Want to Be a Pea!* (Ann Bonwill) promises a fun read, *Step Gently Out* (Helen Frost) sounds like a quiet read, and *Noah Webster & His Words* (Jeri Chase Ferris) seems like a more matter-of-fact book. For a title indicating the fable's mood, I'm going with "Oh, Dear! Trouble!"

HINTS AT THE BOOK'S PLOT OR THEME

As long as you've done the work of writing a fascinating story, pick a title that's emblematic of something plot- or theme-related. *Last Stop on Market Street* by Matt de la Peña isn't going to be about a football game or a fight with a bully. It's obviously related to a ride on a bus or train. As for *Zero the Hero* by Joan Holub, we can safely say it isn't about the number seven. If you wanted to hint at the fable's content, "One Good Turn Deserves Another" seems fitting.

DOESN'T GIVE AWAY THE ENDING

It's easy to fall in love with a last line, but don't automatically use it as your title. What if Leslie Staub, in *Time for (Earth) School, Dewey Dew*, had used her last line that basically said everything would be okay? You wouldn't have needed to read the story because you would have known everything was going to work out. Avoid giving away so much information that the reader won't need to pick up your book. What about "Double Trouble" for "The Ant and the Dove"?

SUSPENSEFUL

One of the best ways to engage the reader is by creating suspense, and that can start with your title. I think *Oh, No!* (Candace Fleming) and *I Want My Hat Back* (Jon Klassen) are excellent suspenseful titles. The former makes you wonder what causes the speaker to react this way, and the latter raises the question "Will the bear get back his hat?" As a suspenseful title for our fable, I like "If Ant's Call Goes Unheeded."

GIVES THE ARTIST A COVER IDEA

Sophie's Squash by Pat Zietlow Miller certainly falls into this category. The illustrator, Anne Wilsdorf, makes sure her cover includes both Sophie and her squash. Maybe "Excitement at the River" would spark the imagination of an illustrator designing art for Aesop's fable.

A CHILD CAN EASILY SAY IT

It's common sense. If a child is going to ask an adult to read a book, the title has to be something he can say. *Extra Yarn* (Mac Barnett), *Swamp Song* (Helen Ketteman), and *Nellie Belle* (Mem Fox) are all titles that roll right off the tongue. For our fable, let's go with "Save Me!"

INCLUDES THE MAIN CHARACTER'S NAME

Some titles are solely the main character's name, such as *Olivia* by Ian Falconer and *Rotten Ralph* by Jack Gantos. These titles work because the character is strong and distinctive. Each is the first book in a successful series, and each name figures prominently in future books. Other titles, like *The Adventures of Beekle: The Unimaginary Friend* (Dan Santat) and *Kel Gilligan's Daredevil Stunt Show* (Michael Buckley), include the name and some more information about the character. We could call Aesop's fable "Ant and Dove's Adventures."

Obviously not all titles can contain every attribute mentioned above. But in creating a title you should consider these and see how many yours can include.

NAILING DOWN THE PERFECT TITLE

Still having problems coming up with the right title for your book? Here are some strategies that may give you the creative second wind you need.

USE A CATCHY LINE FROM YOUR MANUSCRIPT

Sometimes you can use lines that are repeated several times in the story. I did this in *If Animals Kissed Good Night* and *If Animals Said I Love You*. Jacqueline Woodson uses a repeated line from her text for the title *This Is the Rope: A Story from the Great Migration*. The line you choose should be one that also gives readers a good idea of the book's subject matter. Comb your manuscript looking for such a line.

FREE ASSOCIATION

Referring to each characteristic of a good title, write down every one that pops into your mind. Free-associate brief titles and then catchy titles all the way down that list. Don't judge—some will be terrible. Keep on writing until something hits you. You might have pages of possible titles before one works. If nothing strikes you, put your list aside and go back to it later. And, if necessary, do it again.

TURN TO OUTSIDERS

My writing group has been incredibly helpful with titles. They were the ones who suggested I title my prairie-life manuscript *Once Upon a Time* when I was struggling to come up with something. That title inspired me to call it *Once Upon the Prairie*, which eventually evolved into *Twice Upon the Prairie*, what I'd like to be its final title. Other writers and friends have the advantage of coming to your story new and fresh. They see things you never noticed, and their minds work differently than yours. Before you settle on a title, remember to go online or check *Books in Print* to make sure your idea is original.

A FEW FINAL WORDS

We've looked at what makes a good title and how to create a snappy one. Keep in mind that it's still possible the publisher may change your title for marketing reasons after you've realized what you believe should be its final iteration. Feel free to disagree with her decision. Explain why you chose your title and why you think it works better. Offer alternative titles. However, if your publishing house won't budge on the issue, let it go.

Your book is being published, and you don't want to leave the people working there with sour feelings. Accept the inevitable, just as you accept that your children will be exposed to ideas, activities, and language that doesn't please you. This is the way of the world.

Promote your book, no matter the title, as much as you can. The title is a small, albeit important, part of the manuscript. Focus on what's behind the cover, not what's on the cover.

WHAT'S NEXT?

Now that you're convinced you're really done, there's one more task before you send your story to an editor—sharing it with an outside reader. Why must you do this after the many hours of work you've already done? Your picture-book story is meant to be read by others. Perhaps others won't see what you are trying to say. Do you want your editor to be the first reader who doesn't get it? That's why you need to read the next chapter and let someone (maybe several people) read your story.

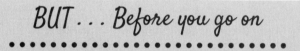

BUT . . . Before you go on

1. Think about your favorite memorable titles. What makes them stick with you?
2. Using the exercises in this chapter, create alternate titles for a popular published book. I did this for *Goodnight Moon* by Margaret Wise Brown. It was revealing to see how many possibilities I could come up with. Some of them were terrible, but others could just as easily have been substituted.
3. Using the exercises in this chapter, create alternate titles for your manuscript. Select one, and give yourself a smiley face or star for each of the characteristics your title possesses. Obviously, the more stars or happy faces, the better.

    a. Brief
    b. Catchy
    c. Unique
    d. Straightforward
    e. Expresses the book's mood
    f. Hints at the book's plot or theme
    g. Doesn't give away the ending

h. Suspenseful
i. Gives the artist a cover idea
j. A child can easily say it
k. Includes the main character's name

4. Could the titles of the manuscripts you typed up be improved? How?
5. Read a new picture book, perhaps one mentioned in this chapter.

Part Six

After Your Story Is Done

20

Sharing Your Story

"Fine writers should split hairs together, and sit side by side, like friendly apes, to pick the fleas from each other's prose."

—LOGAN PEARSALL SMITH

I'm a firm believer in writing groups. Our picture books are meant to be read by others. Think of your picture-book story as a triangle.

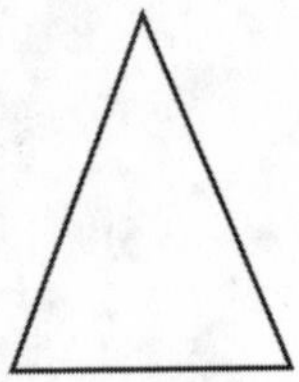

One side is you, the writer. Another side is your words. But it's not a complete triangle until that bottom line—the reader—joins them.

We want our words to reach and move both adults and children. We want to help them through hard times and let them know they're not alone. We want to share our views and enrich lives. If we don't allow others to see our work, we'll never know if our words are received as we intended. Who better than a group of fellow writers to be your first readers?

A word of warning! Your partner, parents, children, and students are not necessarily good readers for your manuscript. My husband loves everything I write, and when my children were young, they couldn't be bothered to hear Mom's stories. The best potential manuscript readers are those who also write picture books. If that is true of your partner, lucky you. If not, you'd better join a writing group.

FINDING MEMBERS

My group evolved from a class I took in picture-book writing through UCLA Extension. After the class ended, several students, whose writing I respected, formed a group that met regularly.

Another writing group I belong to includes members from all over the country. We met in a workshop with Jane Yolen at Centrum (centrum.org) in Port Townsend, Washington, and several of us continue to meet to share our works-in-progress. We also share via e-mail.

Today, the Internet is a wonderful way to contact other writers who might be willing to critique your work. However, don't dive into the first critique group you hear about or that invites you. Choosing a critique group is as important to your work as choosing a mate is to your life. Likewise, you hope that your writing group will last forever.

PERSONAL QUALIFICATIONS

Look for people who share your values about life and writing. A writing group that endures, like mine has for thirty years, evolves into much more than a gathering of professionals. You are going to be discussing your stories with the other group members. Therefore, they will learn intimate things about you, just as a partner does. You need to like these people and feel safe interacting with them because they will become your second family—your writing family.

Each member will hopefully grow into a friend. If someone rubs you the wrong way, sends unpleasant vibes, or makes you uncomfortable, don't invite her to be a part of your group.

In your meetings, you will share the frustrations and disappointments of the field. You'll bring rejections and get emotional support. You'll disseminate publishing information. You'll cry when books go out-of-print and celebrate when stories are accepted and made into books. In my writing group, a sale is marked with champagne and small gifts related to the book.

Friends who don't write can't possibly appreciate the ups and downs of this business like the members of your group. Because they will become such an important part of your life, recognize that adding or subtracting members from an established group can start out smoothly enough but later may cause an earthquake of changes in the relationships.

PROFESSIONAL QUALIFICATIONS

Once I was in a group where everyone's understanding of picture books was that they needed to be short. As you now know, picture books are a unique form and brevity is merely one element. They are a book specialty, the same as orthopedics is a medical specialty. You would never ask an orthopedic surgeon to remove your tonsils. You would not ask your Spanish teacher for help with a math problem. Don't join a writing group that doesn't have members writing picture books.

Also try to find at least one member who has either published or has more knowledge than everyone else. You won't learn much if you're all beginners. That's like letting first graders teach first graders. Find members whose participation will help you grow.

Sometimes you can find a published expert who might require a fee to participate in your group. Pay it. It's money well spent. After a while, you'll learn so much from that person you'll all turn into experts and no longer need to pay anyone.

Make sure you're in a group with writers whose work you respect. Just because a person is published doesn't mean you're bound to like what she writes. If you find yourself in a group with such a person, you might have difficulty accepting her criticisms of your work.

Also, don't join a group where people are not comfortable critiquing. You'll get no help from those who only praise your work. As good as it feels at the time, a steady diet of bravos will not help you get published. Don't tread water in your career. Seek out members who are open, honest, and constructive but not hurtful.

SIZE

You want your group to be large enough so if one person can't attend, your group can still meet. On the other hand, you don't want a group so big that critiques will be rushed and some people's work will not even be looked at because of time constraints. Four people are in my local group, and the number of members in my group across the country has dwindled to three.

The advantage of having more than one group is that after bringing a story to one group several times, members might lose their objectivity—they will be as close to the story as the writer is. A new set of eyes reviewing the work is always beneficial.

MEETING TIME AND PLACE

Plan a regular schedule for your meetings. This allows everyone to block out calendars in advance and ensures a professional commitment. How frequently you do meet will depend on each member's availability, writing schedule, and life demands.

Where you meet can vary greatly. Writing groups meet in coffee shops, at parks, at libraries (they often have rooms available for meetings), and in homes. Sometimes they rotate between homes, and other times they meet only at one home. Your group will need to work out those details in a way that all members find satisfactory.

Some writing groups meet entirely online to share their manuscripts. Often this is just a loose association of people who ask for critiques whenever needed, but such groups may still schedule their meetings.

WHAT HAPPENS IN YOUR MEETINGS?

SHARING NEWS

Make time for sharing news—both good and bad—and for people to pass along upcoming conference information, book recommendations, and publishing business. Don't let the sharing last too long as this could interfere with critiquing. Appoint someone as timekeeper who will say, "Enough! Let's get to work." Alternatively, group members can share news and business after your critiquing time or perhaps during a food break.

THE CRITIQUING PROCESS

Since you are a picture-book group and your stories are meant to be read aloud, include time for that. The story should not be read by the person who wrote it because the writer knows where the emphasis should be and where the drama is supposed to take place. If the author reads, the story might sound fabulous when it actually needs work. Remember, the author will not be there to read or explain nuances to an editor.

You can learn a lot when you hear another person stumble over a sentence, have difficulty pronouncing words, or deliver the story in a flat manner. Hearing a story read aloud will direct you to places that need revision. My group has found it helpful for each member to have a hard copy of the manuscript so they can make notes and study it more carefully during the discussion. Just remember to recycle the paper afterwards.

Some groups might keep time for each critique, allotting a certain amount for every writer. I've found this to be useless. If one manuscript is almost ready to be sent out, the changes to it will be small and the discussion brief. Another manuscript may have many areas that require extensive deliberation. Not every manuscript needs to be critiqued for an equal amount of time, but each participant's manuscript should be critiqued with equal interest and attention. Trust me: Writers will learn from every manuscript discussed, not just their own.

WHEN YOUR MANUSCRIPT IS BEING CRITIQUED ...

During the reading of your story, listen to the sound of your words. Pay attention to when the other members look bored, amused, unbelieving, or uninterested. When the time for commenting begins, understand how this can be an uncomfortable process. You have spilled your blood, sweat, and tears onto the page. You've revised and revised and revised. Every time I bring a new story to my group, I'm *sure* it's ready to be submitted to an editor. Unhappily, in over thirty-five years of sharing new stories with my group, I've heard "It's wonderful. Send it off" only once. I'm sorry to say that story has not yet sold. Maybe it wasn't ready to be seen by an editor.

Getting fantasies squashed is hurtful. No one likes hearing their baby isn't ready for delivery to the world. But don't think you're the only one uncomfortable about sharing. Everyone is, especially in the beginning. I used to suffer terrible stomach cramps before, during, and after my writing group met.

The good news is that discomfort abates. I no longer endure stomach cramps. I have learned, and you will too, that they're not criticizing you as a person but attempting to help make your manuscript the best it can be. You will learn to be grateful for their honesty and constructive comments, and you will look forward to sharing your writing.

When the comments start coming, zip up your mouth, unless you are asked a direct question. Take notes on what you hear; do not argue: "But this really happened."

Do not question: "Why would you think that?"

Do not defend: "My husband loved that part."

Your job is to *listen*. Take in the criticism. Write it down. Later, when everyone is finished, you may ask questions. "Why did you think the character was too passive? How could I tighten my opening? Why wasn't my ending strong?"

Now is also the time to say "You're moving my story in a new direction. What I want my story to say is ... [you fill in the blank]. Why is what I want to say not coming across? How can I change my writing so it's in tune with my theme?"

Then go home with your notes, and carefully consider the comments. You may find yourself feeling exhilarated after your meeting because your story needs few changes before sending it to publishers.

On the other hand, even if you do not feel exhilarated, you may at least be comfortable with the direction you need to go. Perhaps you agreed with the suggestions. Making changes will be work but not a burden. I try to do this kind of revision within a day or two of our meeting so the comments are still fresh and I can remember what my shorthand notes mean.

Must you make all the changes your group suggests? Absolutely not. Each comment is merely an opinion. Some of these comments will feel wrong, and you can discard them immediately. Some comments you won't be so sure about. They may improve your story, or they may not. The only way to find out is to try them. If they're a disaster, go back to your original. Some comments will be so dead-on that you'll make the changes immediately.

Be forewarned, it's not enough to make one change and forget about the rest of the manuscript. Every change, no matter how small, sends ramifications rippling through your entire text. Don't assume one change solves the problem. It usually creates inconsistencies elsewhere. Don't rush your revisions. Watch for unexpected impact throughout.

You may need to take your manuscript back to your group several times before you feel confident it's ready to be sent to an editor. Over time, if your group members become so connected to your story that they become unable to view it objectively, then you need to show it to other writers or put it aside for several weeks or months, as long as it takes, before bringing it back to your group.

Sadly, after your critique, you may not feel exhilarated or comfortable with your group's comments; you might feel discouraged and depressed if your story isn't reaching readers the way you'd hoped. When your group offers ideas that don't sit right with you, you have to go back to the drawing board and rethink everything. This can feel like a Herculean task.

If you think you can push forward immediately, do. But if you're not up to it, put your story away. Let it sit on the shelf, and see if while you're going about your life, your creative mind can come up with a solution.

Also, be willing to accept that some stories won't ever work, and move on. Giving up on a project is not a sign of failure. Rather, it's a sign of maturity to say "I've learned everything I can from this story. I'm ready to apply those lessons to my next project."

WHEN YOU ARE DOING THE CRITIQUING …

It's best, especially in the early time of your group's life, to begin with positive comments. Positive contributions can be as general as "I like the message you're trying to get across" or "You've worked really hard on this revision." However, avoid generalities such as "I like this a lot" or "What a fun story." These comments aren't specific enough to be helpful. Let the writer know exactly what works for you, such as "I like the way your character steps in and takes action" or "Your opening is strong; you dropped me right into the action."

Focusing your comments will help the writer whose manuscript is being critiqued. Specificity also allows everyone to learn from the critiqued manuscript since some comments may be applicable to their own work.

Suppose there are no positives. Not possible. Every manuscript, no matter how bad, comes from a place deep within the writer. Respect that. Begin by asking the writer what he is trying to say. If you hate the manuscript, bite your tongue. Focus on specific parts of the story that didn't work for you: "I found it hard to believe the voice of your main character. You say he's six years old, but he speaks like an adult." Another example would be "Perhaps you have too much setup in the beginning. I wonder if the real opening is actually in the first paragraph of your second page." By pointing to the exact places that don't work, you are giving concrete information to the writer about where and why the story doesn't work.

Refrain from relating personal experiences. The focus here must be on the story, not on remembrances or connections it makes for you. Personal stories waste valuable critiquing time. Divide your comments into the following three areas.

BIG ISSUES

Start with major questions about how the story is working.

1. What's the writer trying to say? Is it more than an incident? Does the main character change or learn something new at the end?
2. Is the main character a child or childlike? Are there superfluous characters who don't advance the story?
3. Is it really a board book? Picture book? Picture storybook? Would this story be better told as a chapter book or as an early reader?
4. Does the story have more than one level? Does it say something? Does it have depth?
5. Is the story new and unique? Is the idea old or overdone? How might the writer add freshness?
6. Is the story tightly focused? Is it about one thing or one aspect of a thing?

When all the questions have been answered satisfactorily, you can move on.

MIDDLING ISSUES OF FORM AND STRUCTURE

1. Is the opening strong and compelling? Has the setup and description gone on too long?
2. Does the plot build to a climax?
3. Does the ending grow out of the story? Does it evoke an emotional response and make the reader want to read it again?
4. How well does the story fit into the thirty-two-page format? Look at the dummy.
    a. Is the problem established by the third spread (at the latest)?
    b. Are there strong page turns?
    c. Does the resolution come on pages thirty to thirty-one or at least close to the end? What about picture variety? Is there a nice twist, punch line, or satisfying *aha* moment on page thirty-two?
5. Does the language fit the story? Does the writer milk the emotion with cadence, rhythm, and tools of poetry, like alliteration, consonance, and assonance?
6. Do the characters speak appropriately?
7. How can this story be best told? In poetry or prose?

FINE-TUNING

It's wasted time to focus on this too early because the story may change completely. Consider the smaller issues of grammar and tight writing only after everything above is resolved.

1. Is the writer using passive instead of active verbs?
2. Does the writer tell, rather than show?
3. Are there excess words that don't advance the story?

    a. Qualifying words such as *almost, really, nearly, seemed*
    b. Adjectives and adverbs: Find the strong verb that says it all.
    c. Action details that don't advance the story
    d. Purple prose
    e. Attributions of dialogue—*said* plus an action

IF YOUR GROUP DISBANDS

I would not be the writer I am today without my critique groups. While I have improved on the versions I first brought and revision now moves faster, I still could not write without them.

Unfortunately, not all critique groups survive. Sometimes they die a slow natural death as members move away, stop writing, or personalities clash. If this is the case, find another group. Don't be afraid to say goodbye. Create a new writing family.

OTHER GROUPS HELPFUL TO WRITERS

A critique group is not the only kind that may help further your education and career. Here are some other types you might consider joining or starting.

READING GROUP

Several years ago, I was fortunate to sit in on a monthly meeting sponsored by the Cooperative Children's Book Center at the University of Wisconsin-Madison (ccbc.education.wisc.edu/), where teachers, librarians, and other children's book lovers discussed recently published works. It was so eye-opening. I was thrilled to form a similar group upon my return to Los Angeles. Once a month, our group of teachers, librarians, writers, and illustrators gather to nibble snacks, sip wine, and discuss one picture book and one longer book.

Check out our blog, which summarizes our discussions: bookchatthursday.blogspot.com. Besides exposing me to newly published books and making me consider what works and what doesn't in each one, the group has helped me discover what teachers and librarians look for when selecting books and how they'll be used in the classroom.

WRITE-IN GROUP

Another group I highly encourage you to create is a write-in group, where writers get together to do nothing but write. Every Monday I meet with fellow writers in a neighborhood coffee shop. We grab a corner table near an electrical outlet and write.

We don't talk until lunch. You'd be surprised how much one can get done even with music and chatter going on all around. Something about having to force yourself to concentrate sparks creativity. At home, too many distractions—laundry that needs doing, a phone that demands answering, the cat begging for a snuggle, a book tempting you to read one more chapter—pull you away from your work.

In a coffee shop with like-minded writers who aren't too chatty, you can accomplish a lot. And it's a win for the owners of the coffee shop. All of us have both breakfast and lunch, and because the place we go to has a bakery, we often purchase goodies to take home. I even contracted with the owner to make gorilla-shaped cookies available at my book signings.

GET TO KNOW THE PUBLISHERS GROUP

This group was started by a friend and newbie, Colleen Paeff, who wanted to become familiar with the different imprints and publishing houses. Each month she collects books from a specific house to share with attendees. When at all possible, she tries to find out who edited each book. At the meetings, members take turns reading the books and discussing them. This group not only keeps members aware of the newest titles but also helps them come up with a submission plan for their stories. You can read their blog here: pbpublishers101.blogspot.com/.

SHARING-FRUSTRATIONS GROUP

I belong to yet another group that meets monthly. We're not all picture-book writers, but we all are children's-book writers in roughly the same stage of our careers. We meet to discuss all aspects of creating, business, and the writer's life. Sometimes we alternate between people sharing their expertise, assigning writing exercises, discussing promotion—whatever suits our fancy.

PROMOTION GROUP

While I've never been in a group of this kind, I know they exist. For those wanting to learn about promotion and perhaps share ideas and work together to cross-promote every member's books, these groups can be extremely helpful, not only for shy promoters like myself but also for those go-getters who are looking for new ways to get the word out about their books.

A FEW FINAL WORDS

All these groups nudge hermit-type writers to get out into the world, interact, and learn from others. My groups are essential to my writing life. Try forming one of your own. You may feel the same way, too.

WHAT'S NEXT?

After you've shared your story, you really are done. Now it's time to submit your work and consider whether you need an agent. We'll do that in chapter twenty-one.

BUT . . . Before you go on

1. Share your story with another writer or with a writing group.
2. Revise if necessary.
3. If you've revised, repeat steps one and two until you and your group feel the story is the best it can be.
4. Read a new picture book.

21

Submitting Your Manuscript

"First of all, you must have an agent, and in order to get a good one, you must have sold a considerable amount of material. And in order to sell a considerable amount of material, you must have an agent. Well, you get the idea."

—STEVE MCNEIL

With apologies to William Shakespeare and Hamlet, let's start with "To have an agent or not: That is the question." When I first began in the business, this question had no predictable answer. Many houses accepted manuscripts submitted without an agent. I sold my first two books and represented myself (badly, I admit) for both contracts.

Now with smaller editorial staffs and writers submitting to several publishers simultaneously—commonly known as multiple submissions—more and more houses won't read manuscripts unless they are submitted by an agent. Busy editors count on agents to save them time by weeding out inappropriate manuscripts.

IF YOU GO THE AGENT ROUTE

Although I've been represented by several different agents over the course of my career, I am not commitment averse. As proof, I point to my marriage; I've been with the same wonderful man for nearly fifty years. Divorcing an agent is never easy, and searching for a new one can be painful, time-consuming, and discouraging. Hopefully, this section will help you avoid my mistakes and find an agent you can work with happily throughout your career.

WHAT'S IMPORTANT TO YOU IN AN AGENT?

Think carefully about these questions:

1. **DO YOU WANT AN AGENT WHO'S ALSO AN EDITOR?** Many agents formerly worked as editors. They enjoy and have the expertise to discuss what works and what doesn't in a manuscript. I'm grateful my agent does this. Anything I can do to improve my story before an editor sees it is a plus. Some agents don't feel comfortable doing this. They may sense a manuscript isn't ready, but they can't tell you why. However, if you have a strong critique group or are a good judge of your writing, you may not need or want editorial service.
2. **DOES THE AGENT REPRESENT PICTURE BOOKS?** This may seem obvious, but many beginning writers send queries helter-skelter without first checking. Even with agents who say they represent picture books, check further. Some only take on clients who both write and illustrate their stories. If that's not you, cross them off your list.
3. **DO YOU NEED A LOT OF SUPPORT AND HAND-HOLDING?** We could all do with both, but some writers require more than others. Many agents are good at this. Others don't understand our insecurities and perhaps don't have the time. They primarily envision their job as facilitating connections between writers and publishers.
4. **HOW OFTEN DO YOU NEED UPDATES?** Is your agent receptive and available to keep you informed regarding submissions, rejections, and editorial comments?
5. **WHAT PUBLISHING HOUSES ARE YOU INTERESTED IN WORKING WITH?** Does the agent have connections with these houses, or does he mostly submit to others?
6. **IS THE AGENT RESPECTED BY PUBLISHING HOUSES?** Do editors eagerly await his submissions, or do they push them aside to read later?
7. **WILL THE AGENT BE A STRONG ADVOCATE FOR YOU WHEN NEGOTIATING YOUR CONTRACTS?**
8. **IS THIS AGENT MORE INTERESTED IN CAREER BUILDING OR IN SELLING AS MANY MANUSCRIPTS AS POSSIBLE?** Do you share those goals?
9. **DOES THE AGENT RESPECT YOU AND YOUR WRITING?** Will your agent encourage experimentation in uncharted waters?
10. **DO YOU AND YOUR AGENT AGREE TO WORK TOGETHER TO COME UP WITH A SUBMISSION PLAN?**

You may have other issues that are important to you. Add those questions to this list.

SEARCHING FOR AN AGENT

The more you write, the more you will hear scuttlebutt from agented writers. Pay attention. Do their agents refuse to submit some stories or insist on revision after revision, rarely expressing satisfaction? Are their agents easy to talk to and available to address their concerns? Ask them specific questions related to what you require in an agent. You may come out of this process with a small list, but there are many other fish in the sea. It behooves you to cast your net further online.

Check out SCBWI, the Society of Children's Book Writers and Illustrators. If you're not yet a member of this excellent organization representing children's writers, shame on you. Go to www.scbwi.org, and join immediately. Once you're a member, check out their publication *The Book* with its up-to-date list of agents and what they are looking for. Add the most promising names to your list. Writers who are members of SCBWI may also find an agent by attending their conferences. Often agents will be on the program and will consider manuscripts submitted by attendees.

Don't stop there, though. Many agents tweet—a good way to learn about their personalities. Also, look at *Publishers Marketplace*. You can sign up for one month for a nominal fee and research, research, research. Google *children's book agents*, and you'll find scads of resources—articles, blogs, and more lists. If you are new to this field, don't just search for well-known and established agents.

There are advantages and disadvantages to approaching those who have just begun agenting. The advantages are

1. They're hungry and eager for clients.
2. They have more time to focus on you and your needs.

The disadvantages are

1. Depending on their backgrounds, they may not be knowledgeable about writing and the publishing industry.
2. If they're not part of a larger agency, they may not have the connections with publishing houses that established agents have.

3. This is a volatile and difficult industry. Sadly, not everyone has the stamina to remain an agent, so newer agents are not always a sure thing.

Make sure you visit each potential agent's website to check out books they represent. If they're not in line with your writing, don't submit to them.

After all this research, you'll end up with a list of agents to rank in order of preference. On their agency websites, you'll learn if they're closed to submissions. Delete such agents. Some will accept multiple submissions, but some will not. Some read only snail-mail submissions, and others insist on fax or e-mail. Some want manuscripts attached to the e-mails, but others want them pasted into the body of the message.

They'll differ on how many manuscripts they'll consider and on whether they want only a query letter or a query letter and the manuscript. Some want no query at all, just the manuscript. Make copious notes about each agency's requirements. Now choose your best, most remarkable, ready-to-publish manuscript (and a second or third if the agent wants more), and write your query letter.

WHAT SHOULD A QUERY INCLUDE?

1. **THE CORRECT SPELLING OF THE AGENT'S NAME:** This sounds obvious, but you'd be surprised how often it is misspelled. Also, if the agent's name is Chris, make sure you know whether Chris is male or female.
2. **DO YOU HAVE A CONNECTION TO THE AGENT?** Does she represent a friend? Did you meet her at a writing conference? Do you love books she represents? Mention that.
3. **IF YOU HAVE ANY PUBLISHING CREDITS, LIST THEM ALONG WITH THE PUBLISHER'S NAME AND DATE OF PUBLICATION.** Any publishing credit is valid. When I first started, I wrote about being published in my local paper, the *Los Angeles Times*. I didn't say that it was merely a letter to the editor.
4. **WRITE A BRIEF LINE OR TWO ABOUT YOUR MANUSCRIPT.** Don't bog down the agent with details. Let your manuscript speak for itself.
5. **SOME AGENTS MAY WANT SYNOPSES OF OTHER MANUSCRIPTS YOU DEEM READY FOR SUBMISSION.**
6. **DON'T FORGET TO THANK THE AGENT FOR HER TIME AND CONSIDERATION.**

Avoid a flat recitation of the above material. Your query is not just an opportunity to introduce your writing; it's a chance for the agent to meet you and get a sense of your personality. In the same way your uniqueness will come through in every story, let your voice shine in your query letter.

Rebecca Colby generously offered to let me share a successful query letter she wrote to an agent who agreed to represent her. The manuscript was eventually published in 2015.

> Dear Ms. Rushall,
>
> I was thrilled to read your tweet yesterday stating that you love little witches. I love little witches too and have written a humorous picture book about witches entitled *It's Raining Bats and Frogs*.
>
> *It's Raining Bats and Frogs* was written first as a picture-book manuscript and later as a storybook app. I've attached only the picture-book manuscript, but please know the storybook app text is available upon request. A synopsis follows:
>
> *It's Raining Bats and Frogs* (450 words)—It's raining on the Witch Parade, and the witches are wet and miserable, so Delia decides to change the rain to cats and dogs, then hats and clogs, and finally bats and frogs. But each new type of rain brings its own problems. Eventually, Delia magics the rain back, and the parade proceeds, with the witches showing a great appreciation for real rain.
>
> My writing credits include winning the 2011 Society of Children's Book Writers and Illustrators (SCBWI) Barbara Karlin Grant. This is an international award given out each year to one aspiring picture-book writer. In 2012, I won first place in the Winchester Writers' Conference "Writing for Children 4–7 Years" category. I also won the 2012 Margaret Carey SCBWI British Isles Conference Scholarship for picture-book writers and illustrators.
>
> Before writing for children, I worked for the Russian comedian Yakov Smirnoff, taught English in Taiwan, traveled the world as a tour director, and worked as a librarian. Born in America, I now live in England.
>
> Thank you for your time and consideration of my work. I look forward to your reply.
>
> Sincerely,
> Rebecca Colby

Note how Rebecca addresses the agent by name. In the first paragraph, she connects the agent's interests with her own writing. Her summary of the manuscript is concise (just three sentences). Then she mentions her writing credits and gives some personal information about herself in two sentences. Most importantly, she thanks Ms. Rushall for her time and consideration. Her succinct, straightforward letter demonstrates her professionalism.

Just like a manuscript needs to be fine-tuned and revised, so does your query letter. Don't dash it off. Once you're satisfied, it's time to submit. And then wait. And wait.

Often the agent's website will state how long it will be before he gets back to you. If you don't hear from the agent within the designated time, you can drop him a note. However, my feeling is if he takes his time responding, I'm probably not interested in working with him.

IF NO AGENT CONNECTS WITH YOUR WRITING

Confession: This recently happened to me. Why am I telling you this?

Because I don't want you to get discouraged during this process. Getting turned down happens, no matter one's track record. I had nearly twenty books to my credit, but established agents already had full rosters, and unless my writing blew them away (which it obviously didn't), they weren't taking.

I had more work to do. I went back to the Internet, and after more research, discovered a new agent offering a webinar about pacing picture books. I'm always open to discovering new approaches, as you should be, so I signed up. Besides learning plenty, I liked her and her approach and especially respected her comments about my manuscripts. I ended up signing with her. It turned out that agent didn't love the submission side of agenting, so after a year she paired with another agent who prefers that part over the editing side. The three of us work together, and it's a happy arrangement. This story is meant to encourage you to not give up.

There's a caveat, though: If no agent is interested in your work, perhaps you have more learning to do. Read more picture books. Go to more conferences. Find yourself a critique group, and keep writing. But let's suppose your agent search has a happy ending. Someone wants to represent you, and because you've researched, you're excited about working with him.

SIGNING WITH AN AGENT

Some agents are content with a verbal agreement. Others require a contract covering the services you can expect the agent to perform, such as submitting your manuscript, not entering into agreements without consultation, and collecting moneys owed from the publisher. It will spell out the percentage they earn from any sale (normally around 15 percent). Just as we enter marriage hoping it will last forever, we hope our agent relationship will as well. Sadly, it may not, so contracts contain terms for easing any breakup.

Now you're off. While your agent is submitting your manuscripts, you'll be writing more picture books. A few words of advice:

1. **REMEMBER: YOUR AGENT WORKS FOR YOU *AND* THE PUBLISHER.** If he submits too many unpublishable stories, editors may lose enthusiasm for his future submissions. Respect that he must consider both his reputation and yours. It's disappointing if he feels a manuscript isn't ready, but consider things from his point of view.
2. **DON'T LET ISSUES BETWEEN YOU TWO FESTER.** If you have a story he's not enthusiastic about, perhaps you know an editor who might love it. Would he be willing to submit it to her or let you submit it? Working with an agent requires good listening and empathy. You both stand to gain from an open and comfortable relationship.
3. **DON'T EXPECT HAVING AN AGENT TO GUARANTEE SALES.** You'll still get rejections, only now you'll have someone to share your disappointment with. A sale may be a long time coming. This is not a business for those who require instant gratification. It's for those who have a story to tell and the drive and passion to tell it in the best possible way. Since you're reading this book, I already know that's you.

SUBMITTING DIRECTLY TO PUBLISHERS

Some writers don't and never have worked with an agent. Many have connections with editors who've published them before. Some nonfiction writers whose work is directed more toward the educational market than high-concept nonfiction-for-trade publishers (we'll cover these differences in the next chapter) also might not need agents. Some don't want to share their earnings with an agent. If this is you, researching publishing houses is your job.

Finding the right publisher for your book will require a new workplace. Walk, ride, bike, bus, or drive to the nearest library or bookstore, and page through as many picture books as you can. Make a list of the companies that publish books you like. Write those book titles next to the name of the house for future reference.

Watch out for published books similar to yours. If one publishing house has had great success with a book about a pig with illustrations that seem like they could easily be from your pig story, hold back. Chances are, they won't want another book in a similar vein. However, if you've written a funny book about a pig and you find a house that publishes funny books, put that name at the top of your submissions list.

Unless a book is dedicated to the editor or is under a specific editor's imprint, gleaning the name of the person who worked on the book can be difficult. Sometimes a call to the publisher's office can reveal that information, but some publishers don't share that. You may have to contact other writers to get the scoop. Every August the SCBWI updates their "Publishers of Books for Young Readers" market survey with publishers' areas of focus and the names of their editors. They also make available to members a list of editors and the books on which they've worked titled "Edited By."

Writer's Digest Books publishes a yearly update of markets for children's stories called *Children's Writer's & Illustrator's Market*. It's packed with up-to-date information on publishing houses, including names of editors, whether they're taking unsolicited submissions, and their manuscript preferences. You can find this book in a library, a bookstore, or online.

Another way to get information is through contact with other writers. If you don't have other children's writers nearby, you're only a mouse-click away from a community who is willing to share their knowledge about publishing. Search for children's writers in Yahoo groups, and see if there's a group you'd like to join. While you're on the Internet, check out each publisher's website. Peruse their catalog, and look at the books. With so many sources of information available, there's no excuse for getting back a manuscript with this note: "Sorry, we don't publish picture books."

USING PERSONAL CONTACTS

In any business, who you know means a lot. Go to every writing conference you can, especially those with editors in attendance. You'll learn about the different publishing houses and discover which editors are probably compatible with you and your work. If part of the conference's program includes an opportunity to submit a manuscript for critique, do it. You might be lucky and get an editor or agent to read your manuscript. An agent might offer to represent you. The editor might like your manuscript and even buy it! Organizers of conferences are thrilled to be able to announce the sale of a manuscript.

But suppose you don't sell your manuscript or find an agent at the conference. All isn't lost. A good friend of mine once received great revision suggestions from an editor. She did revise and ... happy ending! The editor later bought the story. If your manuscript isn't assigned to an editor, there's still hope. At the SCBWI Annual Summer Conference in Los Angeles (held every August), the writers, agents, and editors who critique are allowed to submit manuscripts for the Sue Alexander Most Promising New Work Award, which rewards a writer with a trip to New York and meetings with editors.

Even if your story doesn't merit any of the above, you will still go out a winner because you received additional feedback on your story from a publishing professional or a knowledgeable author. And there's always another conference around the corner. Polish your manuscript, and attend.

At most conferences, editors in attendance offer to read manuscripts submitted by the attendees, even if their company doesn't normally take unsolicited manuscripts. If you like the editor and the picture books her house publishes, send your story to her.

Try not to be too shy at conferences. This advice is coming from a writer who would rather sing naked in a bar than approach an editor about a project, so do as I say, *not* as I do. Tell yourself editors are people, just like you. Some of them are shy, too, and insecure. If you honestly liked an editor's talk, introduce yourself and send an e-mail or a snail-mail note telling her so. If you have a project you think might appeal to her, mention it. An editor's job depends on discovering the next great book. That could be yours.

The bigger your community of writing friends, the bigger your network of information. Obviously, don't become friends with other writers just to pick their brains, but true friendship includes sharing of publishing news. Children's writers are especially generous when it comes to that.

ENTER CONTESTS

Another way to get your name out there and your writing recognized is to enter contests. Many of the local SCBWI local events offer an opportunity to enter a contest. If you win or receive an honorable mention, include that in your submission letter.

Every year, through SCBWI, a one-thousand-dollar grant donated by yours truly and Writer's Digest Books will be given to the recipient of the Most-Promising Picture Book Manuscript Award. Make sure you enter, and look online and in writing magazines for other contests.

SUBMISSION FORM

Regardless of whether you're submitting to an agent or editor or whether you're doing so via snail mail or online form, your manuscript should be double-spaced and not in a fancy font or colored ink.

A few agents and publishing houses still request a hard copy. If so, your manuscript should look like the following one.

The title and the author's name (three spaces between each line) go midway down the page and are centered. In the lower right-hand corner, place your contact information.

IF ANIMALS KISSED GOOD NIGHT . . .

By

Ann Whitford Paul

Ann Whitford Paul
1234 Swamp Street
Los Angeles, CA 90027
phone 555 555-5555
e-mail ann@annwhitfordpaul.com
web-site www.annwhitfordpaul.com

The first page of your manuscript should be modeled after the following example.

Place contact information in the upper left-hand corner and start the story halfway down the page. Type in your title and then three double-space skips before you start the manuscript. Keep one-inch (25mm) margins on all sides, except at the top—use only half an inch (13mm). You will understand why when you look at the second page.

> Ann Whitford Paul
> 1234 Swamp Street
> Los Angeles, CA 90027
> phone 555 555-5555
> e-mail ann@annwhitfordpaul.com
> web-site www.annwhitfordpaul.com
>
> IF ANIMALS KISSED GOOD NIGHT . . .
>
> If animals kissed
> like we kiss good night,
> Sloth and her cub
> in late afternoon's light
> would hang from a tree
> and start kissing soooooo sloooowwwwwww . . .,
> the sky would turn pink
> and the sun sink down low.

Ann Whitford Paul 2
IF ANIMALS KISSED GOODNIGHT . . .

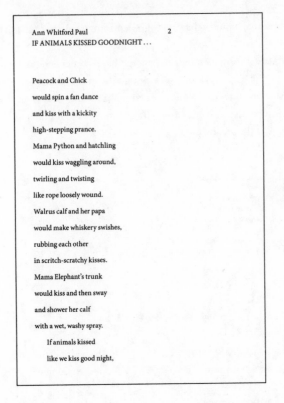

Peacock and Chick
would spin a fan dance
and kiss with a kickity
high-stepping prance.
Mama Python and hatchling
would kiss waggling around,
twirling and twisting
like rope loosely wound.
Walrus calf and her papa
would make whiskery swishes,
rubbing each other
in scritch-scratchy kisses.
Mama Elephant's trunk
would kiss and then sway
and shower her calf
with a wet, washy spray.
If animals kissed
like we kiss good night,

The header at the top of the page with the writer's name and the title of the manuscript on the left side (facing you), and the page number on the right side are single-spaced, along with four more single spaces before the text starts. Succeeding pages should look identical to this. The only difference will be on your last page. After your last line, double-space and make a line of asterisks so the editor will know the story is over.

but Sloth and her cub?

Still . . .

kissing good night!

****

This manuscript was a poem and was therefore submitted with poetic line lengths, but a prose story would have normal paragraphs. For example, here's the first half page of my manuscript for *Mañana, Iguana.*

> On Monday, *lunes*, Iguana twitched her tail happily. "Let's celebrate spring with a party on Saturday."
>
> Conejo hopped up and down. "Yes! Let's!"
>
> Tortuga poked out of his shell. "A fiesta? On sábado? Count me in."
>
> Culebra shook his rattle. "Me, too!"
>
> "Good!" said Iguana. "We must start right away. Who will help me write the invitations?"
>
> "Yo no. Not I," said Conejo. "I write too fast! No one could read my words!"
>
> "Yo no," said Tortuga. "I write too slow."

Note the great amount of white space due to dialogue and short paragraphs. Your manuscript should have lots, too. Don't write long narrative paragraph clumps in picture books.

If you are unsure about punctuation or paragraphing, grammar, or any other nitpicky detail, refer to a grammar book before submitting your story. Carefully check your manuscript for spelling errors. It's not enough to spell-check in your word processor. That handy program won't catch errors like using the word *sew* for *so* or *there* for *their.* The only way to catch those mistakes is to slowly read your manuscript aloud.

SELF-ADDRESSED STAMPED ENVELOPE

Include one only if the publisher requests it. Nowadays, many publishers prefer electronic submissions. If you've pasted your manuscript into the body of your e-mail, a cover page is unnecessary. However, I would include a cover page when dealing with a publisher who asks for attachments.

TEN COMMANDMENTS FOR SUBMITTING PICTURE-BOOK MANUSCRIPTS

Here is a list of commandments to keep in mind when submitting, whether you do it yourself or with an agent.

1. Thou shalt send out only your best work.
2. Thou shalt inform everyone if you're submitting multiples. Thou shalt immediately inform the other publishing houses and agents if and when your manuscript has been sold.
3. Thou shalt submit all manuscripts according to the publisher's or agent's specifications. Never hand your manuscript to an editor at a conference and expect an immediate response.
4. Thou shalt not skip spaces to show page turns or use fancy fonts or colored inks.
5. Thou shalt not submit your manuscript with illustrations unless *you* are the illustrator or unless you state your willingness to sell your story without the illustrations and vice versa.
6. If your manuscript comes back with a personal rejection letter or a note on a form rejection, thou shalt immediately thank the editor.
7. Thou shalt consider any suggestions seriously. If you still believe in your manuscript, promptly send it out again.
8. After four months, if you have not heard from the publishing house or agent, a follow-up is acceptable. E-mail is fine, but if by snail mail, include a SASE or postcard for a reply. If after six months you still have not heard anything, assume they're not interested and submit your story elsewhere. Sadly, some publishers indicate that if you haven't heard from them in a certain amount of time, they're not interested. This strikes me as slightly rude. Just a quick e-mail saying "Sorry, not for us" would not keep a writer hopefully expectant, waiting six months for a response.
9. Thou shalt remember that a rejection of your manuscript is not a rejection of you. It is merely a business letter and signifies thou art a professional writer who actively submits your work.
10. Thou shalt *never* allow a single rejection to make you give up on a story or on your chosen career of writing picture books.

DEALING WITH REJECTION

Whenever I submit a story, I dream an agent will take me on or an editor will buy it the day she receives it. She'll call to rave how the book will turn me into the new Dr. Seuss. That never happens.

So how do you deal with the disappointment, probably many disappointments, you'll endure during your career? Even best-selling authors receive rejections. Remind yourself what novelist Jane Smiley said: "... a rejection letter is a business letter, not a personal letter." When I was first writing and busy raising four children, I considered rejection letters contact with adults and the outside world. I told myself that at least I was in the game.

Another way of dealing with disappointment is to put on your boxing gloves and leap back into the ring. Tell yourself the publishing house that rejected you will be sorry because you'll sell the story to someone else. That first editor will watch it win awards and appear on top-ten lists and groan, "Why did I reject that story?" That probably won't happen either, but it's important to not allow a stranger to affect your confidence in your work.

Some stories are rejected for reasons unrelated to writing quality. Perhaps the editor who opened your manuscript about the death of a dog had just put her dog to sleep and couldn't bear to read past the first line. In addition, it's possible the publishing house already has a similar book. Or they've decided to cut back on the number of picture books they publish. Don't panic. Not long ago, editors at conferences stated emphatically, "Don't send fantasy" or "Young-adult books are dead." And then came Harry Potter. J.K. Rowling's success coincided with a downturn in picture-book sales; now the pendulum is swinging toward picture books. Kathleen T. Horning, head of the Cooperative Children's Book Center in Madison, Wisconsin, guesstimates that about one third of published children's books are now picture books.

Walter Davenport said, "An editor is a person who knows precisely what he wants but isn't quite sure." Temper your disappointment by reminding yourself that just as people don't agree on a movie's merits, different editors respond differently to different books. Perhaps this editor wasn't the right one for your project.

If a book has been rejected more than half-a-dozen times, put it on the back burner for a while, or at least look at it again to make sure it's the best you can do. If not, take it back to your writing group. Time away from your story while it's circulating can give you the distance you need to be able to see it with a fresh eye.

You may get a personal note from the editor of the publishing house. It might be a brief personal note and may even contain suggestions for revisions.

Jean Cocteau said, "Listen carefully to first criticisms made of your work. Note just what it is about your work that critics don't like—then cultivate it. That's the only part of your work that's individual and worth keeping."

This quote meant a lot when I received rejection letters criticizing the quietness of my stories. Inspired to write after years of bedtime reading to my four children, why wouldn't they be quiet? I wanted to create stories adults and children could share before nap or bedtime.

However, that quietness had to be addressed. I had to learn ways to add tension to every story, no matter how peaceful. If you get suggestions for revisions and they feel right to you, do them. But don't rush. It bears repeating that even the smallest revisions can require tumultuous changes. Take your time. If you're worried the editor or agent might forget your manuscript, relax. When you resubmit, remind her of her previous letter; perhaps include a copy of it.

If the suggestions feel off base, put the manuscript and letter away for a while. Quelling your disappointment is the first step to reading the comments without emotion. It brings your professionalism to the forefront and might even allow you to consider that the editor may be right. If after some time you still don't agree and you feel confident in your story, submit it elsewhere.

A FEW FINAL WORDS

Hopefully this chapter has given you the information you'll need to make important decisions regarding how you want to manage your career and whom, if anyone, you want to accompany you on this writing journey.

Pay close attention to different publishers' submission policies, and show you're a professional by following them.

WHAT'S NEXT?

Time to look more deeply at the business side of writing picture books. How big is this business? What is a publisher's responsibility, and for what work and expenses are they responsible? We'll explore that in chapter twenty-two.

BUT . . . Before you go on

1. Decide whether you want to go solo or work with an agent.
2. Research agents or publishing houses to find those that feel most compatible with you and your work.
3. Polish two manuscripts to perfection.
4. Write a query letter.
5. Submit your story.
6. Read a new picture book.

22

The Business of Publishing

"You know how it is in the kid's book world: It's just bunny eat bunny."

—ANONYMOUS

You've done it! You've written a fabulous story and spent hours, days, or weeks, even months or years, revising it. You're confident, and your writing group agrees it will make a fabulous book. You've submitted it to publishers or to an agent. Now turn off the creative side of your brain, and turn on the practical side so you can consider the business of publishing—a huge business it is! According to PublishersGlobal, as of this printing, there are 280 trade book publishers in the United States.

WHAT IS A TRADE PUBLISHER?

These publishers create books for the general reading public. Their sales are mostly through bookstores, although some of their books cross over to schools and libraries. Trade publishers can be huge because they have purchased other publishing companies and have several independent and separate imprints. These imprints can publish a certain type of book—early readers, nonfiction, poetry, etc.—or may have been started by an editor who publishes books that reflect his tastes. Many of these larger publishers aren't open to unagented, unsolicited submissions.

Small trade publishers, who are not part of a conglomerate, are generally more open to new writers. Some of these smaller publishers have a specific focus. There are also small-niche trade publishers. If you've written a book about California, a small publisher in that state might be right for your book. If your main character has autism, see if one of the many organizations that deals with this issue has a publishing department. If your book is about the care and feeding of gorillas, you might do better searching for a publisher who specializes in those amazing animals.

MASS-MARKET AND EDUCATIONAL PUBLISHERS

These publishers sell books in budget retail establishments and grocery stores. Their books usually cost significantly less than trade books, often have movie or television tie-ins, or are brand-name spin-offs. Most of their books are produced "in house," meaning their staffs create their content.

Mass-market publishers may also publish less-expensive versions of trade books. *If Animals Kissed Good Night* is a good example of this. The manuscript was initially sold to a trade publisher who subsequently went out of business. My editor took it to her new trade publishing house. After decent hardcover traditional-picture-book sales, the decision was made to print it as a board book. That board book can now be found in both bookstores and budget retail stores.

Lastly, we have the educational market, whose books sell mostly to schools and libraries. These books are specially produced to withstand the frequent and rough use they'll receive. These publishers look for manuscripts that will fit into a series, perhaps one on presidents of the United States or jungle animals, or individual books that might fill holes in school curriculums.

MORE ABOUT TRADE PUBLISHERS

Since many of you are writing books that will appeal to these publishers, they deserve a closer look. Their variety is remarkable. Some publishers produce only adult books. Some are further specialized, publishing only cooking, historical, romance, nonfiction, or how-to books. Immediately cross off all those who solely publish adult books. You may think your manuscript is so brilliant everyone will jump at it. Not so! Even if an adult publishing company were to release it, they would not have the sales and marketing departments to get your book into the hands of your specific audience.

Of those trade publishers, nearly half publish children's books. Many of those focus on chapter books or novels. Around twenty publish picture books. But there's room for still more specificity. Some houses want a manuscript with potential for distinctive and detailed art. Other publishers love biographies but not other nonfiction. To say it's discouraging is an understatement. But if it's discouraging for writers and illustrators submitting to publishers, it's also discouraging for the publishing house. Why?

Publishers invest a lot of time and money when taking on a book. They have much to gain if a book does well and much to lose if it doesn't. Most publishers, when signing a contract with an author, offer an advance on future royalties. This varies depending on the house and the author's sales records. Yes, you read that correctly. They keep track of how many books each author has sold, which behooves us all to submit only our best work. Royalties are typically 10 percent if the author and illustrator are the same person. If not, they're usually split so each one gets 5 percent. This may vary under special circumstances.

We like to imagine that publishing houses and those who work in them are earning humongous amounts of money, all off the backs of struggling writers and illustrators. According to Rubin Pfeffer, who has worked for over thirty years as an art director, editor-in-chief, and president in several different publishing companies and is now an agent, a minor percentage of titles published actually break even or make a profit for the publisher. Some houses may see a small percentage of their titles (10–20 percent) making a profit and compensating for the other 80–90 percent of the unprofitable titles. Other houses may have a better balance, with 40–50 percent of their titles in the black and the balance in the red. It varies by house, by season, and over time. To keep publishing books, at least a few books have to make it big. *Really* big! Wouldn't it be wonderful if predicting which book will be the next blockbuster were possible? Unfortunately, it's not. That's why, when a publisher decides to take on a book, she is not unlike a Las Vegas gambler betting chips in a game of blackjack. Sometimes she wins. Most of the time, she loses.

But you may wonder, if we creators earn so little on each book and publishers charge so much, how is it possible they aren't raking in money? Again, with appreciation to Rubin Pfeffer, let's imagine a picture book sells at your neighborhood bookstore for $15. The discount to the bookstore is usually 50 percent, leaving $7.50 to cover the publisher's expenses. Of that, if you are like me—a writer only—your take of that sale is a mere $.75, with an equally puny sum going to the illustrator. Those two add up to $1.50, leaving $6.00 to cover publishing expenses like paper, printing, binding, shipping, warehousing, unsold and damaged inventory, unearned advances, marketing, and general overhead of staff and facilities. This will combine to approximately $4.50, yielding a $1.50 or 10 percent net profit. This varies widely—some titles will be big success stories; others not so much. But on an overall seasonal list, this expenses breakdown is a reasonable model.

I don't want to turn this into a pity party for publishers, but every writer or illustrator should consider their pressures. To stay in business, a publisher must at least break even. Likewise, if your editor wants to keep her job, she must take on books that will sell. Don't think your editor doesn't feel the pressure to discover bestsellers.

WHAT ARE EDITORS LOOKING FOR?

This question comes up at every conference, and the answer is invariably "a good book" or some variation of this. As of this writing, narrative nonfiction is doing particularly well. Editors are asking for books that are "edgy," but press them for a definition, and you'll hear fumbles and mumbles. My advice is to ignore trends. Just like a pendulum swings back and forth on a tall grandfather clock, so do trends in publishing. Readers will get tired of edginess and beg for relative serenity. Editors will see so many talking-animal books that they'll long for talking kids. Don't try to write to trends. By the time you finish polishing your story, the current trend will be history. Write the best, most compelling story you can. The story that tugs at your heartstrings will tug at your editor's and readers' heartstrings.

WHEN AN EDITOR LIKES YOUR MANUSCRIPT

My editor, Janine O'Malley, gave me the following rundown on what happens at Farrar, Straus & Giroux. Other houses may vary on the details, but this is generally the process across the industry. Your story has either been submitted by you or your agent, and the editor loves it. Maybe so much she may not ask for any revisions. Or maybe she might.

Decision time! Are you willing to do revisions in line with the suggestions offered? Do you agree with them? Then by all means, go ahead and make the changes, knowing there's no guarantee of a contract. But suppose the editor's comments make you uncomfortable. In that case, trust your instincts and submit your story to another publisher *after* you send a letter to the first editor, thanking her for her time and trouble with your manuscript. Indicate you will think about her suggestions. She doesn't have to know that you've already thought about them ... negatively.

Let's assume, though, your editor thinks your manuscript is in fine shape. She will then share it either informally with other editors or at a meeting attended by everyone in the editorial department. They will discuss your text's merits and visual possibilities and consider different illustrators for the project.

They'll also toss around selling points for the upcoming acquisition meeting with sales and marketing people, such as the audience for the book, whether it will stand out from other published books, and whether it fills a niche for booksellers and has tie-ins for schools' curriculums.

In preparation for the acquisition meeting, the editor will prepare a guesstimate of the book's production costs and how many copies it will sell over its lifetime. The hope is that in the first eighteen months, it will sell between fifteen- and twenty-thousand copies. Remember: Picture books cost more to produce than novels because of their color art.

At this larger acquisition meeting, in addition to discussing the book, they consider hooks the text presents for reaching a wider audience. Is the book timely? They're thrilled if the writer blogs or has other platforms to spread the word. If there is general agreement and support for the manuscript, the editor makes an offer. There is usually negotiation regarding the terms of the contract.

Picture books need to be acquired around two years before publication because so many people are involved in the production of the book. Besides your editor, there is the copyeditor who checks the story's spelling, punctuation, etc. The art director or designer (often with the editor) will determine the print style, trim size, number of pages, and look of the endpapers.

Assuming the artist doesn't have other projects, he will have six months to submit a rough dummy. After everyone comments and agrees to move forward, he will need to finish the final art around eighteen months before the publication date. Why so long before the book is published? There's still much to do!

It takes about four months for the final art to be passed around for comments and corrections from all interested parties. After the art is okayed, the designer lays out the mechanicals (first combinations of text and pictures) and the jacket copy and then sends everything out for color proofs. When those come back, more tweaking may be required.

Finally, your book is ready to be printed, often overseas. In the meantime, the final proofs are passed on to marketing and sales departments, who start promoting and creating buzz. The last step, about six months before publication, is the sharing of the book with sales reps from around the country, who will begin showing it to booksellers.

A FEW FINAL WORDS

This is a quick overview of what happens at the publishing house. Chapter twenty-five will offer more details regarding your part after a publishing house makes an offer.

WHAT'S NEXT?

Chapter twenty-three is about taking an alternative path to getting your book into readers' hands.

BUT . . . Before you go on

1. Research as much as you can about the life of an editor and its pressures.
2. Read a new picture book.

23

Self-Publishing?

"The good news about self-publishing is you get to do everything yourself. The bad news about self-publishing is you get to do everything yourself."

—LORI LESKO

Should you self-publish? The above quote sums up all you need to know about the process. If you decide to go this route, you will have to edit and design your book; find an illustrator; determine how to publish the book (e-book, hardcover, softcover); and promote, distribute, and sell it. If you don't do these things yourself, you'll have to hire people to do them for you.

Probably the most famous self-publishing story in picture books is *The Tale of Peter Rabbit* by Beatrix Potter. She first wrote it as a letter to the child of a former governess and then sent the story to several publishers. Her story was rejected, so she self-published it, and a year later it was picked up by Frederick Warne & Co. The rest is history. Will that self-publishing success be repeated? Maybe ...

I ended this chapter's title with a question mark because self-publishing is a big *if*. I speak from experience. In 2013, I self-published *'Twas the Late Night of Christmas*. The book originated as a poem sent out as my holiday card to friends and family. The comments were generous and supportive. Several people said it should be published. The problem was that the story wasn't specifically directed at kids; my intended audience was parents who are exhausted by the Christmas holidays. After several rejections and because I had been dealing with family issues that interfered with my creativity (which was probably the reason I had not had a sale for several years), I thought self-publishing might be the way to go. In addition, a talented friend and published illustrator, Nancy Hayashi, agreed to do the art.

Because we were novices about the necessary requirements, we hired a company specializing in self-publishing. They, in turn, hired a designer who chose the print style and worked on the layout. They took care of registering the copyright info and researching the best ways to print. We ended up partnering with both Barnes & Noble and Amazon for print-on-demand books, so we didn't have to fill our garages with boxes.

All of that was wonderful. None of it was free. Nevertheless, we were pleased with the way the book turned out. Then came the problem.

SPREADING THE WORD

Neither of us were in-your-face, come-buy-my-book, rah-rah promoters. While some creative people love the hustle, hype, and hoopla of calling attention to themselves and their work, I suspect their numbers are low. Creative people mostly work alone. We enjoy debating with ourselves and shaping ideas and experimenting on our own. Tooting one's horn is not one of our basic skills. So what did we do? We hired a publicist. That meant more money.

The publicist got us some signings and sent out calls for people to review our book on Amazon, but the word about our book didn't stretch far beyond our circle of acquaintances and Facebook friends. We did make a YouTube promo video for the book (another expense), which starred my sister-in-law, Jane Kaczmarek, of *Malcolm in the Middle* fame. You can watch it here: www.youtube.com/watch?v=s9unMBhrehY. As of this writing, it's had over 2,500 views, which is nothing to sneeze at but not enough to sell a decent number of books.

For two years, I did a Christmas blog that was a small financial outlay compared to other expenses but a big outlay of time. Time I could have spent writing new stories. I believe in what Bella Andre, who broke out by self-publishing, wrote: "The best self-promotion is your next book. And the book after that and after that ..." So although I shared how to make Christmas decorations, gifts, and cookies and provided helpful suggestions for surviving the holidays, I didn't do much—no, let's be honest—I didn't do *any* story writing. I was one frustrated author.

Would this have mattered if our efforts had resulted in a blockbuster sale? Probably not. But it didn't. After all was said and done, we lost money. I still like the book. I like the words. I love the illustrations. Would I self-publish again? Definitely not.

Although you earn more money per book by self-publishing, what you lose are all those people at the publishing house who have the expertise to make a book the best possible—editors, art directors, book designers, copyeditors, marketing people, and sales reps. Granted, you will sometimes feel frustrated with mainstream publishers. You will wish they were more responsive and worked faster. You won't agree with their editorial comments, and you'll wonder about their marketing, but believe me: Once you have done everything yourself, you will forever be grateful for their support.

ARE THERE HAPPY STORIES ABOUT SELF-PUBLICATION?

Of course, but most successes come to people like Lucas Miller, who sings and performs about scientific issues at schools and has a built-in audience for his books. Success comes to someone who has passion, like Linda Liukas, who strives to interest children in computer programming.

Successful self-publishers are not overwhelmed by book promotion like I was. If you are one of those promo people, go for it! If your book turns out to be successful, an agent may contact you or a publishing house may hop on your bandwagon. Here are some self-published authors' websites.

- Linda Liukas at www.helloRuby.com
- Kara Van Kirk Levin at www.littlewoodenflute.com
- Lucas Miller at www. singingzoologist.com

INSTANCES WHERE SELF-PUBLISHING MAKES SENSE

Suppose your book, like my *Hello Toes! Hello Feet!*, went out of print due to closure of the publishing house. Suppose you want to produce a book only for your children, extended family, or descendants. Or perhaps you want to produce a remembrance for a special occasion or for an organization you're involved with. Then it would be foolish to approach a trade publisher.

A FEW FINAL WORDS

I encourage everyone to consider the time and commitment necessary to make your book a success (i.e., at least break even with your expenses) before you decide to self-publish.

WHAT'S NEXT?

You've made a decision about what direction you want to go. That doesn't mean you get to sit on your laurels until the book comes out. You need to start on another story. In chapter twenty-four, we'll consider ways to find ideas for your next picture book.

BUT . . . Before you go on

1. If you're not sure whether you're going to go with a publishing house or self-publish, investigate online or in bookstores and make a list of pros and cons to facilitate your decision.
2. Read a new picture book.

24

Priming Your Idea Pump

"Any productive writer learns that you can't wait for inspiration."

—SUSAN SONTAG

You've sent off your manuscript to your agent or publishing house with high hopes for acceptance. Or maybe you've settled on self-publishing. Now what do you do?

a. Mope around and worry it might get lost in the stratosphere?
b. Rewrite your story over and over again in your mind?
c. Take a vacation from writing?
d. None of the above?

If you chose *d*, you're correct.

Specifically, the answer should be "Get back to work." The best way to make time pass while waiting for a response to your story (which could take months) is to jump into another project. Don't say "It's too hard." Quit complaining "I don't have any good ideas." Don't think "If I can just sell my manuscript, I'll have the confidence to write another." As my grandfather would have said, "Hogwash!"

Let's be honest. Rarely do manuscripts sell the first time out ... or I'm sad to say, the second, third, or maybe even the tenth. No matter how much you've revised and polished, it's a minor miracle if a story gets bought right away.

I recently heard author Tod Goldberg say "If a writer's sales to manuscripts submitted were calculated like a baseball player hitting a ball compared to times at bat, we writers would look pretty pathetic." As of this writing, baseball star Justin Turner (go Dodgers!) is hitting .345, which means he gets a hit in more than one-third of his times at bat. A writer, on the other hand, would be a star with a selling average of 15 percent, i.e., selling a little over one out of seven submissions.

Five years passed, and 180 "not-interested" notes arrived in my mailbox before I sold my first manuscript. This isn't meant to discourage you. I want to *encourage* you. The struggle, work, and rejections are all dues one must pay to enter the published-author club. You may get admitted earlier than I did. Maybe it will be later, but if you have the passion and are temporarily depressed, know you're not the only one who receives bad news from a publishing house. And once you've sold a manuscript, that doesn't mean a career is made. *Do not give up your day job!*

In my chapter on self-publishing, I mentioned I had gone a while without a sale. The actual figure was *eight* years! And this came after a year when I had published three books. One of my writing-group members had said, "Ann, you've really arrived."

Being in this business requires patience, persistence, and rhinoceros-thick skin so you won't give up when the going gets tough. That said, there is a way to improve your odds of selling a manuscript.

1. Write more stories.
2. Revise each story to the best of your ability.
3. Submit your story to an editor you've researched who publishes your kind of book.

We've already covered steps two and three. This chapter is about the first step—writing more stories.

Say your mind is blank. You're exhausted from the many hours spent creating and revising your last story. You'd prefer to sit a while and bask in the warm feelings of having completed and submitted your manuscript. Don't! Find a new idea, and start writing. But how do you find that idea? Where does inspiration come from?

I was an insecure writer (I still am), but I used to be especially insecure about ideas. Other writers seemed to come up with wonderful, zany ideas, but mine felt flat and boring. There are two schools of thought about getting ideas. James Dickey, a poet and novelist, wrote: "A poet is someone who stands outside in the rain hoping to get struck by lightning." This may work for him and for other writers, but personally, the idea of getting soaked until lightning strikes is not appealing.

I'm more of a Jack London kind of writer. He said, "You can't wait for inspiration. You have to go after it with a club" or, as I would put it, with a pump. Years ago, when visiting my grandparents' farm, my favorite task was bringing up water from the outdoor well. We didn't need the water since they had modernized the house with indoor plumbing and turning a spigot guaranteed a spew of water. Still, I preferred to do it the old-fashioned way. It took several steps.

First, I had to pour a pitcher of water from the kitchen to prime the pump. Then I had to lift the pump's handle up and push it down, up and down, up and down, until my arms ached. Just when I thought I couldn't do it one more time, cold, clear water splattered into my pail and onto my legs and feet. That's a water pump. How do you prime your writing pump?

Bear with me while I tell another story. You'll understand the connection shortly. Several years ago, a tomato plant sprouted in the middle of my flower garden. My husband and I debated how the plant might have gotten there.

1. Did the tomato plant come from a seed floating in the air?
2. Did someone or some animal plant the tomato seed there?
3. Did I plant it there and not remember?
4. Was the seed hidden in the earth until, after much time, it reached the surface?

What do tomato seeds have to do with writing? They help explain how people get their creative juices running in their writing pumps.

WRITING IDEAS ARE FLOATING IN THE AIR

Like tomato seeds, they're everywhere, waiting to be grabbed and planted in our brains. Find them by paying close attention to the world around you. Look at your newspaper or news sites, not just to read about our world but to find something that might spark a story. Right now I'm writing safe and secure in my California home while those in Texas, Florida, and Puerto Rico have been hit by record hurricanes. *The New York Times* had an article about a young child clinging to her dead mother when rescuers arrived. There must be uncountable stories around this event that are just waiting to be told. Perhaps, by the time this book is published, one will already be on the shelf of your local bookstore.

When you read an article, let your mind wander through story possibilities. Could I write about a child surviving Irma? Or another disaster? I've lived through several California earthquakes and a fire that threatened my house. Maybe I should write about one of those. On the other hand, thinking about animals during a hurricane might inspire me to write an animal story that has nothing to do with natural disasters.

FLIP THROUGH A MAGAZINE

The sheer variety of photos in a magazine can get story juices flowing. I love pictures of children, but even a picture of a snow-covered mountain can spark a writing session. Use pictures as a jump-start. Let free association lead you to the story idea that strikes your fancy. Still no story? Don't give up.

REWRITE A CLASSIC CHILDREN'S STORY

Remember how you loved "Goldilocks and the Three Bears" or "Three Billy Goats Gruff"? Move it to a different location, change the time period, or even turn female characters into males. I did this with *Tortuga in Trouble,* placing Red Riding Hood in a Southwest setting with characters appropriate to that location. Helen Ketteman, the master of retellings, gives readers a version of "The Little Red Hen" with Texas twang in *Armadilly Chili.* Her book *Señorita Gordita* is a Tex-Mex take on "The Gingerbread Man." Read her work not only for the retellings but for her rollicking, musical language.

TRY A CHANGE OF SCENE

Go for a walk. My book *Mañana, Iguana* came to me while I was on a stroll around the block. I was frustrated with revisions for another story and needed to get away from my computer. Passing a car with a license plate that read "MAÑANA," *iguana* popped into my head as a fun near-rhyming word. "The Little Red Hen" seemed like the story that belonged with the Spanish word, which translates to "tomorrow." I began to think about moving that story to a Southwest setting and completed the first draft in my head before I returned home.

What about going to the zoo? Pick out a favorite animal, then give it an ability it couldn't possibly have in the real word. Ask yourself, *What if?* Remember how Dumbo the elephant could fly? You could write about an alligator who can't swim. Or a giraffe whose neck is short. Or a hippopotamus who hates vegetables. Come up with your own what-ifs, and perhaps you'll create a story from one of them.

While you're at the zoo, linger close to a group of kids and listen to them talk. Of course, you can eavesdrop on children anywhere … at the mall, at a playground, a restaurant, just walking down the street. Listening will keep you in tune with how today's kids view the world and express themselves. Art Linkletter had a radio and television show called *House Party* that ran for twenty-five years, and it included a segment called "Kids Say the Darnedest Things." Check them out on YouTube, and be prepared to laugh as you learn how kids think.

WHEN SOMEONE ELSE PLANTS A TOMATO SEED

Ask someone to give you an assignment. Ask me! Here's one: A child opens a door. What does she see in this new room? How does she react? Why? Make up a story about it.

Here's another assignment: Write a story about a hippo and an elephant. I guarantee even if every person who reads this book writes a story about a hippo and an elephant, each one will be different. You have your own style, background, and ideas about plotting.

Want another assignment? Check out these books:

- *Poemcrazy* by Susan Goldsmith Wooldridge
- *Story Sparkers: A Creativity Guide for Children's Writers* by Debbie Dadey and Marcia Thornton Jones
- *I'd Rather Be Writing* by Marcia Golub
- *A Year of Creative Writing Prompts* by Love in Ink

Now ask your friends or your writing group to give you a writing prompt. Here are some online resources for writing prompts:

- www.creativewritingprompts.com
- www.writersdigest.com/prompts
- thinkwritten.com/365-creative-writing-prompts
- www.journalbuddies.com/journal_prompts__journal_topics/creative-writing-prompts-for-kids (because kids are our target audience)

WHEN YOU PLANT YOUR OWN TOMATO SEED

There are two writing assignments I often give myself. First, I open a children's dictionary at random, close my eyes, and point to a word. I write down that word. I flip to another page and repeat this until I have six words. Then I write a story using all of them. I may delete some of those words from the final version, but they have already done their job, forcing me to think creatively.

When I studied children's poetry with Myra Cohn Livingston, our class did this multi-word exercise. The resulting poems were so unique and powerful she collected them into a book titled *I'm Writing a Poem About … A Game of Poetry.*

The other assignment I give myself is to choose an object to observe. It can be anything: a pencil, a scrap of cloth, an old ball, a penny, a snail, a leaf, a twig, a stamp. Let's take a look at how this is done.

I'm going to observe a stuffed monkey. I write *Monkey* at the top of a piece of paper. Then I draw four columns. Over the first column, I write *Facts*. Under this fact column, I write all of the objective things I see and know about this monkey:

- Brown fur
- Plastic green eyes
- Black felt nose
- Head harder than body and stuffed with something smooth
- Body, arms, and legs stuffed with sand or grains of rice
- Can't stand but can sit
- Eight inches tall
- Black thread at the seams
- Brown ears

The heading of the second column is *Fantasy*. Here I allow myself to go wild.

- What if the monkey came to life and leapt about my bed and chair?
- What if this monkey had superpowers and fought crime in the animal kingdom?
- What if this monkey could compose like Mozart?
- What if I could take a real monkey to school?

The heading of my third column is *Feelings*. These are the feelings and memories monkeys bring to mind.

- How sad it was to visit the zoos of my childhood, where monkeys were kept in small cages
- The joy I felt on first seeing monkeys in the wild, swinging free
- How much I loved sleeping with the stuffed monkey my high-school boyfriend gave me
- How excited I was when I changed the main character in a story from a boy to a monkey, eventually resulting in *Little Monkey Says Good Night*

The fourth column is headed *Fuzzy Connections*. This is where I think in metaphor and simile.

- Brown as penny loafers
- Brown as dirt
- Arm fur soft as the satin on my favorite blanket
- Still as a statue
- Silent as a secret
- Active as a can of soup
- Smile as wide as a Cheshire cat

In this column many of my connections like *brown as dirt* and *still as a statue* are tired and overused. I wrote them down anyway. When filling in these columns, forget about editing. Now is the time for spilling guts, not passing judgment.

Note the crossover in the columns. Some observations belong in different columns; I don't worry about it. The column headings are there to focus my creative flow. Once my mind starts traveling, I let it journey wherever it desires. When my mind is finally blank, I go back and think about possible writing ideas.

In my list, I like the idea of a monkey superhero solving problems in the animal kingdom. Maybe that could be a fun series. I love remembering my high-school romances. If I changed my boyfriends to animals, that might be a picture-book idea. "Still as a statue" reminds me of the recent conflicts over statues commemorating Confederate soldiers. I could write an op-ed piece or perhaps a picture book exploring a child's discovery of what those statues represented.

When I'm void of ideas, these two assignments usually give me something to write about. Experiment with what gets your story juices flowing. If you've found an exercise from a book that helps plant seeds, then make regular use of it.

WHEN YOUR TOMATO SEED IS HIDDEN UNDERGROUND

What story ideas lurk inside your mind? Often ideas stare at us, stomping up and down and yelling, "Write me!" but we ignore them. Why is it so hard to write about the things that matter most to us?

It's human nature to have self-doubt. We don't find our own ideas interesting. They're such a part of our life they feel mundane. We squash them before they get a chance to sprout because we don't believe others will care about them.

Here's a true story: At an SCBWI conference in 1985, I attended a Saturday evening nonfiction talk. The speaker, Ross Olney, was tall, thin, and imposing. He spoke with self-assuredness, leaning over the podium and shaking his finger at the audience. "Write about what you know," he intoned.

That's easy for him, I thought. He skydives. He races motorcycles. His life is full of exciting adventures. I slumped into my seat, feeling snail-small.

Probably most of you are like me and don't lead dramatic lives. I've never saved anyone from drowning. I've never lived in a foreign country or hiked Kilimanjaro Mountain. My parents never divorced. My husband and I are about to celebrate our fiftieth wedding anniversary. My children haven't spent any time in jail ... yet!

Where's the drama in my life? Who would buy a book, I wondered, about the shortest carpool route between home and school, how to make Play-Doh, how to stretch a pound of hamburger into dinner for six, or how to sew? *How to sew!*

Just like in cartoons, a lightbulb switched on in my head. Sewing! I don't sew buttons. I don't sew hems or mend rips. I sew patchwork—quilts and pillows, dresses and toys, curtains and Christmas decorations. Once I even covered an entire room in tiny fabric squares.

I couldn't wait to get home and start on *Eight Hands Round: A Patchwork Alphabet.* Before that night in 1985, I thought the lack of drama in my life was a detriment. Now I accept and cherish my normal life and celebrate it in my writing. Do not, I beg you, discount your life. It's uninteresting to you because it's so familiar. To others it may be exotic.

I am constantly bewildered when people rave about my patchwork and say how talented and artistic I am. I look at my quilts and can see only uneven stitches and pieces that don't exactly fit at the corners. I know my quilts too well. To me, my quilts are ordinary. To others, they are extraordinary. Trust that others will find beauty in your writing, too. Accepting that I have something valuable to impart from my own life was the single most important realization in my career because it led me to write heartfelt stories that didn't receive form rejections and would eventually become books.

How do you find what interests you? You don't have to visit a therapist or delve into Freudian analysis. But you do need to spend time thinking about yourself, your past, your present, and even your future.

One way to do this is to keep a journal. It's not necessary to write in it every day. Write when inspiration hits you and about whatever you want—activities, dreams, observations, frustrations. Maybe add newspaper clippings. Quotes or pictures might also find their way into your journal. The crucial thing, though, isn't to keep a journal but to periodically read it. You'll discover certain themes and subjects that pop up frequently, begging to be written. By *you!*

Don't want to keep a journal? Too time-consuming? Too much of a commitment? Here's a shortcut: Tap into your childhood memories by completing the following sentence fragments. Don't ponder your answers. Write whatever comes to mind. Don't stop to edit. Write or type until you've exhausted each phrase and can't say anything more. Does something you wrote tug at your heart? Then stop. Write that story. If not, do another until something inspires you. The list will still be there for you whenever you need to jog your memory.

a. The first thing I remember was—
b. When I was a kid, I got so mad at—
c. I hated it when Mother asked me to—
d. I loved it when Mom and I went—
e. I hated it when Dad got mad at me because—
f. I loved it when my father took me to work because—
g. I've always wanted to learn how to—
h. My favorite foods as a child—
i. When I was young, I especially hated—
j. I liked pretending to be—

k. I'll never forget the time my best friend—
l. It really bothered me when—
m. I was scared of—
n. I got in trouble with my teacher because—
o. The things I hated about growing up in the city/country/etc. were—
p. At recess time, I usually—
q. The most embarrassing moment of my life was—
r. The saddest thing that happened to me was—
s. The best vacation I ever went on was—
t. I hated winter because—
u. The most fun thing I did each summer was—
v. Each summer, I hated—
w. When it rained, I usually—
x. Growing up, my mother always made me—
y. My favorite part of fall was—
z. I felt especially shy when—
aa. When I was young, my parents made me—
ab. The most fun thing I did with my grandparents was—
ac. My best memory of my siblings is—
ad. It made me furious when my sibling—
ae. Other than family, the most important adult in my life influenced me by—
af. The thing I loved best about my favorite pet was—
ag. The reason I loved/hated sports was—
ah. The thing I worried about most when I was a child was—
ai. My happiest/unhappiest birthday celebration was—
aj. Sometimes I felt different because—
ak. If I could change anything from my childhood, it would be—
al. My favorite books were—
am. As a child, my favorite TV shows and movies were—
an. My favorite video and board games are—
ao. The best thing that ever happened to me was—
ap. The moment in my life that seems like something from a movie is—
aq. The argument that felt the most uncomfortable occurred—
ar. Any special family traditions—
as. I've always loved the color______ because—
at. December memories are—

au. I always laugh when—

av. My favorite subject in school was_______ because—

aw. I love the song________ because—

ax. My childhood home was—

ay. Of all the animals, I would like to be ______because—

az. I always felt shy when—

If you think of other sentence fragments that inspire you, follow each train of thought to its logical conclusion. A story in my early-reader book *Silly Sadie, Silly Samuel* came out of my list. Filling it out reminded me how much I hated listening to my grandparents arguing. One would say, "The sky is blue." The other would say, "Not really blue. I see a bit of gray." I cringed at their bickering, but years later, thanks to that memory, I was able to write about their arguing in a way that made children laugh.

Another thing to do is think about your interests, passions, and curiosities. Make a list of at least ten.

1. Things I love to do—
2. Things I'd like to do but haven't—
3. Things I want to know more about—
4. Things I enjoy reading about—

Notice numbers two and three are not things you have firsthand knowledge of but things you'd like to do and explore. My books *Mañana, Iguana; Fiesta Fiasco; Count on Culebra*; and *Tortuga in Trouble* were all inspired by my desire to learn Spanish.

A FEW FINAL WORDS

Now you have four ways to prime your pump. Everything depends on your being open to the new ideas that either come your way or that you cultivate. Don't be a bud, closed and tight. Be a blossom open to the sun, wind, rain, and any idea that comes your way.

WHAT'S NEXT?

While you've been busy writing new stories, a publishing house was discussing your story … favorably. In chapter twenty-five, we'll learn what lies ahead.

BUT . . . Before you go on

1. Experiment with each of the ways to prime your creative pump.
2. Choose an idea that grabs you.
3. Write that story.
4. Revise your story to publication.
5. Keep reading new picture books.

25

When Your Dreams Turns into Reality

A Publisher Makes an Offer

"Of course no writers ever forget their first acceptance. One fine day when I was seventeen, I had my first, second, and third, all in the same morning's mail. Oh, I'm here to tell you, dizzy with excitement is no mere phrase."

—TRUMAN CAPOTE

If you're fortunate to sell your manuscript the first time out, or maybe many times out, celebrate. Call your husband, wife, or partner and friends, children, and neighbors. Kiss the postal delivery person. Hug the grocery-store clerk. Tell everyone your fabulous news. Then treat yourself. Get a massage. Buy that watch you've had your eye on for months. Pop open champagne. You deserve it.

The joy of a sale never dissipates. I was as thrilled for my twentieth as for my first. In chapter twenty-two, I gave a quick overview of what happens on the publisher's end after a sale. Now let's look at what happens on the writer's end.

When I first began writing, back in the dark ages, editors usually offered a contract even though revisions were still needed. Nowadays it's more likely the editor will require your manuscript be in near-final shape before taking it to an acquisition meeting or offering a contract.

THE CONTRACT

When your feet have come back to Earth, write or ask the editor to e-mail, snail-mail, or fax the details. Tell her that you're thrilled but you'd still like to look over your contract. If you have an agent, she may have already negotiated the terms of it for you. If not, a law degree or an entire book would be required to understand a contract's fine print, so ask the advice of published writers or organizations like the Authors Guild or SCBWI to help you navigate the unfamiliar terms and complicated language.

MORE REVISIONS

Unless you perfected the manuscript with your editor before you put your signature on that dotted line, you will need to do more revisions now. Some editors are hands-on and go through your manuscript with an eagle eye. They may notice big issues that need to be rethought. They may want to strengthen the trajectory of your plot, revise the ending, or change the main character. They make these suggestions by sending you an editorial letter via snail mail or e-mail. Don't be surprised if this letter is longer than your manuscript.

Your manuscript, with lots of questions, corrections, and comments, will be included with the editorial letter. When I showed my teenage son one story with all the editorial writings, he responded, "Mom, if I got a school paper back like that, I'd know I'd gotten a *D*."

Isn't it nice we don't get graded in publishing?

Throughout this book I've emphasized how important it is to experiment with one's manuscript, to try different manners of telling, to come up with unique language, play around with openings, etc. You're exhausted from all your work up to this point. How can there be more? Easy!

Your editor is another fresh eye for your story. She brings with her a publishing and marketing background you probably haven't tapped into yet. Be grateful! Consider this time with your editor another opportunity to revisit, revise, and improve.

Of course, sometimes you'll disagree. If the issue is important for you, state calmly and clearly why you want to keep the writing as is. When faced with a reasonable explanation, editors will usually defer to you, as they should. After all, your name goes on the cover, and you are the one who will feel the brunt of the reviews.

Be reasonable, however. Don't let your hair stand on end at every comment. Don't slam down the phone or stop talking. That wouldn't be the way to resolve issues in a marriage, and it won't work here. Graciously honest communication is always the best policy. Note the word *graciously.* You want your editor to buy future manuscripts. Keep the relationship calm and happy.

When you are done working with the editor, the copyeditor—a whiz at grammar, punctuation, etc.—will have his turn with your manuscript. He might be rigid about these issues and suggest changes that dilute your text's poetic language, but everything is negotiable if you make your points calmly and professionally. After copyediting, your words will be printed in the font style and size they'll be in the future book. Then your illustrator goes to work.

CHOOSING AN ILLUSTRATOR

Alas, that is not your job.

The editor, often in consultation with the art director and others, has that responsibility. He probably will not even seek your opinion. In fact, the illustrator may have been chosen before you were even offered a contract.

Now that I'm well-published, editors occasionally ask me if I have strong feelings about an illustrator or maybe even let me suggest one for them. This, however, is sometimes qualified with "I can't guarantee I'll pay any attention to you."

When you first hear the name of your illustrator, you'll probably rush to your local bookstore or library or pop online to see his work. Maybe you'll be thrilled; maybe you'll be disappointed. Most likely you'll need time to adapt to the artist's style.

This concept of handing over one's manuscript to an artist one did not choose calls for a huge amount of trust and faith. Let me ease your mind. Although I've known writers (not many) who've been disappointed in the art for their books, my experience has been the opposite, even in those instances where an editor named an illustrator whose established style appeared diametrically opposed to what I'd envisioned.

Life and books both have a way of working out for the best. In one case, the editor was correct in her selection and the book turned out better than I could have imagined. Another time, the editor finally saw the light and removed the artist from the project.

Illustrators are chosen for a myriad of reasons unknown to the writer. Perhaps the illustrator has a famous name that the publishing house hopes will translate to strong sales. Although you might be distressed by the artist's style in previous books, she may be eager to try something new and your story offers her that opportunity. Perhaps the editor wants to defy artistic expectations for your story. Her first choice artist may be booked up through the next few years. Maybe the publishing house is afraid an up-and-coming artist might start working with another house if she doesn't get a new project soon. Whatever the cause, the result is the same. You have an illustrator. Congratulations!

Will you get to see the evolution of the artist's vision for your story (i.e., a dummy, sample art, and finished art)? That varies from house to house. Some editors make sure I see and comment on the illustrations. Other editors keep it a closely guarded secret. Why would they do that?

Let me tell you another true story. An artist friend of mine received a manuscript about a child's relationship with her two grandfathers. She sent in her rough sketches, and the editor, being generous, showed them to the writer, who was immediately upset because the grandfathers didn't look at all like her grandfathers. She even offered to share photos with the illustrator. *No! No! No!* Imagine if an illustrator told you how to write your story. Writing is not (unless she does both) her field of expertise. In the same way, we can't tell artists how to illustrate our books.

Picture books are collaborations. Just as we writers struggle to tell our story in the best possible way, so do artists. They are expected to bring their unique personality, style, and talent to each project. Telling my friend how the grandfathers should look is as inappropriate as insisting your child go to law school when his dream is to be a pop singer. Wise parents permit children to follow their dreams (assuming they can support themselves). Let your illustrator follow hers.

If your manuscript is a nonfiction or historical story, you can rightfully request to verify the illustrations' veracity. Often in these circumstances, the illustrator might even contact you through the editor to ask for some research guidance. When the art comes, text changes may be necessary. Certain words may be eliminated if the pictures have done their work, unless cutting will interfere with the music of your words.

When the final art and text are combined, you will be given one last look. This is when I fall into a pit of anxiety. Help! My story is truly going to be published, exposed to all the world (well, considering sales numbers, probably a small part of it), and I have to make sure it's right. I'm like Konrad Lorenz, who said, "During the final stages of publishing a paper or book, I always feel strongly repelled by my own writing ... it appears increasingly hackneyed and banal and less worth publishing."

Let those self-criticisms wash over you like a spring shower. This is fear and self-loathing talking. What you have written is fine. Your group agrees. Your editor agrees. So does the publishing house. They wouldn't have bought your manuscript if they didn't.

Your job as a professional is to go over the text and make sure every *i* is dotted and every *t* is crossed. Sue Alexander used to read her manuscripts backward to ensure the careful attention required to pick up errors in a text she knew too well. I've never done that, but I do read mine aloud several—okay, *many*—times. Major changes at this stage may cost money, but if you're convinced of the necessity, go for it.

WAITING FOR PUBLICATION

The time between your manuscript's sale and your book's publication may be as long or longer than an elephant's pregnancy (twenty-two months). In fact, this is almost always the case. I've had several books published in a year and a half, but that's fast. Others took two years; one book took five! What do you do during that period? Certainly not sit around and wait! You need to start a new story, which we covered in the previous chapter.

When you're not working at your computer, use the time to get a leg up on promoting your book. The marketing people will usually have you complete a questionnaire about possible contacts and what you're willing to do to support your book. Be honest. If you can't speak to an auditorium of seven-hundred squirming kindergarteners, say so.

Promotion requires writers to hone skills that may be new to them. Many of us are drawn to creating stories because we prefer to be alone, to mull over issues and share our views of the world while hiding behind the covers of books. However, chances are excellent your book will not be the only one released by your publisher that season. They will be pushing your book along with all the others on their list. So here are some things you might do to get the word out about your work.

1. **UPDATE YOUR MAILING LIST.** Perhaps you will want to send a snail-mail or e-mail announcement about your book. Don't be shy. I suspect few people would consider me pushy or aggressive, but I've come to feel that, just as I like to hear friends' good news, they probably want to hear

mine. And if they don't, they can just drop my letter in the recycle bin or press the delete button.

2. **MAKE A LIST OF NEWSPAPERS OR WEBSITES THAT MIGHT BE INTERESTED IN DOING AN ARTICLE ON YOUR BOOK.**
3. **INTRODUCE YOURSELF TO BOOKSELLERS.** If you'd like to do a signing when the book comes out, tell them. They will be more apt to host such an event if you provide a list of people to invite.
4. **GET TO KNOW YOUR LIBRARIAN (IF YOU DON'T ALREADY).** Attend their story hours. Offer to present at one.
5. **CHECK OUT BLOGS ABOUT PICTURE BOOKS.** Follow them. Comment. See if they'd interview you about your book.
6. **THINK ABOUT MAKING A TRAILER FOR YOUR BOOK.** You may have to hire someone for this.
7. **START PRACTICING YOUR PEOPLE AND PERFORMANCE SKILLS.** Sometime in your career, you'll be invited to talk to children and/or a wide range of adults—teachers, librarians, and other writers. You may be terrified of public speaking and prefer taking out trash or eating liver (both of which I hate!), but during this lag time before publication, work on improving your comfort level for these appearances. Take an acting or public-speaking class. Deliver a talk to your mirror.
8. **CREATE A WEBSITE.** Do it fast. Teachers, students, and authors will want to find out about you. If you can do this yourself, go for it. However, I want to focus on creating new books, so I hired a web designer.
9. **IF YOUR BOOK HAS POTENTIAL FOR THE SCHOOL MARKET AND YOU'RE A TEACHER, CREATE A TEACHER'S GUIDE.** If the only connection you have with the educational world is the fact that you were once a student, hire a teacher to do this.
10. **THINK ABOUT HAVING A LAUNCH PARTY.** Be creative.

For a bookstore event for my newest book, *If Animals Said I Love You,* because gorillas are ongoing characters, I asked a bakery to make me gorilla-shaped cookies. Ethan Long, my illustrator, created line drawings of the characters in our English-Spanish Iguana Series books for kids to color. Alexis O'Neill did her book launch for *The Kite That Bridged Two Nations* in the mausoleum where her subject is buried. She invited VIPs and served wine and cheese. A good time was had by all.

REVIEWS

Ahhhh, those bugaboo reviews! They start arriving a couple months before the book's publication date. Some are wonderful. Some are not so wonderful. Maybe you even get a horrible review—one so bad, you want to climb into bed and bury your head under your pillow for weeks.

The amazing thing about reviews is their variety. My early-reader, *Silly Sadie, Silly Samuel*, received the most fantastic review of my career. I was sure it would be a winner. Then it received a terrible review from *School Library Journal*. An early-reader obviously needs the school and library market, and the book died quickly and quietly.

The easiest way to deal with reviews, good or bad, is to not pay attention to them. Going into a funk for days or weeks is a waste of time and emotional energy. You can't change the world by complaining or withdrawing, but you can write another story.

PUBLICATION DATE

Here! At last! The day you've been dreaming about. You've already received the catalog announcing your book and your author's copies, but this is that magic moment when booksellers will finally have your baby in hand. You may anticipate the day, but I'm sorry to disillusion you; the world probably won't. It will most likely come and go unnoticed by everyone but your immediate family and close friends.

Years ago, when my beloved grandfather died, I was furious the world didn't stop to recognize its loss and my pain. Eventually I understood that *my* world may have been forever changed, but the *whole* world didn't know my grandfather and my sadness. His death prepared me for what was to come in my career. While I still have fantasies that firecrackers will go off and TV reporters will knock at my door, I'm more realistic. I don't let that insight stop me from enjoying my proud moment. You shouldn't either. Be like James M. Barrie who said, "For several days after my first book was published, I carried it about in my pocket and took surreptitious peeps at it to make sure that the ink had not faded." Carry your book around, read it over and over, and then go back to your computer. Start writing another wonderful book.

A FEW FINAL WORDS

After years of struggle and hard work, nothing is better than achieving your dream and selling a book. However, as you've learned here, there's more work to be done. In this career of writing picture books, you'll discover there's always more work—writing, revising, submitting, editing, promoting, and so on. My wish for you is that you enjoy the process, no matter what the activity.

WHAT'S NEXT?

Nothing ... except for an epilogue, acknowledgments, and a bibliography.

Epilogue

"All good writing is swimming under water and holding your breath."

—F. SCOTT FITZGERALD

If you've taken your time reading this book and doing the exercises, you've discovered writing picture books is not as easy as you'd imagined. While I'm from the school of the-more-effort-one-puts-in, the-more-satisfying-the-outcome, you may worry that every story is going to require the same kind of attention to detail. Years ago, Clyde Bulla wrote this to me: "Sometimes when I look back on the seventy odd [books] published under my name, I think someone else must have written them. If I *did* write them, why haven't I learned something from the writing? Why does each book seem to pose a new set of problems? And what's with beginnings? Why is each one so nearly impossible?"

So if you ask me if you're going to have to struggle through each story you write, I would answer, "Yes and no." *Yes* because no two stories will be the same. Every new writing project will create problems, some big, some little, some you've faced before and others that might throw you for a loop. Each story requires expanding your creative approaches to solve those problems. It's an exciting, challenging process.

But the answer is also *no* because the more you write, the more you will pay attention to the subjects covered in this book, read in the field, and acquire knowledge. Because I've been doing this so long, I rarely color highlight my openings. The 6 *W*s are so ingrained in me I don't need to anymore. But I still make sure those 6 *W*s are all in the front of my story. As you write and do these exercises, they will eventually become second nature to you, too.

Writing will never be easy. Struggle is part of the game. However, if you're discouraged and looking for a reason to keep going, I'd like to close with this story.

Years ago, my surgeon husband and I dined with another physician and his wife. We didn't know them well but thought we might have something in common. The evening was a disaster. This doctor, whom I'll call Dr. Full-of-Himself, kept trying to impress me by reiterating what important work he and my husband do.

Don't get me wrong: I believe my husband's work is incredibly vital, especially to his patients. But Dr. Full-of-Himself wouldn't give up. At one point, he leaned forward and stared directly into my eyes. "Think about it," he said in a low and serious voice, cupping his hands. "Every day your husband holds life in his hands."

It was all I could do not to burst into laughter and spew food into his face. Talk about self-importance! That phrase about holding life in his hands has now become a standing joke whenever my husband starts acting cocky or self-important, but it got me thinking about what you and I do.

We picture-book writers don't hold children's lives in our hands. Thank goodness! I couldn't stand the stress. However, we do introduce children to the pleasures of reading. If we give them good stories, they want to delve into early-readers and then chapter books, middle-grade and young-adult novels, adult fiction and nonfiction, textbooks, newspapers, computer screens, and magazines. We help children take the first steps to becoming lifelong readers.

Without a thoughtful, educated, and well-read population, how can we solve the many problems—environment, healthcare, schools, wars, climate change—facing us? How can we make important decisions, like whom to vote for, if we don't know the facts—facts that are revealed only after careful reading. We picture-book writers hold something important in our hands: We hold the world's future.

So keep going. Keep writing and revising, no matter the struggle. Walter de la Mare said, "Only the rarest kind of best in anything can be good enough for the young." That best must be our goal with each story we write.

You're on your own now, but this book is always available for your reference. I wish you not only happy writing but challenging writing and the publication of memorable books for children … stories that will inspire them to read more and more. You can do it!

Acknowledgments

"My friends are my estate."

—EMILY DICKENSON

Although I wrote this book alone in my office, in the library, and in different coffee shops, people in spirit hovered over my shoulder, prodding me on, reminding me of lessons learned, and sharing their expertise.

Linda Zuckerman, my dear friend and former editor, invited me to Portland for ten straight years to speak each July at her Pacific Northwest Children's Book Conference. Many of those talks have been adapted into this book.

More than forty years ago, I discovered UCLA Extension Writers' Program and it was a timid, doubtful young mother who first walked into Sonia Levitin's class. Without her encouragement, I wouldn't have signed up for future classes with her and other fine teachers like Sue Alexander and Myra Cohn Livingston. Sue and Myra, both from the school of tough love, never held back in their criticisms. While their comments were often painful, I appreciated how they prodded me to do my best. Although they have both died, I still hear their admonitions in my head. I can't thank them enough.

UCLA Extension Writers' Program also gave me the opportunity to teach about my passion. I thank Linda Venis for trusting a novice. In addition, I'm grateful to my students. Their questions and works-in-progress inspired some of this book's exercises and forced me to articulate my writing process. More gratitude than she will ever know goes to former student Molli Nickell, who suggested I write this book and kept after me when I dragged my feet.

When I started writing, I was introduced to the Society of Children's Book Writers and Illustrators. Their publications, conferences, and advice have helped make me the published writer I am today. Many speakers at their meetings and workshops have shared wisdom that has crept into this book. Some of their exercises were refined and adapted for picture-book writing.

Over the years I've learned much from my editors. It's always surprising how a story I'd thought ready for publication still needed work. I thank Janine O'Malley, Mary Cash, Nora Cohen, Dianne Hess, Ruth Katcher, Melanie

Kroupa, Kevin Lewis, and Linda Zuckerman for making each of my books better than I could have imagined.

Thanks to Alice Pope, who first edited this book. For someone who was used to writing 350-word manuscripts, the jump to 250 pages was terrifying, but Alice couldn't have been more calm and helpful. Special appreciation goes to Cris Freese. What a pleasant surprise to get his e-mail suggesting an update to this book! Although it's been more work than I envisioned, I learned much more in the process and became acquainted with many wonderful new books. Cris is also an incredible editor. His suggestions were helpful and clarifying, and I'm especially grateful for his crash course in the use of commas, which I somehow missed back in high-school English classes. After Cris changed jobs, Amy Jones has stepped in beautifully to make the transition smooth. I also owe a big thanks to my copyeditor Michael Hanna whose close, careful reading of this manuscript saved me from many embarrassing mistakes and awkward sentences.

Writing would be a lonely task without the fabulously talented writers in my critique groups. In Los Angeles, I work with Erica Silverman, Karen Winnick, and Michelle Markel. Evolving from a ten-day workshop, Centrum Port Townsend Writers' Conference (www.centrum.org) with Jane Yolen, my other group's members live scattered across the United States. We call ourselves "The Write Sisters." Although thirty years have passed and several members have gone off in new directions, Mary Nethery, Kirby Larson, and I still try to meet and share manuscripts.

PJ Lutz, Brian Rocklin, Rebecca Delfino, Armineh Manookian, Cindy Moussas-Holmes, and Sheri Linden are writing friends who worked with me on the beginning chapters and proposal for this book's first edition. Thanks to all my other writing buddies who have shared their talents and wisdom with me over the years. I've learned so much from you.

I could not begin to list all of the librarians and bookstore owners who have supported my career, tracked down hard-to-find references, and introduced me to new and exciting books. Special thanks to the wonderful staff at Children's Book World in Los Angeles (www.childrensbookworld.com), who, no matter what question I brought regarding examples for this book, have the answer at their fingertips. Thanks to Ronna Mandel and Erica Silverman for helping me find new book examples, to Janine O'Malley for taking time out of her busy day to talk about an editor's work, and to Rebecca Colby for sharing her agent query letter. Also, much appreciation goes to my agent, Jill Corcoran, for reading my agent chapter, Nancy Hayashi for helping with my self-publishing chapter, Rubin Pfeffer for his comments on my publishing-business chapter, and Joe Taylor and Karol Silverstein for sharing their critique process.

My interest in picture books would never have been born without my four children, Henya, Jon, Alan, and Finn. Our bedtime readings inspired me to write.

Now my grandchildren, Hazel, Lena, Tade, Ellie, Owen, and Thea, listen to my stories and spark new story ideas.

My biggest thanks go to my beloved husband, Ron, who insists on washing the dinner dishes because "You have important work to do." I would still be unpublished were it not for his understanding, support, and encouragement.

Bibliography

". . . a man will turn over half a library to make one book."

—SAMUEL JOHNSON

PICTURE BOOKS

*=rhymed picture book
O=strong opening
E=strong ending
L=lyrical writing

Adams, Jennifer, and Greg Pizzoli. *My Little Cities: Paris.* San Francisco: Chronicle Books, 2015.

Aesop. *Aesop's Fables Online Collection.* Edited by John R. Long. Translated by Ambrose Bierce, Jean De La Fontaine, and George Fyler Townsend. John R. Long/Star Systems, 2014. http://aesopfables.com/cgi/aesop1.cgi?1&TheAntandtheDove&&antdove2.ram.

Alko, Selina, and Sean Qualls. *The Case for Loving; The Fight for Interracial Marriage.* New York: Arthur A. Levine Books, 2015.

Appelt, Kathi, and Bob Dunlavey. *Counting Crows.* New York: Atheneum Books for Young Readers, 2015.

(*) Ashman, Linda, and Christine Davenier. *Samantha on a Roll.* New York: Farrar, Straus and Giroux, 2011.

(*) Ashman, Linda, and Chuck Groenink. *William's Winter Nap.* Los Angeles: Disney-Hyperion, 2017.

(*) Aylesworth, Jim, and Brad Sneed. *Cock-a-doodle-doo, Creak, Pop-Pop, Moo.* New York: Holiday House, 2012.

Baker, Keith. *Hap-pea All Year.* La Jolla, CA: Beach Lane Books, 2016.

(O, E, L) Bakos, Lisa M., and Anna Raff. *The Wrong Side of the Bed.* New York: G.P. Putnam's Sons Books for Young Readers, 2016.

Bang, Molly, and Penny Chisholm. *Rivers of Sunlight: How the Sun Moves Water Around the Earth.* New York: Blue Sky Press, 2017.

(L) Barnett, Mac, and Jon Klassen. *Extra Yarn*. New York: Balzer and Bray, 2012.

Barton, Byron. *My Bus*. New York: Greenwillow, 2014.

Bateman, Teresa, and Paul Meisel. *The Leprechaun Under the Bed*. New York: Holiday House, 2012.

Baum, L. Frank, and W. W. Denslow. *The Wonderful Wizard of Oz*. New York: HarperCollins, 2000.

(*) Beaty, Andrea, and David Roberts. *Ada Twist, Scientist*. New York: Harry N. Abrams, 2016.

(*) Beaty, Andrea, and David Roberts. *Happy Birthday Madame Chapeau*. New York: Harry N. Abrams, 2014.

(*) Beaumont, Karen, and David Catrow. *Doggone Dogs!* New York: Dial Books, 2008.

(*) Beaumont, Karen, and LeUyen Pham. *Hats Off to You!* New York: Scholastic Press, 2017.

(L) Becker, Bonny, and Kady MacDonald Denton. *A Library Book for Bear*. Somerville, MA: Candlewick, 2014.

(*) Bemelmans, Ludwig. *Madeleine*. New York: Viking Press, 1939.

(*) Berger, Samantha, and Kristyna Litten. *Snoozefest*. New York: Dial Books, 2015.

Bingham, Kelly, and Paul O. Zelinsky. *Z is for Moose*. New York: Greenwillow, 2012.

(E) Birdsall, Jeanne, and Harry Bliss. *My Favorite Pets: By Gus W. for Ms. Smolinski's Class*. New York: Knopf Books for Young Readers, 2016.

(O) Boelts, Maribeth, and Lauren Castillo. *Happy Like Soccer*. Somerville, MA: Candlewick, 2012.

Bonwill, Ann, and Simon Rickerty. *I Don't Want to Be a Pea!* New York: Atheneum Books for Young Readers, 2012.

Boynton, Sandra. *Happy Hippo, Angry Duck: A Book of Moods*. New York: Little Simon, 2011.

(L) Bryant, Jen, and Melissa Sweet. *A River of Words: The Story of William Carlos Williams*. Grand Rapids, MI: Eerdman's Publishing Co., 2008.

Buckley, Michael, and Dan Santat. *Ken Gilligan's Daredevil Stunt Show*. New York: Harry N. Abrams, 2012.

Bunting, Eve, and Lauren Castillo. *Yard Sale*. Somerville, MA: Candlewick, 2015.

(*) Bunting, Eve, and Sergio Ruzzier. *Have You Seen My New Blue Socks?* New York: Clarion Books, 2013.

(O, E) Cannon, A.E., and Lee White. *Sophie's Fish.* New York: Viking Books for Young Readers, 2012.

(O) Carbone, Elisa, and Jen Hill. *Diana's White House Garden.* New York: Viking Books for Young Readers, 2016.

(O) Carnesi, Mônica. *Little Dog Lost: The True Story of a Brave Dog Named Baltic.* New York: Paula Wiseman Books, 2012.

Casanova, Mary, and Nick Wroblewski. *Wake Up, Island.* Minneapolis: University of Minnesota Press, 2016.

(*) Clarke, Jane, and Charles Fuge. *Who Woke the Baby?* London: Noisy Crow, 2016.

(L) Colby, Rebecca, and Steven Henry. *It's Raining Bats and Frogs.* New York: Feiwel and Friends, 2015.

(*, E) Collins, Ross. *There's a Bear on My Chair.* London: Nosy Crow, 2016.

(L) Cuyler, Margery, and David Catrow. *That's Good! That's Bad!* New York: Henry Holt and Company, LLC, 1991.

Cuyler, Margery, and Michael Garland. *That's Good! That's Bad! On Santa's Journey.* New York: Henry Holt/Macmillan, 2009.

De la Peña, Matt, and Christian Robinson. *Last Stop on Market Street.* New York: G.P. Putnam's Sons, 2015.

Diesen, Deborah, and Dan Hanna. *Sweet Dreams, Pout-Pout Fish.* New York: Farrar, Straus & Giroux, 2014.

Dodd, Emma. *I Love Bugs!* New York: Holiday House, 2010.

Edwards, Michelle, and G. Brian Karas. *A Hat for Mrs. Goldman: A Story about Knitting and Love.* New York: Schwartz and Wade, 2016.

Falconer, Ian. *Olivia.* New York: Atheneum Books for Young Readers, 2000.

(L) Ferber, Brenda A., and Tedd Arnold. *The Yuckiest, Stinkiest, Best Valentine Ever.* New York: Dial Books, 2012.

(O, L) Ferris, Jeri Chase, and Vincent X. Kirsch. *Noah Webster and His Words.* Boston: Houghton Mifflin Harcourt, 2012.

Fleming, Candace, and Nancy Carpenter. *Imogene's Last Stand.* New York: Schwartz & Wade, 2009.

(L) Fleming, Candace, and Eric Rohmann. *Oh, No!* New York: Schwartz & Wade, 2012.

(L) Fleming, Candace, and Eugene Yelchin. *Seven Hungry Babies.* New York: Atheneum Books for Young Readers, 2010.

(L) Floca, Brian. *Locomotive.* New York: Richard Jackson Books, Atheneum, 2013.

Forler, Nan, and Peter Etril Snyder. *Winterberries and Apple Blossoms: Reflections and Flavors of a Mennonite Year.* Plattsburgh, NY: Tundra Books, 2011.

(*) Fox, Mem, and Mike Austin. *Nellie Belle.* La Jolla, CA: Beach Lane Books, 2015.

(O) Frazee, Marla. *The Boss Baby.* La Jolla, CA: Beach Lane Books, 2010.

Frazee, Marla. *The Farmer and the Clown.* La Jolla, CA: Beach Lane Books, 2014.

(*) Frost, Helen, and Rick Lieder. *Step Gently Out.* Somerville, MA: Candlewick, 2012.

(*) Frost, Helen, and Rick Lieder. *Wake Up!* Somerville, MA: Candlewick, 2017.

Funk, Josh, and Rodolfo Montalvo. *Dear Dragon: A Pen Pal Tale.* New York: Viking Books for Young Readers, 2016.

Gallion, Sue Lowell, and Joyce Wan. *Pug Meets Pig.* La Jolla, CA: Beach Lane Books, 2016.

Gantos, Jack, and Nicole Rubel. *Rotten Ralph.* Boston, MA: Houghton Mifflin, 1976.

Gomi, Taro, and Amanda Mayer Stinchecum. *Everyone Poops.* La Jolla, CA: Kane Miller Books, 1993.

(L) Gottesfeld, Jeff, and Peter McCarty. *The Tree in the Courtyard: Looking Through Anne Frank's Window.* New York: Knopf Books for Young Readers, 2016.

(*) Green, Katie May. *Seen and Not Heard.* Somerville, MA: Candlewick, 2015.

(*) Haber, Tiffany Strelitz, and Kirstie Edmunds. *The Monster Who Lost His Mean.* New York: Henry Holt and Company, 2012.

Hall, Michael. *Perfect Square.* New York: Greenwillow Books, 2011.

(O) Hanlon, Abby. *Ralph Tells a Story.* New York: Two Lions, 2012.

Harris, Robie H., and Nadine Bernard Westcott. *Who Has What?: All About Girls' Bodies and Boys' Bodies.* Somerville, MA: Candlewick Books, 2011.

Hershenhorn, Esther, and Zachary Pullen. *S is for Story: A Writer's Alphabet.* Ann Arbor, MI: Sleeping Bear Press, 2009.

Hoban, Russell, and Garth Williams. *Bedtime for Frances.* New York: Harper & Row Publishers, 1960.

Hoffman, Ian, Sarah Hoffman, and Chris Chase. *Jacob's New Dress.* Parkridge, IL: Albert Whitman & Company, 2014.

Hoffmann, Heinrich. *Struwwelpeter.* Richmond, VA: Robert Godwin-Jones/Virginia Commonwealth University, 1999. germanstories.vcu.edu/struwwel/struwwel.html.

Holub, Joan, and Tom Lichtenheld. *Zero the Hero.* New York: Henry Holt and Company, 2012.

(O) Howe, James, and Chris Raschka. *Otter and Odder: A Love Story.* Somerville, MA, Candlewick, 2012.

Isadora, Rachel. *Old Mikamba Had a Farm.* New York: Nancy Paulsen Books, 2013.

(L) Jenkins, Emily, & Sophie Blackall. *A Fine Dessert: Four Centuries, Four Families, One Delicious Treat.* New York: Schwartz & Wade Books, 2015.

Jenkins, Steve, and Robin Page. *Creature Features.* New York: Houghton Mifflin, 2015.

(L) Jenson-Elliott, Cindy, and Carolyn Fisher. *Weeds Find a Way.* La Jolla, CA: Beach Lane Books, 2014.

(O, L) Joosse, Barbara, and Randy Cecil. *Lovabye Dragon.* Somerville, MA: Candlewick, 2012.

(L) Joosse, Barbara, and Jan Jutte. *Old Robert and the Sea-Silly Cats.* New York: Philomel Books, 2012.

(O) Judge, Lita. *Flight School.* New York: Atheneum Books for Young Readers, 2014.

(*) Ketteman, Helen, and Ponder Goembel. *Swamp Song.* Allentown, PA: Two Lions, 2009.

(*) Ketteman, Helen, and Bonnie Leick. *Goodnight, Little Monster.* Allentown, PA: Two Lions, 2010.

(O, L) Khan, Rukhsana, and Sophie Blackall. *Big Red Lollipop.* New York: Viking Books for Young Readers, 2010.

Klassen, Jon. *I Want My Hat Back.* Somerville, MA: Candlewick, 2011.

Klassen, Jon. *This is Not My Hat.* Somerville, MA: Candlewick, 2012.

Klassen, Jon. *We Found a Hat.* Somerville, MA: Candlewick, 2016.

(O) Knudsen, Michelle, and Scott Magoon. *Big Mean Mike.* Somerville, MA: Candlewick, 2012.

Kontis, Alethea, and Bob Kolar. *Alpha Oops!: The Day Z Went First.* Somerville, MA: Candlewick, 2006.

Krauss, Ruth, and Maurice Sendak. *A Hole Is to Dig.* New York: Harper & Row Publishers, 1952.

(L) Krensky, Stephen, and Josée Bisaillon. *The Great Moon Hoax.* Minneapolis: Carolrhoda Books, 2011.

Kunhardt, Dorothy. *Pat the Bunny.* New York: Golden Books, 1940.

Laden, Nina. *Peek-a Boo!* San Francisco: Chronicle Books, 2015.

Leaf, Munro, and Robert Lawson. *The Story of Ferdinand.* New York: Viking Press, Inc., 1936.

Leathers, Philippa. *The Black Rabbit.* Somerville, MA: Candlewick, 2013.

Levine, Arthur A., and Julian Hector. *Monday is One Day.* New York: Scholastic Press, 2011.

(L) Levy, Debbie, and Elizabeth Baddeley. *I Dissent: Ruth Bader Ginsburg Makes Her Mark.* New York: Simon and Schuster Books for Young Readers, 2016.

(E) Liu, Cynthea, and Kristyna Litten. *Bike On, Bear!* New York: Aladdin, 2015.

Lobel, Arnold. *Fables.* New York: HarperCollins, 1980.

(L) Logue, Mary, and Pamela Zagarenski. *Sleep Like a Tiger.* Boston: Houghton Mifflin Harcourt Books for Young Readers, 2012.

(L) Loh-Hagan, Virginia, and Renné Benoit. *PoPo's Lucky Chinese New Year.* Ann Arbor, MI: Sleeping Bear Press, 2016.

(O, E) Manley, Curtis, and Kate Berube. *The Summer Nick Taught His Cats to Read.* New York: Paula Wiseman Books, Simon & Schuster, 2016.

(*) Manushkin, Fran, and Lauren Tobia. *Happy in Our Skin.* Somerville, MA: Candlewick, 2015.

(L) Markel, Michelle, and Nancy Carpenter. *Balderdash!: John Newbery and the Boisterous Birth of Children's Books.* San Francisco: Chronicle Books, 2017.

(O, L) Markel, Michelle, and LeUyen Pham. *Hillary Rodham Clinton: Some Girls Are Born to Lead.* New York: Balzer and Bray, 2016.

(L) Markel, Michelle, and Melissa Sweet. *Brave Girl: Clara and the Shirtwaist Makers' Strike of 1909.* New York: Balzer and Bray, 2013.

Maynor, Megan, and Rosalinde Bonnet. *Ella and Penguin Stick Together.* New York: HarperCollins, 2016.

McPike, Elizabeth, and Patrice Barton. *Little Bitty Friends*. New York: G.P. Putnam's Sons Books for Young Readers, 2017.

Messner, Kate, and Christopher Silas Neal. *Over and Under the Snow*. San Francisco: Chronicle Books, 2011.

(O) Miller, Pat Zietlow, and Anne Wilsdorf. *Sophie's Squash*. New York: Schwartz & Wade, 2013.

(*) Mortensen, Lori, and Michael Allen Austin. *Cowpoke Clyde Rides the Range*. New York: Clarion Books, 2016.

(E) Mortensen, Lori, and Nina Victor Crittenden. *Chicken Lily*. New York: Henry Holt and Company, 2016.

(*) Mortensen, Lori, and Betsy Lewin. *Mousequerade Ball: A Counting Tale*. New York: Bloomsbury USA, 2016.

Nagara, Innosanto. *A is for Activist*. Salem, OR: Triangle Square, 2013.

Numeroff, Laura, and Felicia Bond. *If You Give a Cat a Cupcake*. New York: HarperCollins Children's Books, 2008.

Numeroff, Laura, and Felicia Bond. *If You Give a Dog a Doughnut*. New York: HarperCollins Children's Books, 2011.

Numeroff, Laura, and Felicia Bond. *If You Give a Moose a Muffin*. New York: HarperCollins Children's Books, 1991.

Numeroff, Laura, and Felicia Bond. *If You Give a Mouse a Brownie*. New York: HarperCollins Children's Books, 2016.

Numeroff, Laura, and Felicia Bond. *If You Give a Mouse a Cookie*. New York: HarperCollins Children's Books, 1985.

O'Brien, Anne Sibley. *I'm New Here*. Watertown, MA: Charlesbridge, 2015.

O'Connor, Jane, and Robin Preiss Glasser. *Fancy Nancy*. New York: HarperCollins, 2005.

(L) O'Neill, Alexis, and Terry Widener. *The Kite that Bridged Two Nations: Homan Walsh and the First Niagara Suspension Bridge*. Honesdale, PA: Calkins Creek, 2013.

Parker, Jake. *Little Bot and Sparrow*. New York: Roaring Brook, 2016.

Paul, Ann Whitford, and Ethan Long. *Count on Culebra: Go from 1 to 10 in Spanish*. New York: Holiday House, 2008.

Paul, Ann Whitford, and Ethan Long. *Fiesta Fiasco*. New York: Holiday House, 2007.

Paul, Ann Whitford, and Ethan Long. *Mañana, Iguana.* New York: Holiday House, 2004.

Paul, Ann Whitford, and Ethan Long. *Tortuga in Trouble.* New York: Holiday House, 2009.

Paul, Ann Whitford, and Michael McCurdy. *The Seasons Sewn: A Year in Patchwork.* San Diego: Harcourt Brace & Company, 1996.

(*) Paul, Ann Whitford, and Maggie Smith. *Everything to Spend the Night: From A to Z.* New York: DK Publishing, Inc., 1999.

(*) Paul, Ann Whitford, and David Walker. *If Animals Kissed Good Night.* New York: Farrar, Straus and Giroux, 2008.

(*, O) Paul, Ann Whitford, and David Walker. *If Animals Said I Love You.* New York: Farrar, Straus and Giroux, 2017.

(E) Paul, Ann Whitford, and David Walker. *Little Monkey Says Good Night.* New York: Farrar, Straus and Giroux, 2003.

(*) Paul, Ann Whitford, and Nadine Bernard Westcott. *Hello Toes! Hello Feet!* New York: DK Publishing, Inc., 1998.

Paul, Ann Whitford, and Jeanette Winter. *Eight Hands Round: A Patchwork Alphabet.* New York: HarperCollins Publishers, 1991.

Perrault, Charles. *Perrault's Mother Goose Tales.* Edited by D.L. Ashliman. Pittsburgh: D. L. Ashliman/University of Pittsburgh, 2013. www.pitt.edu/~dash/perrault01.html.

(L) Phi, Bao, and Thi Bui. *A Different Pond.* Mankato, MN: Capstone Publishers, 2017.

Platt, Cynthia, and Veronica Vasylenko. *Panda-Monium!* Wilton, CT: Tiger Tales, 2011.

(O) Portis, Antoinette. *Best Frints in the Whole Universe.* New York: Roaring Brook Press, 2016.

Portis, Antoinette. *Not a Box.* New York: HarperCollins, 2006.

Portis, Antoinette. *Not a Stick.* New York: HarperCollins, 2007.

Potter, Beatrix. *The Tale of Peter Rabbit.* London: Frederick Warne & Co., 1902.

(L) Rappaport, Doreen, and Matt Tavares. *Helen's Big World: The Life of Helen Keller.* New York: Disney-Hyperion, 2012.

(L) Rex, Adam, and Christian Robinson. *School's First Day of School.* New York: Roaring Brook Press, 2016.

Rey, H.A., and Margret Rey. *Curious George Gets a Medal.* Boston: Houghton Mifflin Company, 1957.

(O) Reynolds, Aaron, and Sara Varon. *President Squid.* San Francisco: Chronicle Books, 2016.

(L) Rockliff, Mara, and William Low. *Me and Momma and Big John.* Somerville, MA: Candlewick, 2012.

Santat, Dan. *The Adventures of Beekle: The Unimaginary Friend.* New York: Little, Brown, 2014.

Sauer, Tammi, and Goro Fujita. *Your Alien.* New York: Sterling Publishers, 2015.

Sauer, Tammi, and Scott Magoon. *Mostly Monsterly.* New York: Simon & Schuster Books for Young Readers, 2010.

(L) Sayre, April Pulley, and Steve Jenkins. *Eat Like a Bear.* New York: Henry Holt and Company, 2013.

Scheffler, Axel. *Cuddly Cow.* London: Nosy Crow, 2017.

(*) Schertle, Alice, and Jill McElmurry. *Little Blue Truck.* New York: Houghton, Mifflin, Harcourt, 2008.

(*) Schwartz, Corey Rosen, and Deborah Marcero. *Twinderella: A Fractioned Fairy Tale.* New York: G.P. Putnam's Sons Books for Young Readers, 2017.

Scieszka, Jon, and Lane Smith. *The True Story of the 3 Little Pigs.* New York: Viking, 1989.

Sendak, Maurice. *Chicken Soup with Rice: A Book of Months.* New York: Harper & Row Publishers, 1962.

Sendak, Maurice. *Where the Wild Things Are.* New York: Harper & Row Publishers, 1963.

Seuss, Dr. *Yertle the Turtle and Other Stories.* New York: Random House, 1958.

Shannon, David. *No, David!* New York: Blue Sky Press, 1998.

(*) Sierra, Judy, and Tim Bowers. *Suppose You Meet a Dinosaur: A First Book of Manners.* New York: Knopf Books for Young Readers, 2012.

(*) Sierra, Judy, and G. Brian Karas. *Make Way for Readers.* New York: Paula A. Wiseman Books, 2014.

(*) Silverman, Erica, and Laure Fournier. *Wake Up, City!* New York: Little Bee Books, 2016.

Slade, Suzanne, and Stacy Innerst. *The Music in George's Head: George Gershwin Creates Rhapsody in Blue.* Honesdale, PA: Calkins Creek/Boyds Mills Press, 2016.

(L) Slater, Dashka, and Terry Fan. *The Antlered Ship*. La Jolla, CA: Beach Lane Books, 2017.

(L) Smith, Cynthia Leitich, Cornelius Van Wright, and Ying-Hwa Hu. *Jingle Dancer*. New York: Morrow Junior Books, 2000.

(E) Staub, Leslie, and Jeff Mack. *Time for (Earth) School, Dewey Dew*. Honesdale, PA: Boyds Mills Press, 2016.

Stead, Philip C., and Erin E. Stead. *Bear Has a Story to Tell*. New York: Roaring Brook Press, 2012.

Stein, David Ezra. *Love, Mouserella*. New York: Nancy Paulsen Books, 2011.

Sullivan, Tom. *I Used to Be a Fish*. New York: Balzer and Bray, 2016.

Twohy, Mike. *Wake Up, Rupert!* New York: Paula Wiseman Books/Simon & Schuster, 2014.

Ultman, Suzy. *Tiny Town*. San Francisco: Chronicle Books, 2017.

Underwood, Deborah, and Laura Rankin. *A Balloon for Isabel*. New York: Henry Holt and Company, 2016.

(O) Vail, Rachel, and Jeremy Tankard. *Piggy Bunny*. New York: Feiwell and Friends, 2012.

(L) Van Slyke, Rebecca, and Chris Robertson. *Where Do Pants Go?* New York: Sterling Children's Books, 2016.

(L) Waddell, Martin, and Patrick Benson. *Owl Babies*. Somerville, MA: Candlewick, 1992.

Wahl, Phoebe. *Sonya's Chickens*. Toronto: Tundra Books, 2015.

Walker, Sally M., and Jonathan D. Voss. *Winnie: The True Story of the Bear Who Inspired Winnie-the-Pooh*. New York: Henry Holt and Company, 2015.

Ward, Lindsay. *When Blue Met Egg*. New York: Dial Books, 2012.

(O) Wayland, April Halprin, and Katie Kath. *More Than Enough: A Passover Story*. New York: Dial Books, 2016.

Wenzel, Brendan. *They All Saw a Cat*. San Francisco: Chronicle Books, 2016.

(L) Wheeler, Lisa, and Jerry Pinkney. *The Christmas Boot*. New York: Dial Books, 2016.

Willems, Mo. *Knuffle Bunny: A Cautionary Tale*. New York: Hyperion, 2004.

(L) Willems, Mo. *Nanette's Baguette*. New York: Disney-Hyperion, 2016.

Willems, Mo, and Jon J. Muth. *City Dog, Country Frog.* New York: Disney-Hyperion, 2010.

(L) Winnick, Karen B., and Laura Watkins. *Good Night, Baby Animals You've Had a Busy Day.* New York: Henry Holt, 2017.

Wolff, Ashley. *Baby Bear Sees Blue.* La Jolla, CA: Beach Lane Books, 2012.

Woodson, Jacqueline, and James Ransome. *This is the Rope: A Story from the Great Migration.* New York: Nancy Paulsen Books, 2013.

Zagarenski, Pamela. *Henry & Leo.* New York: Houghton Mifflin Harcourt, 2016.

POETS

Alexander, Kwame, Chris Colderley, Marjory Wentworth, and Ekua Holmes. *Out of Wonder: Poems Celebrating Poets.* Somerville, MA: Candlewick, 2017.

Belle, Jennifer, and David McPhail. *Animal Stackers.* New York: Hyperion Books for Children, 2005.

Benét, Rosemary, Stephen Vincent Benét, and Charles Child. *A Book of Americans.* New York: Henry Holt and Company, 1933.

Chandra, Deborah, and Leslie Bowman. *Balloons and Other Poems.* New York: Farrar, Straus Giroux, 1990.

Clifton, Lucille, and Ann Grifalconi. *Everett Anderson's Goodbye.* New York: Henry Holt and Company, 1983.

Dotlich, Rebecca Kai, and Jan Spivey Gilchrist. *Lemonade Sun and Other Summer Poems.* Honesdale, PA: Wordsong/Boyds Mills Press, 1998.

Elya, Susan Middleton, and Juana Martinez-Neal. *La Madre Goose: Nursery Rhymes for Los Niños.* New York: G.P. Putnam's Sons Books for Young Readers, 2016.

Fleischman, Paul, and Eric Beddows. *Joyful Noise: Poems for Two Voices.* New York: Harper & Row Publishers, 1988.

Florian, Douglas. *On the Wing.* San Diego: Harcourt, Inc., 1996.

Frank, John, and London Ladd. *Lend a Hand: Poems about Giving.* New York: Lee and Low, 2014.

Frost, Robert. *The Poetry of Robert Frost: The Collected Poems, Complete and Unabridged.* New York: Henry Holt and Company, 1969.

George, Kristine O'Connell, and Kate Kiesler. *Old Elm Speaks: Tree Poems.* New York: Clarion Books. 1998.

Giovanni, Nikki, and George Martins. *Spin A Soft Black Song: Poems for Children*. New York: Farrar, Straus and Giroux, 1985.

Graham, Joan Bransfield, and Kyrsten Brooker. *The Poem That Will Not End: Fun with Poetic Forms and Voices*. Allentown, PA: Two Lions, 2014.

Gunning, Monica, and Ken Condon. *America, My New Home*. Honesdale, PA: Wordsong/Boyds Mills Press, 2004.

Hoban, Russell, and Lillian Hoban. *The Pedaling Man and Other Poems*. New York: W. W. Norton & Company, Inc., 1968.

Holman, Felice, and Jim Spanfeller. *The Song in My Head and Other Poems*. New York: Charles Scribner's Sons, 1985.

Hopkins, Lee Bennett, and Charlene Rendeiro. *Been to Yesterdays: Poems of a Life*. Honesdale, PA: Wordsong/Boyds Mills Press, 1995.

Hosford, Kate, and Cosei Kawa. *Feeding the Flying Fanellis and Other Poems from a Circus Chef*. Minneapolis: Carolrhoda Books, 2015.

Hovey, Kate, and Murray Kimber. *Ancient Voices*. New York: Margaret K. McElderry, 2004.

Hughes, Langston, and Brian Pinkney. *The Dream Keeper and Other Poems*. New York: Alfred A. Knopf, Inc., 1994.

Johnston, Tony, and Ted Rand. *It's About Dogs*. San Diego: Harcourt, Inc., 2000.

Kumin, Maxine, and Pamela Zagarenski. *Mites to Mastodons: A Book of Animal Poems*. Boston: Houghton Mifflin Company, 2006.

Lewis, J. Patrick, and Keith Graves. *The World's Greatest: Poems*. San Francisco: Chronicle Books, 2008.

Livingston, Myra Cohn, and Leonard Everett Fisher. *Celebrations*. New York: Holiday House, 1985.

McCord, David, and Henry B. Kane. *One at a Time: His Collected Poems for the Young*. Boston: Little, Brown and Company, 1986.

Merriam, Eve, and Walter Gaffney-Kessell. *A Sky Full of Poems*. New York: Dell Publishing, 1986.

Moore, Clement C., and Charles Santore. *The Night Before Christmas*. New York: Applesauce Press/Simon & Schuster, 2011.

Moore, Lilian, and Jill McElmurry. *I'm Small and Other Verses*. Cambridge, MA: Candlewick, 2001.

Oliver, Lin, and Tomie dePaola. *Little Poems for Tiny Ears.* New York: Nancy Paulsen Books, 2014.

Paul, Ann Whitford, and Michael Steirnagle. *All by Herself.* San Diego: Browndeer Press/ Harcourt Brace & Company, 1999.

Phi, Bao, and Thi Bui. *A Different Pond.* North Mankato, MN: Capstone Young Readers, 2017.

Prelutsky, Jack, and Arnold Lobel. *Tyrannosaurus Was a Beast.* New York: Greenwillow Books, 1988.

Raczka, Bob. *Wet Cement: A Mix of Concrete Poems.* New York: Roaring Brook Press, 2016.

Roberts, Elizabeth Madox. *Under the Tree.* Whitefish, MT: Kessinger Publishing, LLC, 2007.

Rosenthal, Betsy R., and Margaret Chodos-Irvine. *My House Is Singing.* San Diego: Harcourt, Inc., 2004.

Rosenthal, Betsy R., and Jago. *An Ambush of Tigers: A Wild Gathering of Collective Nouns.* Brookfield, CT: Millbrook, 2015.

Saltzberg, Barney. *All Around the Seasons.* Sommerville, MA: Candlewick, 2010.

Schertle, Alice, and Amanda Schaffer. *How Now, Brown Cow?* San Diego: Browndeer Press, Harcourt Brace & Company, 1994.

Sidman, Joyce, and Pamela Zagarenski. *Red Sings from Treetops: A Year in Colors.* Boston: Houghton Mifflin Books for Young Readers, 2009.

Silverstein, Shel. *A Light in the Attic.* New York: HarperCollins, 1981.

Singer, Marilyn, and Josée Masse. *Mirror, Mirror: A Book of Reverso Poems.* New York: Dutton Books for Young Readers, 2010.

Smith, Hope Anita, and E.B. Lewis. *Keeping the Night Watch.* New York: Henry Holt and Company, 2008.

Sones, Sonya. *Saving Red.* New York: Harper Teen, 2016.

Stevenson, James. *Candy Corn.* New York: Greenwillow Books, 1999.

Stevenson, Robert Louis, and Tasha Tudor. *A Child's Garden of Verses.* Rev. ed. New York: Simon & Schuster Children's Publishing, 1999.

VanDerwater, Amy Ludwig, and Dylan Metrano. *Every Day Birds.* New York: Orchard Books, 2016.

Viorst, Judith, and Lynne Cherry. *If I Were in Charge of the World and Other Worries.* New York: Atheneum Books for Young Readers, 1981.

Wardlaw, Lee, and Eugene Yelchin. *Won Ton: A Cat Tale Told in Haiku.* New York: Henry Holt and Company, 2011.

Wayland, April Halprin, and Elaine Clayton. *Girl Coming in for a Landing: A Novel in Poems.* New York: Alfred A. Knopf, 2002.

Wheeler, Lisa, and Sophie Blackall. *Spinster Goose: Twisted Rhymes for Naughty Children.* New York: Atheneum Books for Young Readers, 2011.

Whitman, Walt, and Charles Mikolaycak. *Voyages.* Edited by Lee Bennett Hopkins. San Diego: Harcourt Brace Jovanovich Publishers, 1988.

Wong, Janet S. *Good Luck Gold and Other Poems.* New York: Margaret K. McElderry Books, 1994.

Worth, Valerie, and Natalie Babbitt. *All the Small Poems and Fourteen More.* New York: Farrar, Straus and Giroux, 1987.

Zolotow, Charlotte, and Margot Tomes. *Everything Glistens and Everything Sings: New and Selected Poems.* San Diego: Harcourt, 1987.

BOOKS ABOUT WRITING

GENERAL

Alderson, Martha. *The Plot Whisperer: Secrets of Story Structure Any Writer Can Master.* Avon, MA: Adams Media, 2011.

Bayles, David, and Ted Orland. *Art & Fear: Observations on the Perils (and Rewards) of Artmaking.* Santa Cruz, CA: Image Continuum Press, 2001.

Bickham, Jack M. *Scene & Structure.* Cincinnati: Writer's Digest Books, 1999.

Booker, Christopher. *The Seven Basic Plots: Why We Tell Stories.* New York: Continuum, 2004.

Cron, Lisa. *Wired for Story: The Writer's Guide to Using Brain Science to Hook Readers from the Very First Sentence.* Berkeley, CA: Ten Speed Press, 2012.

Egri, Lajos. *The Art of Dramatic Writing.* New York: Simon & Schuster, 1946.

Gilbert, Elizabeth. *Big Magic: Creative Living Beyond Fear.* New York: Riverhead Books, 2015.

Golub, Marcia. *I'd Rather Be Writing.* Cincinnati: Writer's Digest Books, 2001.

Kaufman, Scott Barry, and Carolyn Gregoire. *Wired to Create: Unraveling the Mysteries of the Creative Mind.* New York: Perigee, 2015.

King, Stephen. *On Writing: A Memoir of the Craft.* New York: Scribner, 2000.

Lamott, Anne. *Bird by Bird: Some Instructions on Writing and Life.* New York: Pantheon Books, 1994.

McPhee, John. *Draft No. 4: On the Writing Process.* New York: Farrar, Straus and Giroux, 2017.

See, Carolyn. *Making a Literary Life: Advice for Writers and Other Dreamers.* New York: Random House, 2002.

Shapiro, Dani. *Still Writing: The Perils and Pleasures of a Creative Life.* New York: Atlantic Monthly Press, 2013.

Snyder, Blake. *Save the Cat!: The Last Book on Screenwriting You'll Ever Need.* Studio City, CA: Michael Wiese Productions, 2005.

VanDerwater, Amy Ludwig. *Poems Are Teachers: How Studying Poetry Strengthens Writing in All Genres.* Portsmouth, NH: Heinemann, 2017.

Vorhaus, John. *The Comic Toolbox: How to Be Funny Even If You're Not.* Los Angeles: Silman-James Press, 1994.

WRITING FOR CHILDREN

Ashman, Linda. *The Nuts and Bolts Guide to Writing Picture Books.* Chapel Hill, NC: Slow Lane Productions, 2013.

Bird, Betsy, Julie Danielson, and Peter D. Sieruta. *Wild Things!: Acts of Mischief in Children's Literature.* Somerville, MA: Candlewick, 2014.

Dadey, Debbie, and Marcia Thornton Jones. *Story Sparkers: A Creativity Guide for Children's Writers.* Cincinnati: Writer's Digest, 2000.

Epstein, Connie C. *The Art of Writing for Children: Skills and Techniques of the Craft.* Hamden, CT: Archon Books, 1991.

Handy, Bruce. *Wild Things: The Joy of Reading Children's Literature as an Adult.* New York: Simon & Schuster, 2017.

Horning, Kathleen T. *From Cover to Cover: Evaluating and Reviewing Children's Books.* New York: HarperCollins Publishers, 1997.

Karl, Jean E. *How to Write and Sell Children's Picture Books.* Cincinnati: Writer's Digest Books, 1994.

Lamb, Nancy. *The Writer's Guide to Crafting Stories for Children.* Cincinnati: Writer's Digest Books, 2001.

Litowinsky, Olga. *It's a Bunny-Eat-Bunny World: A Writer's Guide to Surviving and Thriving in Today's Competitive Children's Book Market.* New York: Walker & Company, 2001.

Marcus, Leonard S. *Margaret Wise Brown: Awakened by the Moon.* Boston: Beacon Press, 1992.

Marcus, Leonard S., ed. *Dear Genius: The Letters of Ursula Nordstrom.* New York: HarperCollins Publishers, 1998.

Mogilner, Alijandra. *Children's Writer's Word Book.* 2nd ed. Cincinnati: Writer's Digest Books, 2006.

Morgan, Judith, and Neil Morgan. *Dr. Seuss & Mr. Geisel: A Biography.* New York: Random House, 1995.

Roberts, Ellen E.M. *The Children's Picture Book: How To Write It—How To Sell It.* Cincinnati: Writer's Digest Books, 1981.

Shulevitz, Uri. *Writing with Pictures: How to Write and Illustrate Children's Books.* New York: Watson-Cuptill Publications, 1985.

Suen, Anastasia. *Picture Writing: A New Approach to Writing for Kids and Teens.* Cincinnati: Writer's Digest Books, 2003.

Underdown, Harold D. *The Complete Idiot's Guide: Publishing Children's Books.* New York: Alpha Books, 2008.

Wallin, Luke, and Eva Sage Gordon. *The Everything Guide to Writing Children's Books: How to Write, Publish, and Promote Books for Children of All Ages!* 2nd ed. Avon, MA: Adams Media, 2011.

Willard, Nancy. *Telling Time: Angels, Ancestors, and Stories.* San Diego: Harcourt, Brace & Company, 1993.

WRITING POETRY

Fry, Stephen. *The Ode Less Travelled: Unlocking the Poet Within.* New York: Gotham Books, 2006.

Janeczko, Paul B., ed., and Cathy Bobak. *Poetry from A to Z: A Guide for Young Writers.* New York: Simon & Schuster Books for Young Readers, 2012.

Kennedy, X.J., and Dana Gioia. *An Introduction to Poetry.* 9th ed. New York: Longman, 1998.

Kennedy, X.J., and Dorothy M. Kennedy. *Knock at a Star: A Child's Introduction To Poetry.* Boston: Little, Brown and Company, 1982.

Koch, Kenneth. *Making Your Own Days: The Pleasures of Reading and Writing Poetry.* New York: Scribner, 1998.

Livingston, Myra Cohn. *Poem-Making: Ways to Begin Writing Poetry.* New York: HarperCollins Publishers, 1991.

Livingston, Myra Cohn, ed. *I Am Writing a Poem About … A Game of Poetry.* New York: Margaret K. McElderry Books, 1997.

Oliver, Mary. *A Poetry Handbook: A Prose Guide to Understanding and Writing Poetry.* San Diego: Harcourt Brace & Company, 1994.

Oliver, Mary. *Rules for the Dance: A Handbook for Writing and Reading Metrical Verse.* New York: Houghton Mifflin Company, 1998.

Padgett, Ron, ed. *The Teachers & Writers Handbook of Poetic Forms.* New York: Teachers & Writers Collaborative, 1987.

Pinsky, Robert. *The Sounds of Poetry: A Brief Guide.* New York: Farrar, Straus and Giroux, 1998.

Rilke, Rainer Maria. *Letters to a Young Poet.* Novato, CA: New World Library, 2000.

Ryan, Margaret. *How to Write a Poem.* New York: Franklin Watts, 1996.

Stafford, William. *Writing the Australian Crawl: Views on the Writer's Vocation.* Ann Arbor: University of Michigan Press, 1978.

Wooldridge, Susan G. *Poemcrazy: Freeing Your Life with Words.* New York: Three Rivers Press, 1997.

Index